A BRAND-NEW YEAR—
A PROMISING NEW START

With expert readings and forecasts, you can chart a course to romance, adventure, good health, or career opportunities while gaining valuable insight into yourself and others. Offering a daily outlook for 18 full months, this fascinating guide shows you:

- The important dates in your life
- What to expect from an astrological reading
- How the stars can help you stay healthy and fit
  And more!

Let this sound advice guide you through a year of heavenly possibilities—for today and for every day of 2010!

SYDNEY OMARR'S® DAY-BY-DAY
ASTROLOGICAL GUIDE FOR

ARIES—March 21–April 19
TAURUS—April 20–May 20
GEMINI—May 21–June 20
CANCER—June 21–July 22
LEO—July 23–August 22
VIRGO—August 23–September 22
LIBRA—September 23–October 22
SCORPIO—October 23–November 21
SAGITTARIUS—November 22–December 21
CAPRICORN—December 22–January 19
AQUARIUS—January 20–February 18
PISCES—February 19–March 20

IN 2010

SYDNEY OMARR'S®

DAY-BY-DAY ASTROLOGICAL GUIDE FOR

CAPRICORN

DECEMBER 22–JANUARY 19

2010

by Trish MacGregor
with Carol Tonsing

A SIGNET BOOK

SIGNET
Published by New American Library, a division of
Penguin Group (USA) Inc., 375 Hudson Street,
New York, New York 10014, USA
Penguin Group (Canada), 90 Eglinton Avenue East, Suite 700, Toronto,
Ontario M4P 2Y3, Canada (a division of Pearson Penguin Canada Inc.)
Penguin Books Ltd., 80 Strand, London WC2R 0RL, England
Penguin Ireland, 25 St. Stephen's Green, Dublin 2,
Ireland (a division of Penguin Books Ltd.)
Penguin Group (Australia), 250 Camberwell Road, Camberwell, Victoria 3124,
Australia (a division of Pearson Australia Group Pty. Ltd.)
Penguin Books India Pvt. Ltd., 11 Community Centre, Panchsheel Park,
New Delhi - 110 017, India
Penguin Group (NZ), 67 Apollo Drive, Rosedale, North Shore 0645
New Zealand (a division of Pearson New Zealand Ltd.)
Penguin Books (South Africa) (Pty.) Ltd., 24 Sturdee Avenue,
Rosebank, Johannesburg 2196, South Africa

Penguin Books Ltd., Registered Offices:
80 Strand, London WC2R 0RL, England

First Printing, June 2009
10   9   8   7   6   5   4   3   2   1

First published by Signet, an imprint of New American Library,
a division of Penguin Group (USA) Inc.

CONTENTS

INTRODUCTION

Seize the Moment

"Timing is everything" is a saying worth repeating this year. Astrology is the art of interpreting moments in time, and astrology fans from the rich and famous to the readers of daily horoscope columns realize that some moments are more favorable for certain actions than others. Knowing that they can plan their actions in tune with the rhythm of the cosmic cycles gives them confidence that they are making wise choices. This could be a challenging year for many, so let this guide help you seize the moment and turn those challenges into opportunities by using the tools astrology provides.

In our toolbox for 2010, you'll find secrets of astrological timing—how to find the most auspicious dates this year. For those who are new to astrology or would like to know more about it, we offer easy techniques to start using astrology in your daily life. You'll learn all about your sun sign and how to interpret the mysterious symbols on a horoscope chart. You can use the convenient tables in this book to look up other planets in your horoscope, each of which sheds light on a different facet of your personality.

Many people turn to astrology to help them find love or figure out what went wrong with a relationship. At your service is the world's oldest dating and mating coach, ready to help you decide whether that new passion has potential or might burn out fast. We'll go through the pros and cons of all the possible sun-sign combinations, with celebrities to illustrate the romantic chemistry.

Contemplating a career change? Our sun-sign chapters can help you build your confidence and focus your job search in

1

the most fulfilling direction by highlighting your natural talents and abilities.

Many readers have explored astrology on the Internet, where there are a mind-boggling variety of sites. Our suggestions are well worth your surfing time. We show you where to get free horoscopes, connect with other astrology fans, find the right astrology software for your ability, and even find an accredited college that specializes in astrological studies.

Whether it's money matters, fashion tips, or ideas for vacation getaways, we'll provide ways to use astrology in your life every day. Before giving yourself or your home a makeover, be sure to consult your sun sign, for the colors and styles that will complement your personality.

To make the most of each day, there are eighteen months of on-target daily horoscopes. So here's hoping this year's guide will help you use your star power wisely to make 2010 a happy, successful year!

CHAPTER 1

The Top Trends of 2010: Transition Times

Astrologers judge the trends of a year by following the slow-moving planets, from Jupiter through Pluto. A change in sign indicates a new cycle, with new emphasis. The farthest planets (Uranus, Neptune, and Pluto) which stay in a sign for at least seven years, cause a very significant change in the atmosphere when they change signs. Shifts in Jupiter, which changes every year, and Saturn, every two years, are more obvious in current events and daily lives. Jupiter generally brings a fortunate, expansive emphasis to its new sign, while Saturn's two-year cycle is a reality check, bringing tests of maturity, discipline, and responsibility. This year, Jupiter in Pisces and Saturn in Libra are in auspicious signs for most of the year, which should act as a balance to more volatile elements in the comos.

Little Pluto—The Mighty Mite

Though astronomers have demoted tiny Pluto from being a full-fledged planet to a dwarf planet, astrologers have been tracking its influence since Pluto was discovered in 1930 and have witnessed that this minuscule celestial body has a powerful effect on both a personal and global level. So Pluto, which moved into the sign of Capricorn in 2008, will still be called a "planet" by astrologers and will be given just as much importance as before.

Until 2024, Pluto will exert its influence in this practical, building, healing earth sign. Capricorn relates to structures, institutions, order, mountains and mountain countries, mineral rights, issues involving the elderly and growing older—all of which will be emphasized in the coming years. It is the sign of established order, corporations, big business—all of which will be accented. Possibly, it will fall to business structures to create a new sense of order in the world.

You should now feel the rumblings of change in the Capricorn area of your horoscope and in the world at large. The last time Pluto was in Capricorn was the years up to and during the Revolutionary War; therefore this should be an important time in the U.S. political scene, as well as a reflection of the aging and maturing of American society in general. Both the rise and the fall of the Ottoman Empire happened under Pluto in Capricorn.

The Pisces Factor

This year, Jupiter moves from experimental, humanitarian Aquarius to creative, imaginative Pisces. Jupiter is the coruler of Pisces, along with Neptune, so this is a particularly auspicious place for the planet of luck and expansion to be. During the year that Jupiter remains in a sign, the fields associated with that sign are the ones that currently arouse excitement and enthusiasm, usually providing excellent opportunities.

Jupiter in Pisces expands the influence of Neptune in Aquarius; there should be many artistic and scientific breakthroughs. International politics also comes under this influence, as Neptune in Aquarius raises issues of global boundaries and political structures not being as solid as they seem. This could continue to produce rebellion and chaos in the environment. However, with the generally benevolent force of Jupiter backing up the creative side of Neptune, it is possible that highly original and effective solutions to global problems will be found, which could transcend the current social and cultural barriers.

Another place we notice the Jupiter influence is in fashion,

horoscope

By HOLIDAY MATHIS

Your birthday today: You become even more like those you admire. Your growing skills put you in the running for different kinds of jobs. Jump into career changes wholeheartedly — you have every reason to be optimistic. The early success of a venture in June will be followed by hard work and then another big win in September. Gemini and Leo people adore you. Your lucky numbers are: 5, 25, 40, 1 and 18.

ARIES (March 21-April 19). Often, the closer you get to finishing a project the more difficult it seems. You will be tempted to put off for tomorrow what you can do today. Either way, you will get it done, but today you have rhythm on your side.

TAURUS (April 20-May 20). Despite the moments of self-doubt that every human experiences from time to time, you are more than competent to cope with the basic challenges of life. Keep reminding yourself that you are powerful.

GEMINI (May 21-June 21). There are a hundred ways to relate to your kin, and all of them are good as long as you come from a loving space. You'll accept someone's unusual brand of love, and

you'll contribute in unexpected ways yourself.

CANCER (June 22-July 22). Relationships take work. It feels like you're doing all the heavy lifting, but it's just that way sometimes. It's not even worth bringing up, since tomorrow things shift and you'll feel differently about the situation.

LEO (July 23-Aug. 22). Everyone has opinions, but today you'll hear too many. Know when to pull back, find a quiet place and look into yourself. Silence recharges your wisdom and renews your energy.

VIRGO (Aug. 23-Sept. 22). You like the story in which the caterpillar goes to sleep and wakes up a monarch butterfly. Go with that sleepy feeling for now. Soon, in some way, you are about to wake up.

LIBRA (Sept. 23-Oct. 23). Free your inner athlete. Regardless of how long you stick with it, playing a new sport will help you break old routines. You like to mix things up — activities, friends, rhythms — so this is just you being you.

SCORPIO (Oct. 24-Nov. 21). A bold spirit often exerts itself to the detriment of true generosity, but you are one of those rare people who combines an extraordinary ambition with a big heart. You'll make

money and use it to help people.

SAGITTARIUS (Nov. 22-Dec. 21). The fair expression on your face finds its match in your heart and mind: You find it impossible to think anything but the best about everyone you meet. Goodness hovers around you like a perfume.

CAPRICORN (Dec. 22-Jan. 19). No one knows that special loved one like you do. Lately, you've felt a certain distance, but you were wise not to read too much into it. You'll soon be closer than ever.

AQUARIUS (Jan. 20-Feb. 18). There's a fine line between being discerning and being finicky, and you have a friend who crosses it regularly. Normally, you can look the other way, but this time, his or her pickiness directly affects you. Hold your ground.

PISCES (Feb. 19-March 20). Today is a taking-a-bath-in-the-afternoon kind of day. After all, you can't always pick when your quiet time is going to be. Sometimes you just have to sneak it in there.

If you would like to write to Holiday Mathis, please go to www.creators.com and click on "Write the Author" on the Holiday Mathis page.

media

NIELSEN RATINGS

RON TOM • ABC

ABC's "Desperate Housewives" returns with Marcia Cross, Eva Longoria Parker and Felicity Huffman.

critic's picks

Chuck in charge

Prepare yourself for the third season of **"Chu**
isode marathon of reruns (4 p.m., Syfy), whic
pearances from John Larroquette, Chevy Cha
and Scott Bakula. Of course, the real stars are le
Yvonne Strahovski, maybe TV's most likable co

Keeping up with the Joneses

Jennifer Jones, who died last month at age 90,
gotten by the masses, which was probably just
fore going into virtual seclusion, she made some
memorable films, two of which are on display i
starting with 1946's **"Duel in the Sun"** (7 p.m.,
that's also sexy. That's followed by an oft-mis
1954's **"Beat the Devil"** (9:30 p.m., TCM), with
phrey Bogart.

Holidays gone,

Thursday January 7, 2010

| Morning | 6:00am | 6:30am | 7:00am | 7:3 |

which should veer into a Pisces fantasy mood, with more theatrical, dramatic styles and a special emphasis on footwear. Look for exciting beachwear and seaside resorts that appeal to our desire to escape reality.

Those born under Pisces should have many opportunities during the year. However, the key is to keep your feet on the ground. The flip side of Jupiter is that there are no limits. You can expand off the planet under a Jupiter transit, which is why the planet is often called the "Gateway to Heaven." If something is going to burst (such as an artery) or overextend or go over the top in some way, it could happen under a supposedly lucky Jupiter transit, so be aware.

Those born under Virgo may find their best opportunities working with partners this year, as Jupiter will be transiting their seventh house of relationships.

During the summer months, Jupiter dips into Aries, which should give us a preview of happenings next year. In this headstrong fire sign, Jupiter promotes pioneering ventures, start-ups, all that is new and exciting. It can also promote impatience with more conservative forces, especially in early summer, which looks like the most volatile time this year. Jupiter returns to Pisces in September for the rest of the year.

Saturn in Libra

Saturn, the planet of limitation, testing, and restriction, will be moving through Libra, the sign of its exhaltation and one of its most auspicious signs, this year. In Libra, Saturn can steady the scales of justice and promote balanced, responsible judgment. There should be much deliberation over duty, honor, and fairness, which will be ongoing for the next two years, balancing the more impulsive energy of other planets. Far-reaching new legislation and diplomatic moves are possible, perhaps resolving difficult international standoffs. As this placement works well with the humanitarian Aquarius influence of Neptune, there should be new hope of resolving conflicts. Previously, Saturn was in Libra during the early 1920s, the early 1950s, and again in the early 1980s.

Continuing Trends

Uranus and Neptune continue to do a kind of astrological dance called a "mutual reception." This is a supportive relationship where Uranus is in Pisces, the sign ruled by Neptune, while Neptune is in Aquarius, the sign ruled by Uranus. When this dance is over in 2011, it is likely that we will be living under very different political and social circumstances.

Uranus in Pisces and Aries

Uranus, known as the Great Awakener, tends to cause both upheaval and innovation in the sign it transits. This year, it is accompanied by Jupiter, as it is preparing to leave Pisces and dip its toe into Aries from June to mid-August. However, the Pisces influence will predominate, since Jupiter will be in Pisces most of the year.

During previous episodes of Uranus in Pisces, great religions and spiritual movements have come into being, most recently Mormonism and Christian Fundamentalism. In its most positive mode, Pisces promotes imagination and creativity, the art of illusion in theater and film, and the inspiration of great artists.

A water sign, Pisces is naturally associated with all things liquid—such as oceans, oil, and alcohol—and with those creatures that live in the water—fish, the fishing industry, fish habitats, and fish farming. Currently there is a great debate going on about overfishing, contamination of fish, and fish farming. The underdogs, the enslaved, and the disenfranchised should also benefit from Uranus in Pisces. Since Uranus is a disruptive influence that aims to challenge the status quo, the forces of nature that manifest now will most likely be in the Pisces area—the oceans, seas, and rivers. We have so far seen unprecedented rainy seasons, floods, mud slides, and disastrous hurricanes. Note that 2005's devastating Hurricane Katrina hit an area known for both the oil and fishing industries.

Pisces is associated with the prenatal phase of life, which is related to regenerative medicine. The controversy over embryonic stem cell research will continue to be debated, but recent developments may make the arguments moot. Petroleum issues, both in the oil-producing countries and offshore oil drilling, will come to a head. Uranus in Pisces suggests that development of new hydroelectric sources may provide the power we need to continue our current power-thirsty lifestyle.

As in previous eras, there should continue to be a flourishing of the arts. We are seeing many new artistic forms developing now, such as computer-created actors and special effects. The sky's the limit on this influence.

Those who have problems with Uranus are those who resist change, so the key is to embrace the future.

As Uranus prepares to enter Aries, an active fire sign, we should have a preview of coming influences over the summer.

Neptune in Aquarius

Neptune is a planet of imagination and creativity, but also of deception and illusion. Neptune is associated with hospitals, which have been the subject of much controversy. On the positive side, hospitals are acquiring cutting-edge technology. The atmosphere of many hospitals is already changing from the intimidating and sterile environment of the past to that of a health-promoting spa. Alternative therapies, such as massage, diet counseling, and aromatherapy, are becoming commonplace, which expresses this Neptune trend. New procedures in plastic surgery, also a Neptune glamour field, and antiaging therapies are giving the illusion of youth.

However, issues involving the expense and quality of health care, medication, and the evolving relationship between doctors, drug companies, and HMOs reflect a darker side of this trend.

Neptune is finishing up its stay in Aquarius and will begin its transit of Pisces, which it rules, in 2011. So this should be a time of transition into a much more Neptunian era, when Pisces-related issues will be of paramount importance.

Lunar Eclipses Are Movers and Shakers

Eclipses could shake up the financial markets and rock your world in 2010. The eclipses in late June and July are the ones to watch as they coincide with a close contact of Jupiter and Uranus in Aries. This is a potentially volatile time, so it would be wise to be prepared. As several recent studies have shown the stock market to be linked to the lunar cycle, track investments more carefully during this time.

New Celestial Bodies

Our solar system is getting crowded, as astronomers continue to discover new objects circling the sun. In addition to the familiar planets, there are dwarf planets, comets, cometoids, asteroids, and strange icy bodies in the Kuiper Belt beyond Neptune. A dwarf planet christened Eris, discovered in 2005, is now being observed and analyzed by astrologers. Eris was named after a goddess of discord and strife. In mythology, she was a troublemaker who made men think their opinions were right and others wrong. What an appropriate name for a planet discovered during a time of discord in the Middle East and elsewhere! Eris has a companion moon named Dysnomia for her daughter, described as a demon spirit of lawlessness. With mythological associations like these, we wonder what the effect of this mother-daughter duo will be. Once Eris's orbit is established, astrologers will track the impact of this planet on our horoscopes. Eris takes about 560 years to orbit the sun, which means its emphasis in a given astrological sign will affect several generations.

CHAPTER 2

How to Find Your Best Times This Year

It's no secret that some of the most powerful and famous people, from Julius Caesar to Queen Elizabeth I, from financier J. P. Morgan to Ronald Reagan, have consulted astrologers before they made their moves. If astrology helps the rich and famous stay on course through life's ups and downs, why not put it to work for you? Anyone can follow the planetary movements, and once you know how to interpret them, you won't need an expert to grasp the overall trends and make use of them.

For instance, when mischievous Mercury creates havoc with communications, it's time to back up your vital computer files, read between the lines of contracts, and be very patient with coworkers. When Venus passes through your sign, you're more alluring, so it's time to try out a new outfit or hairstyle, and then ask someone you'd like to know better to dinner. Venus timing can also help you charm clients with a stunning sales pitch or make an offer they won't refuse.

In this chapter you will find the tricks of astrological time management. You can find your red-letter days as well as which times to avoid. You will also learn how to make the magic of the moon work for you. Use the information in this chapter and the planet tables in this book and also the moon sign listings in your daily forecasts.

Here are the happenings to note on your agenda:

- Dates of your sun sign (high-energy period)
- The month previous to your sun sign (low-energy time)

- Dates of planets in your sign this year
- Full and new moons (Pay special attention when these fall in your sun sign!)
- Eclipses
- Moon in your sun sign every month, as well as moon in the opposite sign (listed in daily forecast)
- Mercury retrogrades
- Other retrograde periods

Your Most Proactive Time

Every birthday starts off a new cycle of solar energy for you. You should feel a new surge of vitality as the powerful sun enters your sign. This is the time when predominant energies are most favorable to you. So go for it! Start new projects, and make your big moves (especially when the new moon is in your sign, doubling your charisma). You'll get the recognition you deserve now, when everyone is attuned to your sun sign. Look in the tables in this book to see if other planets will also be passing through your sun sign at this time. Venus (love, beauty), Mars (energy, drive), and Mercury (communication, mental sharpness) reinforce the sun and give an extra boost to your life in the areas they affect. Venus will rev up your social and love life, making you seem especially attractive. Mars amplifies your energy and drive. Mercury fuels your brainpower and helps you communicate. Jupiter signals an especially lucky period of expansion.

There are two downtimes related to the sun. During the month before your birthday period, when you are winding up your annual cycle, you could be feeling especially vulnerable and depleted. So at that time get extra rest, watch your diet, and take it easy. Don't overstress yourself. Use this time to gear up for a big push when the sun enters your sign.

Another downtime is when the sun is in the sign opposite your sun sign (six months from your birthday). This is a reactive time, when the prevailing energies are very different from yours. You may feel at odds with the world. You'll have to work harder for recognition because people are not on your wavelength. However, this could be a good time to work on a team, in cooperation with others, or behind the scenes.

Be a Moon Watcher

The moon is a powerful tool to divine the mood of the moment. You can work with the moon in two ways. Plan by the sign the moon is in; plan by the phase of the moon. The sign will tell you the kind of activities that suit the moon's mood. The phase will tell you the best time to start or finish a certain activity.

Working with the phases of the moon is as easy as looking up at the night sky. During the new moon, when both the sun and moon are in the same sign, begin new ventures—especially activities that are favored by that sign. Then you'll utilize the powerful energies pulling you in the same direction. You'll be focused outward, toward action, and in a doing mode. Postpone breaking off, terminating, deliberating, or reflecting— activities that require introspection and passive work. These are better suited to a later moon phase.

Get your project under way during the first quarter. Then go public at the full moon, a time of high intensity, when feelings come out into the open. This is your time to shine—to express yourself. Be aware, however, that because pressures are being released, other people will also be letting off steam. Since confrontations are possible, take advantage of this time either to air grievances or to avoid arguments.

About three days after the full moon comes the disseminating phase, a time when the energy of the cycle begins to wind down. From the last quarter of the moon to the next new moon, it's a time to cut off unproductive relationships, do serious thinking, and focus on inward-directed activities.

You'll feel some new and full moons more strongly than others, especially when they fall in your sun sign. That full moon happens at your low-energy time of year, and is likely to be an especially stressful time in a relationship, when any hidden problems or unexpressed emotions could surface.

Full and New Moons in 2010

All dates are calculated for eastern standard time and eastern daylight time.

New Moon—January 15 in Capricorn (solar eclipse)
Full Moon—January 30 in Leo

New Moon—February 13 in Aquarius
Full Moon—February 28 in Virgo

New Moon—March 15 in Pisces
Full Moon—March 29 in Libra

New Moon—April 14 in Aries
Full Moon—April 28 in Scorpio

New Moon—May 13 in Taurus
Full Moon—May 27 in Sagittarius

New Moon—June 12 in Gemini
Full Moon—June 26 in Capricorn (lunar eclipse)

New Moon—July 11 in Cancer (solar eclipse)
Full Moon—July 25 in Aquarius

New Moon—August 9 in Leo
Full Moon—August 24 in Pisces

New Moon—September 8 in Virgo
Full Moon—September 23 in Aries

New Moon—October 7 in Libra
Full Moon—October 22 in Aries

New Moon—November 5 in Scorpio
Full Moon—November 21 in Taurus

New Moon—December 5 in Sagittarius
Full Moon—December 21 in Gemini (lunar eclipse)

Timing by the Moon's Sign

To forecast the daily emotional "weather," to determine your monthly high and low days, or to synchronize your activities with the cycles of the moon, take note of the moon's sign under your daily forecast at the end of the book. Here are some of the activities favored and the moods you are likely to encounter under each moon sign.

Moon in Aries: Get Moving

The new moon in Aries is an ideal time to start new projects. Everyone is pushy, raring to go, rather impatient, and short-tempered. Leave details and follow-up for later. Competitive sports or martial arts are great ways to let off steam. Quiet types could use some assertiveness, but it's a great day for dynamos. Be careful not to step on too many toes.

Moon in Taurus: Lay the Foundations for Success

Do solid, methodical tasks like follow-through or backup work. Make investments, buy real estate, do appraisals, or do some hard bargaining. Attend to your property. Get out in the country or spend some time in your garden. Enjoy creature comforts, music, a good dinner, or sensual lovemaking. Forget starting a diet—this is a day when you'll feel self-indulgent.

Moon in Gemini: Communicate

Talk means action today. Telephone, write letters, and fax! Make new contacts; stay in touch with steady customers. You can juggle lots of tasks today. It's a great time for mental activity of any kind. Don't try to pin people down—they too are feeling restless. Keep it light. Flirtations and socializing are good. Watch gossip—and don't give away secrets.

Moon in Cancer: Pay Attention to Loved Ones

This is a moody, sensitive, emotional time. People respond to personal attention and mothering. Stay at home, have a family dinner, or call your mother. Nostalgia, memories, and psychic powers are heightened. You'll want to hang on to people and things (don't clean out your closets now). You could have shrewd insights into what others really need and want. Pay attention to dreams, intuition, and gut reactions.

Moon in Leo: Be Confident

Everybody is in a much more confident, warm, generous mood. It's a good day to ask for a raise, show what you can do, or dress like a star. People will respond to flattery and enjoy a bit of drama and theater. You may be extravagant, treat yourself royally, and show off a bit—but don't break the bank! Be careful not to promise more than you can deliver.

Moon in Virgo: Be Practical

Do practical, down-to-earth chores. Review your budget, make repairs, or be an efficiency expert. Not a day to ask for a raise. Tend to personal care and maintenance. Have a health checkup, go on a diet, or buy vitamins or health food. Make your home spotless. Take care of details and piled-up chores. Reorganize your work and life so they run more smoothly and efficiently. Save money. Be prepared for others to be in critical, fault-finding moods.

Moon in Libra: Be Diplomatic

Attend to legal matters. Negotiate contracts. Arbitrate. Do things with your favorite partner. Socialize. Be romantic. Buy a special gift or a beautiful object. Decorate yourself or your surroundings. Buy new clothes. Throw a party. Have an elegant, romantic evening. Smooth over any ruffled feathers. Avoid confrontations. Stick to civilized discussions.

Moon in Scorpio: Solve Problems

This is a day to do things with passion. You'll have excellent concentration and focus. Try not to get too intense emotionally. Avoid sharp exchanges with loved ones. Others may tend to go to extremes, get jealous, or overreact. Great for troubleshooting, problem solving, research, scientific work—and making love. Pay attention to those psychic vibes.

Moon in Sagittarius: Sell and Motivate

A great time for travel, philosophical discussions, or setting long-range career goals. Work out, do sports, or buy athletic equipment. Others will be feeling upbeat, exuberant, and adventurous. Taking risks is favored. You may feel like gambling, betting on the horses, visiting a local casino, or buying a lottery ticket. Teaching, writing, and spiritual activities also get the green light. Relax outdoors. Take care of animals.

Moon in Capricorn: Get Organized

You can accomplish a lot now, so get on the ball! Attend to business. Issues concerning your basic responsibilities, duties, family, and elderly parents could crop up. You'll be expected to deliver on promises. Weed out the deadwood from your life. Get a dental checkup. Not a good day for gambling or taking risks.

Moon in Aquarius: Join the Group

A great day for doing things with groups—clubs, meetings, outings, politics, or parties. Campaign for your candidate. Work for a worthy cause. Deal with larger issues that affect humanity—the environment and metaphysical questions. Buy a computer or electronic gadget. Watch TV. Wear something outrageous. Try something you've never done before. Present an original idea. Don't stick to a rigid schedule; go with the flow. Take a class in meditation, mind control, or yoga.

Moon in Pisces: Be Creative

This can be a very creative day, so let your imagination work overtime. Film, theater, music, and ballet could inspire you. Spend some time resting and reflecting, reading, or writing poetry. Daydreams can also be profitable. Help those less fortunate. Lend a listening ear to someone who may be feeling blue. Don't overindulge in self-pity or escapism. People are especially vulnerable to substance abuse. Turn your thoughts to romance and someone special.

Eclipses Clear the Air

Eclipses can bring on milestones in your life, if they aspect a key point in your horoscope. In general, they shake up the status quo, bringing hidden areas out into the open. During this time, problems you've been avoiding or have brushed aside can surface to demand your attention. A good coping strategy is to accept whatever comes up as a challenge that could make a positive difference in your life. And don't forget the power of your sense of humor. If you can laugh at something, you'll never be afraid of it.

When the natural rhythms of the sun and moon are disturbed, it's best to postpone important activities. Be sure to mark eclipse days on your calendar, especially if the eclipse falls in your birth sign. This year, those born under Capricorn, Cancer, and Gemini should take special note of the feelings that arise. If your moon is in one of these signs, you may be especially affected. With lunar eclipses, some possibilities could be a break from attachments, or the healing of an illness or substance abuse that was triggered by the subconscious. The temporary event could be a healing time, when you gain perspective. During solar eclipses, when you might be in a highly subjective state, pay attention to the hidden subconscious patterns that surface, the emotional truth that is revealed at this time.

The effect of the eclipse can reverberate for some time, often months after the event. But it is especially important to stay cool and make no major moves during the period known as the shadow of the eclipse, which begins about a week before and lasts until at least three days after the eclipse. After three days, the daily rhythms should return to normal, and you can proceed with business as usual.

This Year's Eclipse Dates

January 15: Solar Eclipse in Capricorn
June 26: Lunar Eclipse in Capricorn
July 11: Solar Eclipse in Cancer
December 21: Lunar Eclipse in Gemini

Retrogrades: When the Planets Seem to Backstep

All the planets, except for the sun and moon, have times when they appear to move backward—or retrograde—as it seems from our point of view on Earth. At these times, planets do not work as they normally do. So it's best to "take a break" from that planet's energies in our life and to do some work on an inner level.

Mercury Retrograde: The Key Is in "Re"

Mercury goes into retrograde most often, and its effects can be especially irritating. When it reaches a short distance ahead of the sun several times a year, it seems to move backward from our point of view. Astrologers often compare retrograde motion to the optical illusion that occurs when we ride on a train that passes another train traveling at a different speed—the second train appears to be moving in reverse.

What this means to you is that the Mercury-ruled areas of your life—analytical thought processes, communications, scheduling—are subject to all kinds of confusion. Be prepared. Communications equipment can break down. Schedules may be changed on short notice. People are late for appointments or don't show up at all. Traffic is terrible. Major purchases malfunction, don't work out, or get delivered in the wrong color. Letters don't arrive or are delivered to the wrong address. Employees will make errors that have to be corrected later. Contracts don't work out or must be renegotiated.

Since most of us can't put our lives on "hold" during Mercury retrogrades, we should learn to tame the trickster and make it work for us. The key is in the prefix re-. This is the time to go back over things in your life, reflect on what you've done during the previous months. Now you can get deeper insights, and spot errors you've missed. So take time to review and re-evaluate what has happened. Rest and reward yourself—it's a good time to take a vacation, especially if you revisit a favorite place. Reorganize your work and finish up projects that are backed up. Clean out your desk and closets. Throw away what you can't recycle. If you must sign contracts or agreements, do so with a contingency clause that lets you reevaluate the terms later.

Postpone major purchases or commitments for the time being. Don't get married (unless you're remarrying the same person). Try not to rely on other people keeping appointments, contracts, or agreements to the letter; have several alternatives. Double-check and read between the lines. Don't buy anything connected with communications or transportation (if you must, be sure to cover yourself).

Mercury retrograding through your sun sign will intensify its effect on your life.

If Mercury was retrograde when you were born, you may be one of the lucky people who don't suffer the frustrations of this period. If so, your mind probably works in a very intuitive, insightful way.

The sign in which Mercury is retrograding can give you an idea of what's in store—as well as the sun signs that will be especially challenged.

Mercury Retrogrades in 2010

Mercury has four retrograde periods this year, since it will be retrograde as the year begins. During the retrograde periods, it will be especially important to watch all activities which involve mental processes and communication.

December 26, 2009, to January 15 in Capricorn
April 17 to May 11 in Taurus
August 20 to September 12 in Virgo
December 10 to December 30 from Capricorn to Sagittarius

Venus Retrograde: Relationships Are Affected

Retrograding Venus can cause your relationships to take a backward step, or you may feel that a key relationship is on hold. Singles may be especially lonely, yet find it difficult to connect with someone special. If you wish to make amends in an already troubled relationship, make peaceful overtures at this time. You may feel more extravagant or overindulge in shopping or sweet treats. Shopping till you drop and buying what you cannot afford are bad at this time. It's *not* a good time to redecorate—you'll hate the color of the walls later. Postpone getting a new hairstyle. It only lasts for a relatively short time this year; however, Scorpio and Libra should take special note.

Venus Retrogrades in 2010

Venus retrogrades from October 8 to November 18, from Scorpio to Libra.

Use the Power of Mars

Mars shows how and when to get where you want to go. Timing your moves with Mars on your side can give you a big push. On the other hand, pushing Mars the wrong way can guarantee that you'll run into frustrations around every corner. Your best times to forge ahead are during the weeks when Mars is traveling through your sun sign or your Mars sign (look these up in the planet tables in this book). Also consider times when Mars is in a compatible sign (fire signs with air signs, or earth signs with water signs). You'll be sure to have planetary power on your side.

Mars began a lengthy retrograde in extravagant Leo on December 20, 2009. Your patience may have been tested more than usual during last year's festivities. The Mars retrograde in Leo will last until March 10, during which time there are sure to be repercussions on the international level.

Mars Retrogrades in 2010

Mars turns retrograde in Leo on December 20, 2009, until March 10, 2010.

When Other Planets Retrograde

The slower-moving planets stay retrograde for many months at a time (Jupiter, Saturn, Neptune, Uranus, and Pluto).

When Saturn is retrograde, it's an uphill battle with self-discipline. You may not be in the mood for work. You may feel more like hanging out at the beach than getting things done.

Neptune retrograde promotes a dreamy escapism from reality, when you may feel you're in a fog (Pisces will feel this, especially).

Uranus retrograde may mean setbacks in areas where there have been sudden changes, when you may be forced to regroup or reevaluate the situation.

Pluto retrograde is a time to work on establishing proportion and balance in areas where there have been recent dramatic transformations.

When the planets move forward again, there's a shift in the atmosphere. Activities connected with each planet start moving ahead; plans that were stalled get rolling. Make a special note of those days on your calendar and proceed accordingly.

Other Retrogrades in 2010

The five slower-moving planets all go retrograde in 2010.

Jupiter retrogrades from July 23 in Aries to November 18 in Pisces.

Saturn retrogrades from January 13 in Libra to May 30 in Virgo.

Uranus retrogrades from July 5 in Aries to December 5 in Pisces.

Neptune retrogrades from May 31 to November 7 in Aquarius.

Pluto retrogrades from April 6 to September 13 in Capricorn.

CHAPTER 3

Introduction to Astrology

Astrology is a powerful tool that can help you discover and access your personal potential, understand others and interpret events in your life and the world at large. You don't have to be an expert in astrology to put it to work for you. It's easy to pick up enough basic knowledge to go beyond the realm of your sun sign into the deeper areas of this fascinating subject, which combines science, art, spirituality, and psychology. Perhaps from here you'll upgrade your knowledge with computer software that calculates charts for everyone you know in a nanosecond or join an astrology group in your city.

In this chapter, we'll introduce you to the basics of astrology. You'll be able to define a sign and figure out why astrologers say what they do about each sign. As you look at your astrological chart, you'll have a good idea of what's going on in each portion of the horoscope. Let's get started.

Know the Difference Between Signs and Constellations

Most readers know their signs, but many often confuse them with constellations. *Signs* are actually a type of celestial real estate, located on the *zodiac*, an imaginary 360-degree belt circling the earth. This belt is divided into twelve equal 30-degree portions, which are the *signs*. There's a lot of confusion about the difference between the *signs* and the *constellations* of the zodiac, patterns of stars which originally marked the twelve divisions, like signposts. Though a *sign* is named after the *constellation* that once marked the same area, the constellations are no longer in the same place relative to the earth that they were many centuries ago. Over hundreds of years, the earth's orbit has shifted, so that from our point of view here on earth, the constellations seem to have moved. However, the signs remain in place. (Most Western astrology uses the twelve-equal-part division of the zodiac, though there are some other methods of astrology that still use the constellations instead of the signs.)

Most people think of themselves in terms of their sun sign. A *sun sign* refers to the sign the sun is orbiting through at a given moment (from our point of view here on earth). For instance, if someone says, "I'm an Aries," the sun was passing through Aries when that person was born. However, there are nine other planets (plus asteroids, fixed stars, and sensitive points) that also form our total astrological personality, and some or many of these will be located in other signs. No one is completely "Aries," with all their astrological components in one sign! (Please note that, in astrology, the sun and moon are usually referred to as "planets," though of course they're not. Though there is some controversy over Pluto, it is still called a "planet" by astrologers.)

As we mentioned before, the sun signs are *places* on the zodiac. They do not *do* anything (the planets are the doers). However, they are associated with many things, depending on their location on the zodiac.

How Do We Define a Sign's Characteristics?

The definitions of the signs evolved systematically from four interrelated components: a sign's element, its quality, its polarity or sex, and its order in the progression of the zodiac. All these factors work together to tell us what the sign is like.

The system is magically mathematical: the number 12—as in the twelve signs of the zodiac—is divisible by 4, by 3, and by

2. There are four elements, three qualities, and two polarities, which follow one another in sequence around the zodiac.

The four elements (earth, air, fire, and water) are the building blocks of astrology. The use of an element to describe a sign probably dates from man's first attempts to categorize what he saw. Ancient sages believed that all things were composed of combinations of these basic elements—earth, air, fire, and water. This included the human character, which was fiery/choleric, earthy/melancholy, airy/sanguine, or watery/phlegmatic. The elements also correspond to our emotional (water), physical (earth), mental (air), and spiritual (fire) natures. The energies of each of the elements were then observed to relate to the time of year when the sun was passing through a certain segment of the zodiac.

Those born with the sun in fire signs—Aries, Leo, Sagittarius—embody the characteristics of that element. Optimism, warmth, hot tempers, enthusiasm, and "spirit" are typical of these signs. Taurus, Virgo, and Capricorn are "earthy"—more grounded, physical, materialistic, organized, and deliberate than fire sign people. Air sign people—Gemini, Libra, and Aquarius—are mentally oriented communicators. Water signs—Cancer, Scorpio, and Pisces—are emotional, sensitive, and creative.

Think of what each element does to the others: water puts out fire or evaporates under heat. Air fans the flames or blows them out. Earth smothers fire, drifts and erodes with too much wind, and becomes mud or fertile soil with water. Those are often perfect analogies for the relationships between people of different sun-sign elements. This astrochemistry was one of the first ways man described his relationships. Fortunately, no one is entirely "air" or "water." We all have a bit, or a lot, of each element in our horoscopes. It is this unique mix that defines each astrological personality.

Within each element, there are three qualities that describe types of behavior associated with the sign. Those of cardinal signs are activists, go-getters. These four signs—Aries, Cancer, Libra, and Capricorn—begin each season. Fixed signs, which happen in the middle of the season, are associated with builders and stabilizers. You'll find that Taurus, Leo, Scorpio, and Aquarius are usually gifted with concentration, stamina, and focus. Mutable signs—Gemini, Virgo, Sagittarius, and Pisces—fall at the end of each season and thus are considered catalysts for change. People born under mutable signs are flexible and adaptable.

The polarity of a sign is either its positive or negative "charge." It can be masculine, active, positive, and yang, like air or fire signs, or it can be feminine, reactive, negative, and yin, like the water and earth signs. The polarities alternate, moving energy around the zodiac like the poles of a battery.

Finally, we consider the sign's place in the order of the zodiac. This is vital to the balance of all the forces and the transmission of energy moving through the signs. You may have noticed that your sign is quite different from your neighboring sign on either side. Yet each seems to grow out of its predecessor like links in a chain and transmits a synthesis of energy gathered along the "chain" to the following sign, beginning with the fire-powered positive charge of Aries.

How the Signs Add Up

SIGN	ELEMENT	QUALITY	POLARITY	PLACE
Aries	fire	cardinal	masculine	first
Taurus	earth	fixed	feminine	second
Gemini	air	mutable	masculine	third
Cancer	water	cardinal	feminine	fourth
Leo	fire	fixed	masculine	fifth
Virgo	earth	mutable	feminine	sixth
Libra	air	cardinal	masculine	seventh
Scorpio	water	fixed	feminine	eighth
Sagittarius	fire	mutable	masculine	ninth
Capricorn	earth	cardinal	feminine	tenth
Aquarius	air	fixed	masculine	eleventh
Pisces	water	mutable	feminine	twelfth

Each Sign Has a Special Planet

Each sign has a "ruling" planet that is most compatible with its energies. Mars adds its fiery assertive characteristics to Aries. The sensual beauty and comfort-loving side of Venus rules Taurus, whereas the idealistic side of Venus rules Libra. Quick-moving Mercury rules two mutable signs, Gemini and Virgo. Its mental agility belongs to Gemini while its analytical side is best expressed in Virgo. The changeable emotional moon is associated with Cancer, while the outgoing Leo personality is ruled by the sun. Scorpio originally shared Mars, but when Pluto was discovered in the last century, its powerful magnetic energies were deemed more suitable to the intense vibrations of the fixed water sign Scorpio. Though Pluto has, as of this writing, been downgraded, it is still considered by astrologers to be a powerful force in the horoscope. Disciplined Capricorn is ruled by Saturn, and expansive Sagittarius by Jupiter. Unpredictable Aquarius is ruled by Uranus and creative, imaginative Pisces by Neptune. In a horoscope, if a planet is placed in the sign it rules, it is sure to be especially powerful.

The Layout of a Horoscope Chart

A horoscope chart is a map of the heavens at a given moment in time. It looks like a wheel with twelve spokes. In between each of the "spokes" is a section called a *house*.

Each house deals with a different area of life and is influenced by a special sign and a planet. Astrologers look at the houses to tell in what area of life an event is happening or about to happen.

The house is governed by the sign passing over the spoke (or cusp of the house) at that particular moment. Though the first house is naturally associated with Aries and Mars, it would also have an additional Capricorn influence if that sign was passing over the house cusp at the time the chart was cast. The sequence of the houses starts with the first house located at the left center spoke (or the number 9 position, if you were reading a clock). The houses are then read *counterclockwise* around the chart, with the fourth house at the bottom of the chart, the tenth house at the top or twelve o'clock position.

Where do the planets belong? Around the horoscope, planets are placed within the houses according to their location at the time of the chart. That is why it is so important to have an accurate time; with no specific time, the planets have no specific location in the houses and one cannot determine which area of life they will apply to. Since the signs move across the houses as the earth turns, planets in a house will naturally intensify the importance of that house. The house that contains the sun is naturally one of the most prominent.

The First House: Self

The sign passing over the first house at the time of your birth is known as your ascendant, or rising sign. The first house is the house of "firsts"—the first impression you make, how you initiate matters, the image you choose to project. This is where you advertise yourself, where you project your personality. Planets that fall here will intensify the way you come across to others. It is the home of Aries and the planet Mars.

The Second House: The Material You

This house is where you experience the material world, what you value. Here are your attitudes about money, possessions, and finances, as well as your earning and spending capacity. On a deeper level, this house reveals your sense of self-worth, the inner values that draw wealth in various forms. It is the natural home of Taurus and the planet Venus.

The Third House: Your Thinking Process

This house describes how you communicate with others, how you reach out to others nearby and interact with the immediate environment. It shows how your thinking process works and the way you express your thoughts. Are you articulate or tongue-tied? Can you think on your feet? This house also shows your first relationships, your experiences with brothers and sisters, as well as how you deal with people close to you, such as your neighbors or pals. It's where you take short trips, write letters, or use the telephone. It shows how your mind works in terms of left-brain logical and analytical functions. It is the home of Gemini and the planet Mercury.

The Fourth House: Your Home Life

The fourth house shows the foundation of life, the psychological underpinnings. Located at the bottom of the chart, this house shows how you are nurtured and made to feel secure—your roots! It shows your early home environment and the circumstances at the end of your life (your final "home"), as well as the place you call home now. Astrologers look here for information about the parental nurturers in your life. It is the home of Cancer and the moon.

The Fifth House: Your Self-Expression

The Leo house is where the creative potential develops. Here you express yourself and procreate, in the sense that children are outgrowths of your creative ability. But this house most represents your inner childlike self, who delights in play. If your inner security has been established by the time you reach this house, you are now free to have fun, romance, and love affairs and to give of yourself. This is also the place astrologers look for playful love affairs, flirtations, and brief romantic encounters (rather than long-term commitments). It is the home of Leo and the sun.

The Sixth House: Care and Maintenance

The sixth house has been called the "care and maintenance" department. This house shows how you take care of your body and organize yourself to perform efficiently in the world. Here is where you get things done, where you look after others and fulfill service duties, such as taking care of pets. Here is what you do to survive on a day-to-day basis. The sixth house demands order in your life; otherwise there would be chaos. The house is your "job" (as opposed to your career, which is the domain of the tenth house), your diet, and your health and fitness regimens. It is the home of Virgo and the planet Mercury.

The Seventh House: Your Relationships

This house shows your attitude toward your partners and those with whom you enter commitments, contracts, or agreements. Here is the way you relate to others, as well as your close, intimate, one-on-one relationships (including open enemies—those you "face off" with). Open hostilities, lawsuits, divorces, and marriages happen here. If the first house represents the "I," the seventh or opposite house is the "not I"—the complementary partner you attract by the way you come across. If you are having trouble with partnerships, consider what you are attracting by the energies of your first and seventh house. It is the home of Libra and the planet Venus.

The Eighth House: Your Power House

The eighth house refers to how you merge with something or someone, and how you handle power and control. This is one of the most mysterious and powerful houses, where your energy transforms itself from "I" to "we." As you give up power and control by uniting with something or someone, two kinds of energies merge and become something greater, leading to a regeneration of the self on a higher level. Here are your attitudes toward sex, shared resources, and taxes (what you share with the government). Because this house involves what belongs to others, you face issues of control and power struggles, or undergo a deep psychological transformation as you bond with another. Here you transcend yourself through dreams, drugs, and occult or psychic experiences that reflect the collective unconscious. It is the home of Scorpio and the planet Pluto.

The Ninth House: Your Worldview

The ninth house shows your search for wisdom and higher knowledge: your belief system. As the third house represents the "lower mind," its opposite on the wheel, the ninth house, is the "higher mind," the abstract, intuitive, spiritual mind that asks "big" questions, like "Why we are here?" After the third house has explored what was close at hand, the ninth stretches out to broaden you mentally with higher education and travel. Here you stretch spiritually with religious activity. Since you are concerned with how everything is related, you tend to push boundaries and take risks. Here is where you express your ideas in a book or thesis, where you pontificate, philosophize, or preach. It is the home of Sagittarius and the planet Jupiter.

The Tenth House: Your Public Life

The tenth house is associated with your public life and high-profile activities. Located directly overhead at the "high noon" position on the horoscope wheel, this is the most "visible" house in the chart, the one where the world sees you. It deals with your career (but not your routine "job") and your reputation. Here is where you go public, take on responsibilities (as opposed to the fourth house, where you stay home). This will affect the career you choose and your "public relations." This house is also associated with your father figure or the main authority figure in your life. It is the home of Capricorn and the planet Saturn.

The Eleventh House: Your Social Concerns

The eleventh house is where you extend yourself to a group, a goal, or a belief system. This house is where you define what you really want: the kinds of friends you have, your political affiliations, and the kind of groups you identify with as an equal. Here is where you become concerned with "what other people think" or where you rebel against social conventions. It's where you become a socially conscious humanitarian or a partying social butterfly. It's where you look to others to stimulate you and discover your kinship to the rest of humanity. The sign on this house can help you understand what you gain and lose from friendships. It is the home of Aquarius and the planet Uranus.

The Twelfth House:
Where You Become Selfless

Old-fashioned astrologers used to put a rather negative spin on this house, calling it the "house of self-undoing." When we "undo ourselves," we surrender control, boundaries, limits, and rules. The twelfth house is where the boundaries between yourself and others become blurred and you become selfless. But instead of being self-undoing, the twelfth house can be a place of great creativity and talent. It is the place where you can tap into the collective unconscious, where your imagination is limitless.

In your trip around the zodiac, you've gone from the "I" of self-assertion in the first house to the final house, which symbolizes the dissolution that happens before rebirth. The twelfth house is where accumulated experiences are processed in the unconscious. Spiritually oriented astrologers look to this house for evidence of past lives and karma. Places where we go for solitude or to do spiritual or reparatory work belong here, such as retreats, religious institutions, or hospitals. Here is also where we withdraw from society voluntarily or involuntarily, and where we are put in prison because of antisocial activity. Selfless giving through charitable acts is part of this house, as is helpless receiving or dependence on charity.

In your daily life, the twelfth house reveals your deepest intimacies, your best-kept secrets, especially those you hide from yourself and repress deep in the unconscious. It is where we surrender a sense of a separate self to a deep feeling of wholeness, such as selfless service in religion or any activity that involves merging with the greater whole. Many sports stars have important planets in the twelfth house, which enable them to play in the zone, finding an inner, almost mystical, strength that transcends their limits. The twelfth house is the home of Pisces and the planet Neptune.

Which Are the Most Powerful Houses?

Houses are stronger or weaker depending on how many planets are inhabiting them. If there are many planets in a given house, it follows that the activities of that house will be especially important in your life. If the planet that rules the house is also located there, this too adds power to the house. The most powerful houses are the first, fourth, seventh, and tenth. These are the houses on "the angles" of a horoscope.

CHAPTER 4

The Moon: Your Inner Light

In some astrology-conscious lands, the moon is given as much importance in a horoscope as the sun. Astrologers often refer to these two bodies as the "lights," an appropriate description, since the sun and moon are not planets, but a star and a satellite. But it is also true that these two bodies shed the most "light" on a horoscope reading.

As the sun shines *out* in a horoscope, revealing the personality, the moon shines *in*. The sign the moon was transiting at the time of your birth reveals much about the inner you, secrets like what you really care about, what makes you feel comfortable and secure. It represents the receptive, reflective, female, nurturing self. It also reflects the one who nurtured you, the mother or mother figure in your chart. In a man's chart, the moon position describes his receptive, emotional, yin side, as well as the woman in his life who will have the deepest effect, usually his mother. (Venus reveals the kind of woman who will attract him physically.)

The moon is more at home in some signs than in others. It rules maternal Cancer and is exalted in Taurus—both comforting, home-loving signs where the natural emotional energies of the moon are easily and productively expressed. But when the moon is in the opposite signs—Capricorn and Scorpio—it leaves the comfortable nest and deals with emotional issues of power and achievement in the outside world. If you were born with the moon in one of these signs, you may find your emotional role in life more challenging.

To determine your moon sign, it is worthwhile to have an accurate horoscope cast, either by an astrologer, a computer program, or one of the online astrology sites that offer free charts. Since detailed moon tables are too extensive for this book, check through the following listing to find the moon sign that feels most familiar.

Moon in Aries

This placement makes you both independent and ardent. You are an idealist, and you tend to fall in and out of love easily. You love a challenge but could cool once your quarry is captured. Your emotional reactions are fast and fiery, quickly expressed and quickly forgotten. You may not think before expressing your feelings. It's not easy to hide how you feel. Channeling all your emotional energy could be one of your big challenges.

Celebrity example: Angelina Jolie

Moon in Taurus

You are a sentimental soul who is very fond of the good life and gravitates toward solid, secure relationships. You like displays of affection and creature comforts—all the tangible trappings of a cozy, safe, calm atmosphere. You are sensual and steady emotionally, but very stubborn, possessive, and determined. You can't be pushed and tend to dislike changes. You should make an effort to broaden your horizons and to take a risk sometimes. You may become very attached to your home turf, your garden, and your possessions. You may also be a collector of objects that are meaningful to you.

Celebrity example: Prince Charles

Moon in Gemini

You crave mental stimulation and variety in life, which you usually get via a varied social life, the excitement of flirtation, or multiple professional involvements. You may marry more than once and have a rather chaotic emotional life due to your difficulty with commitment and settling down, as well as your need to be constantly on the go. (Be sure to find a partner who is as outgoing as you are.) You will have to learn at some point to focus your energies because you tend to be somewhat fragmented—to do two things at once, to have two homes, or even to have two lovers. If you can find a creative way to express your many-faceted nature, you'll be ahead of the game.

Celebrity example: Jim Carrey

Moon in Cancer

This is the most powerful lunar position, which is sure to make a deep imprint on your character. Your needs are very much associated with your reaction to the needs of others. You are very sensitive, caring, and self-protective, though some of you may mask this with a hard shell, like the moon-sensitive crab. This placement also gives an excellent memory, keen intuition, and an uncanny ability to perceive the needs of others. All of the lunar phases will affect you, especially full moons and eclipses, so you would do well to mark them on your calendar. Because you're happiest at home, you may work at home or turn your office into a second home, where you can nurture and comfort people. (You may tend to mother the world.) With natural psychic, intuitive ability, you might be drawn to occult work in some way. Or you may get professionally involved with providing food and shelter to others.

Celebrity example: Tom Cruise

Moon in Leo

This warm, passionate moon takes everything to heart. You are attracted to all that is noble, generous, and aristocratic in life (and you may be a bit of a snob). You have an innate ability to take command emotionally, but you do need strong support, loyalty, and loud applause from those you love. You are possessive of your loved ones and your turf and will roar if anyone threatens to take over your territory.

Celebrity example: Paul McCartney

Moon in Virgo

You are rather cool until you decide if others measure up. But once someone or something meets your high standards, you hold up your end of the arrangement perfectly. You may, in fact, drive yourself too hard to attain some notion of perfection. Try to be a bit easier on yourself and others. Don't always act the censor! You love to be the teacher; you are drawn to situations where you can change others for the better, but sometimes you must learn to accept others for what they are—enjoy what you have!

Celebrity example: John F. Kennedy

Moon in Libra

Like other air-sign moons, you think before you feel. Therefore, you may not immediately recognize the emotional needs of others. However, you are relationship-oriented and may find it difficult to be alone or to do things alone. After you have learned emotional balance by leaning on yourself first, you can have excellent partnerships. It is best for you to avoid extremes, which set your scales swinging and can make your love life precarious. You thrive in a rather conservative, traditional, romantic relationship, where you receive attention and flattery—but not possessiveness—from your partner. You'll be your most charming in an elegant, harmonious atmosphere.

Celebrity example: Leonardo DiCaprio

Moon in Scorpio

This is a moon that enjoys and responds to intense, passionate feelings. You may go to extremes and have a very dramatic emotional life, full of ardor, suspicion, jealousy, and obsession. It would be much healthier to channel your need for power and control into meaningful work. This is a good position for anyone in the fields of medicine, police work, research, the occult, psychoanalysis, or intuitive work, because life-and-death situations don't faze you. However, you do take personal disappointments very hard.

Celebrity example: Elizabeth Taylor

Moon in Sagittarius

You take life's ups and downs with good humor and the proverbial grain of salt. You'll love 'em and leave 'em or take off on a great adventure at a moment's notice. "Born free" could be your slogan. Attracted by the exotic, you have mental and physical wanderlust. You may be too much in search of new mental and spiritual stimulation to ever settle down.

Celebrity example: Donald Trump

Moon in Capricorn

Are you ever accused of being too cool and calculating? You have an earthy side, but you take prestige and position very seriously. Your strong drive to succeed extends to your romantic life, where you will be devoted to improving your lifestyle and rising to the top. A structured situation where you can advance methodically makes you feel wonderfully secure. You may be attracted to someone older or very much younger or from a different social world. It may be difficult to look at the lighter side of emotional relationships. Though this moon is placed in the sign to your detriment, the good news is that you tend to be very dutiful and responsible to those you care for.

Celebrity example: Brad Pitt

Moon in Aquarius

You are a people collector with many friends of all backgrounds. You are happiest surrounded by people, and you may feel uneasy when left alone. Though you usually stay friends with lovers, intense emotions and demanding one-on-one relationships turn you off. You don't like anything to be too rigid or scheduled. Though tolerant and understanding, you can be emotionally unpredictable; you may opt for an unconventional love life. With plenty of space, you will be able to sustain relationships with liberal, freedom-loving types.

Celebrity example: Princess Diana

Moon in Pisces

You are very responsive and empathetic to others, especially if they have problems or are the underdog. (Be on guard against attracting too many people with sob stories.) You'll be happiest if you can express your creative imagination in the arts or in the spiritual or healing professions. Because you may tend to escape in fantasies or overreact to the moods of others, you need an emotional anchor to help you keep a firm foothold in reality. Steer clear of too much escapism (especially in alcohol) or reclusiveness. Places near water soothe your moods. Working in a field that gives you emotional variety will also help you be productive.

Celebrity example: Elvis Presley

CHAPTER 5

The Planets: The Power of Ten

If you know a person's sun sign, you can learn some very useful generic information, but when you know the placement of all ten planets (eight planets plus the sun and moon), you've got a much more accurate profile of the person's character. Then the subject of the horoscope becomes a unique individual, as well as a member of a certain sun sign. You'll discover what makes him angry (Mars), pleased (Venus), or fearful (Saturn).

The planets are the doers of the horoscope, each representing a basic force in life. The sign and house where the planet is located indicate how and where its force will operate. For a moment, think of the horoscope as real estate. Prime property is close to the rising sign or at the top of the chart. If two or more planets are grouped together in one sign, they usually operate like a team, playing off each other, rather than expressing their energy singularly. But a loner, a planet that stands far away from the others, is usually outstanding and often calls the shots.

The sign of a planet also has a powerful influence. In some signs, the planet's energies are very much at home and can easily express themselves. In others, the planet has to work harder and is slightly out of sorts. The sign that most corresponds to the planet's energies is said to be ruled by that planet and obviously is the best place for that planet to be. The next best place is a sign where it is exalted, or especially harmonious. On the other hand, there are places in the horoscope where a planet has to stretch itself to play its role, such as the sign opposite a planet's rulership, which embodies the opposite area of life, and the sign opposite its exaltation. However, a planet that must work harder can also be more complete, because it must grow to meet the challenges of living in a more difficult sign. Like world leaders who've had to struggle for greatness, this planet may actually develop strength and character.

Here's a list of the best places for each planet to be. Note that, as new planets were discovered in the last century, they replaced the traditional rulers of signs which best complemented their energies.

ARIES—Mars
TAURUS—Venus, in its most sensual form
GEMINI—Mercury, in its communicative role
CANCER—the moon
LEO—the sun
VIRGO—also Mercury, this time in its more critical capacity
LIBRA—also Venus, in its more aesthetic, judgmental form
SCORPIO—Pluto, co-ruled by Mars
SAGITTARIUS—Jupiter
CAPRICORN—Saturn
AQUARIUS—Uranus, replacing Saturn, its original ruler
PISCES—Neptune, replacing Jupiter, its original ruler

Those who have many planets in exalted signs are lucky indeed, for here is where the planet can accomplish the most and be its most influential and creative.

SUN—exalted in Aries, where its energy creates action
MOON—exalted in Taurus, where instincts and reactions operate on a highly creative level
MERCURY—exalted in Aquarius, where it can reach analytical heights
VENUS—exalted in Pisces, a sign whose sensitivity encourages love and creativity
MARS—exalted in Capricorn, a sign that puts energy to work productively
JUPITER—exalted in Cancer, where it encourages nurturing and growth
SATURN—at home in Libra, where it steadies the scales of justice and promotes balanced, responsible judgment

URANUS—powerful in Scorpio, where it promotes transformation

NEPTUNE—especially favored in Cancer, where it gains the security to transcend to a higher state

PLUTO—exalted in Pisces, where it dissolves the old cycle, to make way for transition to the new

The Personal Planets: Mercury, Venus, and Mars

These planets work in your immediate personal life.

Mercury affects how you communicate and how your mental processes work. Are you a quick study who grasps information rapidly, or do you learn more slowly and thoroughly? How is your concentration? Can you express yourself easily? Are you a good writer? All these questions can be answered by your Mercury placement.

Venus shows what you react to. What turns you on? What appeals to you aesthetically? Are you charming to others? Are you attractive to look at? Your taste, your refinement, your sense of balance and proportion are all Venus-ruled.

Mars is your outgoing energy, your drive and ambition. Do you reach out for new adventures? Are you assertive? Are you motivated? Self-confident? Hot-tempered? How you channel your energy and drive is revealed by your Mars placement.

Mercury Shows How Your Mind Works

Since Mercury never travels far from the sun, read Mercury in your sun sign, and then the signs preceding and following it. Then decide which reflects the way you think.

Mercury in Aries

Your mind is very active and assertive. It approaches a plan aggressively. You never hesitate to say what you think, never shy away from a battle. In fact, you may relish a verbal confrontation. Tact is not your strong point, so you may have to learn not to trip over your tongue.

Mercury in Taurus

This is a much more cautious Mercury. Though you may be a slow learner, you have good concentration and mental stamina. You want to make your ideas really happen. You'll attack a problem methodically and consider every angle thoroughly, never jumping to conclusions. You'll stick with a subject until you master it.

Mercury in Gemini

You are a wonderful communicator with great facility for expressing yourself both verbally and in writing. You love gathering all kinds of information. You probably finish other people's sentences and express yourself with eloquent hand gestures. You can talk to anybody anytime and probably have phone and E-mail bills to prove it. You read anything from sci-fi to Shakespeare and might need an extra room just for your book collection. Though you learn fast, you may lack focus and discipline. Watch a tendency to jump from subject to subject.

Mercury in Cancer

You rely on intuition more than logic. Your mental processes are usually colored by your emotions, so you may seem shy or hesitant to voice your opinions. However, this placement gives you the advantage of great imagination and empathy in the way you communicate with others.

Mercury in Leo

You are enthusiastic and very dramatic in the way you express yourself. You like to hold the attention of groups and could be a great public speaker. Your mind thinks big, so you'd prefer to deal with the overall picture rather than with the details.

Mercury in Virgo

This is one of the best places for Mercury. It should give you critical ability, attention to details, and thorough analysis. Your mind focuses on the practical side of things. This type of thinking is very well suited to being a teacher or editor.

Mercury in Libra

You're either a born diplomat who smoothes over ruffled feathers or a talented debater. Many lawyers have this placement. However, since you're forever weighing the pros and cons of a situation, you may vacillate when making decisions.

Mercury in Scorpio

This is an investigative mind that stops at nothing to get the answers. You may have a sarcastic, stinging wit, a gift for the cutting remark. There's always a grain of truth to your verbal sallies, thanks to your penetrating insight.

Mercury in Sagittarius

You are a super salesman with a tendency to expound. Though you are very broad-minded, you can be dogmatic when it comes to telling others what's good for them. You won't hesitate to tell the truth as you see it, so watch a tendency toward tactlessness. On the plus side, you have a great sense of humor. This position of Mercury is often considered by astrologers to be at a disadvantage because Sagittarius opposes Gemini, the sign Mercury rules, and squares off with Virgo, another Mercury-ruled sign. What often happens is that Mercury in Sagittarius oversteps its bounds and loses sight of the facts in a situation. Do a reality check before making promises that you may not be able to deliver.

Mercury in Capricorn

This placement endows good mental discipline. You have a love of learning and a very orderly approach to your subjects. You will patiently plod through the facts and figures until you have mastered the tasks. You grasp structured situations easily, but may be short on creativity.

Mercury in Aquarius

An independent, original thinker, you'll have more cutting-edge ideas than the average person. You'll be quick to check out any unusual opportunities. Your opinions are so well-researched and grounded that once your mind is made up, it is difficult to change.

Mercury in Pisces

You have the psychic intuitive mind of a natural poet. Learn to make use of your creative imagination. You may think in terms of helping others, but check a tendency to be vague and forgetful of details.

Venus Is the Popularity Planet

Venus tells how you relate to others and to your environment. It shows where you receive pleasure and what you love to do. Find your Venus placement on the chart in this book by looking for the year of your birth in the left-hand column. Then follow the line of that year across the page until you reach the time period of your birthday. The sign heading that column will be your Venus. If you were born on a day when Venus was changing signs, check the signs preceding or following that day to determine if that feels more like your Venus nature.

Venus in Aries

You can't stand to be bored, confined, or ordered around. But a good challenge, maybe even a rousing row, turns you on. Confess—don't you pick a fight now and then just to get someone stirred up? You're attracted by the chase, not the catch, which could cause some problems in your love life, if the object of your affection becomes too attainable. You like to wear red and can spot a trend before anyone else.

Venus in Taurus

All your senses work in high gear. You love to be surrounded by glorious tastes, smells, textures, sounds, and visuals—austerity is not for you. Neither is being rushed. You like time to enjoy your pleasures. Soothing surroundings with plenty of creature comforts are your cup of tea. You like to feel secure in your nest, with no sudden jolts or surprises. You like familiar objects—in fact, you may hate to let anything or anyone go.

Venus in Gemini

You are a lively, sparkling personality who thrives in a situation that affords a constant variety and a frequent change of scenery. A varied social life is important to you, with plenty of mental stimulation and a chance to engage in some light flirtation. Commitment may be difficult, because playing the field is so much fun.

Venus in Cancer

An atmosphere where you feel protected, coddled, and mothered is best for you. You love to be surrounded by children in a cozy, homelike situation. You are attracted to those who are tender and nurturing, who make you feel secure and well provided for. You may be quite secretive about your emotional life or attracted to clandestine relationships.

Venus in Leo

First-class attention in large doses turns you on, and so does the glitter of real gold and the flash of mirrors. You like to feel like a star at all times, surrounded by your admiring audience. The side effect is that you may be attracted to flatterers and tinsel, while the real gold requires some digging.

Venus in Virgo

Everything neatly in its place? On the surface, you are attracted to an atmosphere where everything is in perfect order, but underneath are some basic, earthy urges. You are attracted to those who appeal to your need to teach, be of service, or play out a Pygmalion fantasy. You are at your best when you are busy doing something useful.

Venus in Libra

Elegance and harmony are your key words. You can't abide an atmosphere of contention. Your taste tends toward the classic, with light harmonies of color—nothing clashing, trendy, or outrageous. You love doing things with a partner and should be careful to pick one who is decisive, but patient enough to let you weigh the pros and cons. And steer clear of argumentative types.

Venus in Scorpio

Mysteries intrigue you—in fact, anything that is too open and aboveboard is a bit of a bore. You surely have a stack of whodunits by the bed, along with an erotic magazine or two. You like to solve puzzles. You may also be fascinated with the occult, crime, or scientific research. Intense, all-or-nothing situations add spice to your life, and you love to ferret out the secrets of others. But you could get burned by your flair for living dangerously. The color black, spicy food, dark wood furniture, and heady perfume put you in the right mood.

Venus in Sagittarius

If you are not actually a world traveler, your surroundings are sure to reflect your love of faraway places. You like a casual outdoor atmosphere and a dog or two to pet. There should be plenty of room for athletic equipment and suitcases. You're attracted to kindred souls who love to travel and who share your freedom-loving philosophy of life. Athletics and spiritual or New Age pursuits could be other interests.

Venus in Capricorn

No fly-by-night relationships for you! You want substance in life, and you are attracted to whatever will help you get where you are going. Status objects turn you on. And so do those who have a serious, responsible, businesslike approach, or who remind you of a beloved parent. It is characteristic of this placement to be attracted to someone of a different generation. Antiques, traditional clothing, and dignified behavior are becoming to you.

Venus in Aquarius

This Venus wants to make friends, to be "cool." You like to be in a group, particularly one pushing a worthy cause. You feel quite at home surrounded by people, and could even court fame, yet all the while, you tend to remain detached from intense commitment. Original ideas and unpredictable people fascinate you. You prefer spontaneity and delightful surprises, rather than a well-planned schedule of events.

Venus in Pisces

This Venus loves to give of yourself, and you find plenty of takers. Stray animals and people appeal to your heart and your pocketbook, but be careful to look at their motives realistically once in a while. You are extremely vulnerable to sob stories of all kinds. Fantasy, the arts (especially film, dance, and theater), and psychic or spiritual activities also speak to you.

Mars: The Action Hero

Mars is the mover and shaker in your life. It shows how you pursue your goals, whether you have energy to burn or proceed in a slow, steady pace. It will also show how you get angry. Do you explode, or do a slow burn, or hold everything inside and then get revenge later?

To find your Mars, turn to the chart on pages 82–94. Then find your birth year in the left-hand column and find the line headed by the month of your birth. There you will find an abbreviation of your Mars sign. If the description of your Mars sign doesn't ring true, read the description of the signs preceding and following it. You might have been born on a day when Mars was changing signs, in which case your Mars might fall into the adjacent sign.

Mars in Aries

In the sign it rules, Mars shows its brilliant fiery nature. You have an explosive temper and can be quite impatient. On the other hand, you have tremendous courage, energy, and drive. You'll let nothing stand in your way as you race to be first! Obstacles are met head-on and broken through by force. However, problems that require patience and persistence to solve can have you exploding in rage. You're a great starter, but not necessarily around for the finish.

Mars in Taurus

Slow, steady, concentrated energy gives you the power to last until the finish line. You've great stamina, and you never give up. Your tactic is to wear away obstacles with your persistence. Often you come out a winner because you've had the patience to hang in there. When angered, you do a slow burn.

Mars in Gemini

You can't sit still for long. This Mars craves variety. You often have two or more things going on at once—it's all an amusing game to you. Your life can get very complicated, but that only adds spice and stimulation. What drives you into a nervous, hyper state? Boredom, sameness, routine, and confinement. You can do wonderful things with your hands, and you have a way with words.

Mars in Cancer

You rarely attack head-on. Instead, you'll keep things to yourself, make plans in secret, and always cover your actions. This might be interpreted by some as manipulative, but you are only being self-protective. You get furious when anyone knows too much about you. But you do like to know all about others. Your mothering and feeding instincts can be put to good use, if you work in the food, hotel, or child-care-related businesses. You may have to overcome your fragile sense of security, which prompts you not to take risks and to get physically upset when criticized. Don't take things so personally!

Mars in Leo

You have a very dominant personality that takes center stage—modesty is not one of your traits, nor is taking a back seat. You prefer giving the orders and have been known to make a dramatic scene if they are not obeyed. Properly used, this Mars confers leadership ability, endurance, and courage.

Mars in Virgo

You are the fault-finder of the zodiac, who notices every detail. Mistakes of any kind make you very nervous. You may worry, even if everything is going smoothly. You may not express your anger directly, but you sure can nag. You have definite likes and dislikes, and you are sure you can do the job better than anyone else. You are certainly more industrious and detail-oriented than other signs. Your Mars energy is often most positively expressed in some kind of teaching role.

Mars in Libra

This Mars will have a passion for beauty, justice, and art. Generally, you will avoid confrontations at all costs. You prefer to spend your energy finding diplomatic solutions or weighing pros and cons. Your other techniques are passive aggression or exercising your well-known charm to get people to do what you want.

Mars in Scorpio

This is a powerful placement, so intense that it demands careful channeling into worthwhile activities. Otherwise, you could become obsessed with your sexuality or might use your need for power and control to manipulate others. You are strong-willed, shrewd, and very private about your affairs, and you'll usually have a secret agenda behind your actions. Your great stamina, focus, and discipline would be excellent assets for careers in the military or medical fields, especially research or surgery. When angry, you don't get mad—you get even!

Mars in Sagittarius

This expansive Mars often propels people into sales, travel, athletics or philosophy. Your energies function well when you are on the move. You have a hot temper and are inclined to say what you think before you consider the consequences. You shoot for high goals—and talk endlessly about them—but you may be weak on groundwork. This Mars needs a solid foundation. Watch a tendency to take unnecessary risks.

Mars in Capricorn

This is an ambitious Mars with an excellent sense of timing. You have an eye for those who can be of use to you, and you may dismiss people ruthlessly when you're angry. But you drive yourself hard and deliver full value. This is a good placement for an executive. You'll aim for status and a high material position in life, and keep climbing despite the odds. A great Mars to have!

Mars in Aquarius

This is the most rebellious Mars. You seem to have a drive to assert yourself against the status quo. You may enjoy provoking people, shocking them out of traditional views. Or this placement could express itself in an offbeat sex life. Somehow you often find yourself in unconventional situations. You enjoy being a leader of an active group, which pursues forward-looking studies, politics, or goals.

Mars in Pisces

This Mars is a good actor who knows just how to appeal to the sympathies of others. You create and project wonderful fantasies or use your sensitive antennae to crusade for those less fortunate. You get what you want through creating a veil of illusion and glamour. This is a good Mars for someone in the creative and imaginative fields—a dancer, a performer, a photographer, or an actor. Many famous film stars have this placement. Watch a tendency to manipulate by making others feel sorry for you.

Jupiter Is the Optimist

This big, bright, swirling mass of gases is associated with abundance, prosperity, and the kind of windfall you get without too much hard work. You're optimistic under Jupiter's influence, when anything seems possible. You'll travel, expand your mind with higher education, and publish to share your knowledge widely. On the other hand, Jupiter's influence is neither discriminating nor disciplined. It represents the principle of growth without judgment. Therefore, if not kept in check, it could result in extravagance, weight gain, laziness, and carelessness.

Be sure to look up your Jupiter in the tables in this book. When the current position of Jupiter is favorable, you may get that lucky break. This is a great time to try new things, take risks, travel, or get more education. Opportunities seem to open up easily, so take advantage of them.

Once a year, Jupiter changes signs. That means you are due for an expansive time every twelve years, when Jupiter travels through your sun sign. You'll also have periods every four years when Jupiter is in the same element as your sun sign.

Jupiter in Aries

You are the soul of enthusiasm and optimism. Your luckiest times are when you are getting started on an exciting project or selling an ideal that you really believe in. You may have to watch a tendency to be arrogant with those who do not share your enthusiasm. You follow your impulses, often ignoring budget or other commonsense limitations. To produce real, solid benefits, you'll need patience and the will to follow through wherever this Jupiter falls in your horoscope.

Jupiter in Taurus

You'll spend money on beautiful material things, especially those that come from nature—items made of rare woods, natural fabrics, or precious gems, for instance. You can't have too much comfort or too many sensual pleasures. Watch a tendency to overindulge in good food, or to overpamper yourself with nothing but the best. Spartan living is not for you! You may be especially lucky in matters of real estate.

Jupiter in Gemini

You are the great talker of the zodiac, and you may be a great writer too. But restlessness could be your weak point. You jump around and talk too much; you could be a jack-of-all-trades. Keeping a secret is especially difficult, so you'll also have to watch a tendency to spill the beans. Since you love to be at the center of a beehive of activity, you'll have a vibrant social life. Your best opportunities will come through your talent for language: speaking, writing, communicating, and selling.

Jupiter in Cancer

You are luckiest in situations where you can find emotional closeness or deal with basic security needs, such as food, nurturing, or shelter. You may be a great collector, and you may simply love to accumulate things—you are the one who stashes things away for a rainy day. You probably have a very good memory and love children—in fact, you may have many children to care for. The food, hotel, child-care, and shipping businesses hold good opportunities for you.

Jupiter in Leo

You are a natural showman who loves to live in a larger-than-life way. Yours is a personality full of color that always finds its way into the limelight. You can't have too much attention. Showbiz is a natural place for you, and so is any area where you can play to a crowd. Exercising your flair for drama, your natural playfulness, and your romantic nature brings you good fortune. But watch a tendency to be overextravagant or to monopolize center stage.

Jupiter in Virgo

You actually love those minute details others find boring. To you, they make all the difference between the perfect and the ordinary. You are the fine craftsman who spots every flaw. You expand your awareness by finding the most efficient methods and by being of service to others. Many will be drawn to medical or teaching fields. You'll also have luck in publishing, crafts, nutrition, and service professions. Watch out for a tendency to overwork.

Jupiter in Libra

This is an other-directed Jupiter that develops best with a partner, for the stimulation of others helps you grow. You are also most comfortable in harmonious, beautiful situations, and you work well with artistic people. You have a great sense of fair play and an ability to evaluate the pros and cons of a situation. You usually prefer to play the role of diplomat rather than that of adversary.

Jupiter in Scorpio

You love the feeling of power and control, of taking things to their limit. You can't resist a mystery, and your shrewd, penetrating mind sees right through to the heart of most situations and people. You have luck in work that provides for solutions to matters of life and death. You may be drawn to undercover work, behind-the-scenes intrigue, psychotherapy, the occult, and sex-related ventures. Your challenge will be to develop a sense of moderation and tolerance for other beliefs. You may have luck in handling other people's money—insurance, taxes, and inheritance can bring you a windfall.

Jupiter in Sagittarius

Independent, outgoing, and idealistic, you'll shoot for the stars. This Jupiter compels you to travel far and wide, both physically and mentally, via higher education. You may have luck while traveling in an exotic place. You also have luck with outdoor ventures, exercise, and animals, particularly horses. Since you tend to be very open about your opinions, watch a tendency to be tactless and to exaggerate. Instead, use your wonderful sense of humor to make your point.

Jupiter in Capricorn

Jupiter is much more restrained in Capricorn, the sign of rules and authority. Here, Jupiter can make you overwork and heighten any ambition or sense of duty you may have. You'll expand in areas that advance your position, putting you higher up the social or corporate ladder. You are lucky working within the establishment in a very structured situation, where you can show off your ability to organize and reap rewards for your hard work.

Jupiter in Aquarius

This is another freedom-loving Jupiter, with great tolerance and originality. You are at your best when you are working for a humanitarian cause and in the company of many supporters. This is a good Jupiter for a political career. You'll relate to all kinds of people on all social levels. You have an abundance of original ideas, but you are best off away from routine and any situation that imposes rigid rules. You need mental stimulation!

Jupiter in Pisces

You are a giver whose feelings and pocketbook are easily touched by others, so choose your companions with care. You could be the original sucker for a hard-luck story. Better find a worthy hospital or charity to appreciate your selfless support. You have a great creative imagination and may attract good fortune in fields related to oil, perfume, pharmaceuticals, petroleum, dance, footwear, and alcohol. But beware not to overindulge in alcohol—focus on a creative outlet instead.

Saturn Puts on the Brakes

Jupiter speeds you up with lucky breaks, and then along comes Saturn to slow you down with the disciplinary brakes. It is the planet that can help you achieve lasting goals. Saturn has unfairly been called a malefic planet, one of the bad guys of the zodiac. On the contrary, Saturn is one of our best friends—the kind who tells you what you need to hear, even if it's not good news. Under a Saturn transit, we grow up, take responsibility for our lives, and emerge from whatever test this planet has in store as far wiser, more capable, and mature human beings. After all, it is when we are under pressure that we grow stronger.

When Saturn hits a critical point in your horoscope, you can count on an experience that will make you slow up, pull back, and reexamine your life. It is a call to eliminate what is not working and to shape up. By the end of its twenty-eight-year trip around the zodiac, Saturn will have tested you in all areas of your life. The major tests happen in seven-year cycles, when Saturn passes over the angles of your chart—your rising sign, the top of your chart or midheaven, your descendant, and the nadir or bottom of your chart. This is when the real life-changing experiences happen. But you are also in for a testing period whenever Saturn passes a planet in your chart or stresses that planet from a distance. Therefore, it is useful to check your planetary positions with the timetable of Saturn to prepare in advance, or at least to brace yourself.

When Saturn returns to its location at the time of your birth, at approximately age twenty-eight, you'll have your first Saturn return. At this time, a person usually takes stock or settles down to find his mission in life and assumes full adult duties and responsibilities.

Another way Saturn helps us is to reveal the karmic lessons from previous lives and give us the chance to overcome them. So look at Saturn's challenges as much-needed opportunities for self-improvement. Under a Jupiter influence, you'll have more fun, but Saturn gives you solid, long-lasting results.

Look up your natal Saturn in the tables in this book for clues on where you need work.

Saturn in Aries

Saturn here puts the brakes on Aries's natural drive and enthusiasm. There is often an angry side to this placement. You don't let anyone push you around and you know what's best for yourself. Following orders is not your strong point, nor is diplomacy. You tend to be quick to go on the offensive in relationships, attacking first, before anyone attacks you. Because no one quite lives up to your standards, you often wind up doing everything yourself. You'll have to learn to cooperate and tone down any self-centeredness. Pat Buchanan has this Saturn.

Saturn in Taurus

A big issue is getting control of the cash flow. There will be lean periods that can be frightening, but you have the patience and endurance to stick them out and the methodical drive to prosper in the end. Learn to take a philosophical attitude like Ben Franklin, who also had this placement, and who said, "A penny saved is a penny earned."

Saturn in Gemini

You are a serious student of life, who may have difficulty communicating or sharing your knowledge. You may be shy, speak slowly, or have fears about communicating, like Eleanor Roosevelt. You dwell in the realms of science, theory, or abstract analysis, even when you are dealing with the emotions, like Sigmund Freud, who also had this placement.

Saturn in Cancer

Your tests come with establishing a secure emotional base. In doing so, you may have to deal with some very basic fears centering on your early home environment. Most of your Saturn tests will have emotional roots in those early-childhood experiences. You may have difficulty remaining objective in terms of what you try to achieve, so it will be especially important for you to deal with negative feelings such as guilt, paranoia, jealousy, resentment, and suspicion. Galileo and Michelangelo also navigated these murky waters.

Saturn in Leo

This is an authoritarian Saturn—a strict, demanding parent who may deny the pleasure principle in your zeal to see that rules are followed. Though you may feel guilty about taking the spotlight, you are very ambitious and loyal. You have to watch a tendency toward rigidity, also toward overwork and holding back affection. Joseph Kennedy and Billy Graham share this placement.

Saturn in Virgo

This is a cautious, exacting Saturn, intensely hard on yourself. Most of all, you give yourself the roughest time with your constant worries about every little detail, often making yourself sick. You may have difficulties setting priorities and getting the job done. Your tests will come in learning tolerance and understanding of others. Charles de Gaulle, Mae West, and Nathaniel Hawthorne had this meticulous Saturn.

Saturn in Libra

Saturn is exalted here, which makes this planet an ally. You may choose very serious, older partners in life, perhaps stemming from a fear of dependency. You need to learn to stand solidly on your own before you commit to another. Since you are extremely cautious, you deliberate every involvement—with good reason. It is best that you find an occupation that makes good use of your sense of duty and honor. Steer clear of fly-by-night situations. Both Khrushchev and Mao Tse-tung had this placement.

Saturn in Scorpio

You have great staying power. This Saturn tests you in situations involving the control of others. You may feel drawn to some kind of intrigue or undercover work, like J. Edgar Hoover. Or there may be an air of mystery surrounding your life and death, like Marilyn Monroe and Robert Kennedy, who both had this placement. There are lessons to be learned from your sexual involvements. Often sex is used for manipulation or is somehow out of the ordinary. The Roman emperor Caligula and the transsexual Christine Jorgensen are extreme cases.

Saturn in Sagittarius

Your challenges and lessons will come from tests of your spiritual and philosophical values, as happened to Martin Luther King Jr. and Gandhi. You are high-minded and sincere with this reflective, moral placement. Uncompromising in your ethical standards, you could become a benevolent despot.

Saturn in Capricorn

With the help of Saturn at maximum strength, your judgment will improve with age. And, like Spencer Tracy's screen image, you'll be the gray-haired hero with a strong sense of responsibility. You advance in life slowly but steadily, always with a strong hand at the helm and an eye for the advantageous situation. Like Pat Robertson, you're likely to stand for conservative values. Negatively, you may be a loner, prone to periods of melancholy.

Saturn in Aquarius

Your tests come from relationships with groups. Do you care too much about what others think? Do you feel like an outsider, like Greta Garbo? You may fear being different from others and therefore slight your own unique, forward-looking gifts. Or like Lord Byron and Howard Hughes, you may take the opposite tack and rebel in the extreme. You can apply discipline to accomplish great humanitarian goals, as Albert Schweitzer did.

Saturn in Pisces

Your fear of the unknown and the irrational may lead you to the safety and protection of an institution. You may go on the run like Jesse James to avoid looking too deeply inside. Or you might go in the opposite, more positive direction and develop a disciplined psychoanalytic approach, which puts you more in control of your feelings. Some of you will take refuge in work with hospitals, charities, or religious institutions. Queen Victoria, who had this placement, symbolized an era when institutions of all kinds were sustained. Discipline applied to artistic work, especially poetry and dance, or spiritual work, such as yoga or meditation, might be helpful.

How Uranus, Neptune, and Pluto Influence Your Generation

These three planets remain in signs such a long time that a whole generation bears the imprint of the sign. Mass movements, great sweeping changes, fads that characterize a generation, and even the issues of the conflicts and wars of the time are influenced by these outer three planets. When one of these distant planets changes signs, there is a definite shift in the atmosphere, the feeling of the end of an era.

Since these planets are so far away from the sun—too distant to be seen by the naked eye—they pick up signals from the universe at large. These planetary receivers literally link the sun with distant energies, and then perform a similar function in your horoscope by linking your central character with intuitive, spiritual, transformative forces from the cosmos. Each planet has a special domain and will reflect this in the area of your chart where it falls.

Uranus Is the Surprise Ingredient

Uranus is the surprise ingredient that sets you and your generation apart. There is nothing ordinary about this quirky green planet that seems to be traveling on its side, surrounded by a swarm of moons. Is it any wonder that astrologers assigned it to Aquarius, the most eccentric and gregarious sign? Uranus seems to wend its way around the sun, marching to its own tune.

Significantly, Uranus follows Saturn, the planet of limitations and structures. Often we get caught up in the structures we have created to give ourselves a sense of security. However, if we lose contact with our spiritual roots in the process, Uranus is likely to jolt us out of our comfortable rut and wake us up.

Uranus energy is electrical, happening in sudden flashes. It is not influenced by karma or past events, nor does it regard tradition, sex, or sentiment. Uranus's key words are surprise and awakening. Suddenly, there's that flash of inspiration, that bright idea, or that totally new approach that revolutionizes whatever scheme you were undertaking. A Uranus event takes you by surprise, for better or for worse. The Uranus place in your life is where you awaken and become your own person, leaving the structures of Saturn behind. And it is probably the most unconventional place in your chart.

Look up the sign of Uranus at the time of your birth and see where you follow your own tune.

Uranus in Aries

Birth Dates:
   March 31, 1927–November 4, 1927
   January 13, 1928–June 6, 1934
   October 10, 1934–March 28, 1935

Your generation is original, creative, and pioneering. It developed the computer, the airplane, and the cyclotron. You let nothing hold you back from exploring the unknown, and you have a powerful mixture of fire and electricity behind you. Women of your generation were among the first to be liberated. You were the unforgettable style setters. You have a surprise in store for everyone. As with Yoko Ono, Grace Kelly, and Jacqueline Onassis, your life may be jolted by sudden and violent changes.

Uranus in Taurus

Birth Dates:
   June 6, 1934–October 10, 1934
   March 28, 1935–August 7, 1941
   October 5, 1941–May 15, 1942

The great territorial shakeups of World War II began during your generation. You're independent; you're probably self-employed or you would like to be. You have original ideas about making money, and you brace yourself for sudden changes of fortune. This Uranus can cause shake-ups, particularly in finances, but it can also make you a born entrepreneur, like Martha Stewart.

Uranus in Gemini

Birth Dates:
   August 7, 1941–October 5, 1941
   May 15, 1942–August 30, 1948
   November 12, 1948–June 10, 1949

You were the first children to be influenced by television, and in your adult years, your generation stocks up on answering machines, cell phones, computers, and fax machines—any new way you can communicate. You have an inquiring mind, but your interests may be rather short-lived. This Uranus can be easily fragmented if there is no structure and focus.

Uranus in Cancer

Birth Dates:
   August 30–November 12, 1948
   June 10, 1949–August 24, 1955
   January 28, 1956–June 10, 1956

This generation came at a time when divorce was becoming commonplace, so your home image is unconventional. You may have an unusual relationship with your parents, or come from a broken home or an unconventional one. You'll have unorthodox ideas about parenting, intimacy, food, and shelter. You may also be interested in dreams, psychic phenomena, and memory work.

Uranus in Leo

Birth Dates:
   August 24, 1955–January 28, 1956
   June 10, 1956–November 1, 1961
   January 10, 1962–August 10, 1962

This generation understood how to use electronic media. Many of your group are now leaders in the high-tech industries, and you also understand how to use the new media to promote yourself. Like Isadora Duncan, you may have a very eccentric kind of charisma and a life that is sparked by unusual love affairs. Your children may have traits that are out of the ordinary. Where this planet falls in your chart, you'll have a love of freedom, be a bit of an egomaniac, and show the full force of your personality in a unique way, like tennis great Martina Navratilova.

Uranus in Virgo

Birth Dates:
    November 1, 1961–January 10, 1962
    August 10, 1962–September 28, 1968
    May 20, 1969–June 24, 1969
You'll have highly individual work methods, and many will be finding newer, more practical ways to use computers. Like Einstein, who had this placement, you'll break the rules brilliantly. Your generation came at a time of student rebellions, the civil rights movement, and the general acceptance of health foods. Chances are, you're concerned about pollution and cleaning up the environment. You may also be involved with nontraditional healing methods.

Uranus in Libra

Birth Dates:
    September 28, 1968–May 20, 1969
    June 24, 1969–November 21, 1974
    May 1, 1975–September 8, 1975
Your generation will be always changing partners. Born during the era of women's liberation, you may have come from a broken home and may have no clear image of what a marriage entails. There will be many sudden splits and experiments before you settle down. Your generation will be much involved in legal and political reforms and in changing artistic and fashion looks.

Uranus in Scorpio

Birth Dates:
    November 21, 1974–May 1, 1975
    September 8, 1975–February 17, 1981
    March 20, 1981–November 16, 1981
Interest in transformation, meditation, and life after death

signaled the beginning of New Age consciousness. Your generation recognizes no boundaries, no limits, and no external controls. You'll have new attitudes toward death and dying, psychic phenomena, and the occult. Like Mae West and Casanova, you'll shock 'em sexually.

Uranus in Sagittarius

Birth Dates:
> February 17, 1981–March 20, 1981
> November 16, 1981–February 15, 1988
> May 27, 1988–December 2, 1988

Could this generation be the first to travel in outer space? The new generation with this placement included Charles Lindbergh and a time when the first zeppelins and the Wright Brothers were conquering the skies. Uranus here forecasts great discoveries, mind expansion, and long-distance travel. Like Galileo and Martin Luther, those born in these years will generate new theories about the cosmos and man's relation to it.

Uranus in Capricorn

Birth Dates:
> December 20, 1904–January 30, 1912
> September 4, 1912–November 12, 1912
> February 15, 1988–May 27, 1988
> December 2, 1988–April 1, 1995
> June 9, 1995–January 12, 1996

This generation, now reaching adulthood, will challenge traditions. In these years, we got organized with the help of technology put to practical use. The Internet was born after the great economic boom of the 1990s. Great leaders who were movers and shakers of history, like Julius Caesar and Henry VIII, were born under this placement.

Uranus in Aquarius

Birth Dates:
> January 30, 1912–September 4, 1912
> November 12, 1912–April 1, 1919

August 16, 1919–January 22, 1920
April 1, 1995–June 9, 1995
January 12, 1996–March 10, 2003
September 15, 2003–December 30, 2003

Uranus in Aquarius is the strongest placement for this planet. Recently, we've had the opportunity to witness the full force of its power of innovation, as well as its sudden wake-up calls and insistence on humanitarian values. This was a time of high-tech development, when home computers became as ubiquitous as television. It was a time of globalization, surprise attacks (9/11), and underdeveloped countries demanding attention. The last generation with this placement produced great innovative minds, such as Leonard Bernstein and Orson Welles. The next will become another radical breakthrough generation, much concerned with global issues that involve all humanity.

Uranus in Pisces

Birth Dates:
April 1, 1919–August 16, 1919
January 22, 1920–March 31, 1927
November 4, 1927–January 12, 1928
March 10, 2003–September 15, 2003
December 30, 2003–May 28, 2010

Uranus is now in Pisces, ushering in a new generation. In the past century, Uranus in Pisces focused attention on the rise of electronic entertainment—radio and the cinema—and the secretiveness of Prohibition. This produced a generation of idealists exemplified by Judy Garland's theme, "Somewhere over the Rainbow." Uranus in Pisces also hints at stealth activities, at hospital and prison reform, at high-tech drugs and medical experiments, at shake-ups in the petroleum industry and new locations for Pisces-ruled off-shore drilling. Issues regarding the water and oil supply, water-related storm damage (Hurricane Katrina), sudden hurricanes, droughts, and floods demand our attention.

Neptune Is the Magic Solvent

Neptune is often maligned as the planet of illusions that dissolves reality, enabling you to escape the material world. Under Neptune's influence, you see what you want to see. But Neptune also encourages you to create. It embodies glamour, subtlety, mystery, and mysticism, and governs anything that takes you beyond the mundane world, including out-of-body experiences.

Neptune breaks through and transcends your ordinary perceptions to take you to another level, where you experience either confusion or ecstasy. Its force can pull you off course only if you allow this to happen. Those who use Neptune wisely can translate their daydreams into poetry, theater, design, or inspired moves in the business world, avoiding the tricky con artist side of this planet.

Find your Neptune listed below:

Neptune in Cancer

Birth Dates:

    July 19, 1901–December 25, 1901
    May 21, 1902–September 23, 1914
    December 14, 1914–July 19, 1915
    March 19, 1916–May 2, 1916

Dreams of the homeland, idealistic patriotism, and glamorization of the nurturing assets of women characterized this time. You who were born here have unusual psychic ability and deep insights into basic needs of others.

Neptune in Leo

Birth Dates:

    September 23, 1914–December 14, 1914
    July 19, 1915–March 19, 1916
    May 2, 1916–September 21, 1928
    February 19, 1929–July 24, 1929

Neptune in Leo brought us the glamour and high living of the 1920s and the big spenders of that time. Neptune temptations of gambling, seduction, theater, and lavish entertaining distracted from the realities of the age. Those born in that generation also made great advances in the arts.

Neptune in Virgo

Birth Dates:
   September 21, 1928–February 19, 1929
   July 24, 1929–October 3, 1942
   April 17, 1943–August 2, 1943
   Neptune in Virgo encompassed the 1930s, the Great Depression, and the beginning of World War II, when a new order was born. This was a time of facing what didn't work. Many were unemployed and found solace at the movies, watching the great Virgo star Greta Garbo or the escapist dance films of Busby Berkeley. New public services were born. Those with Neptune in Virgo later spread the gospel of health and fitness. This generation's devotion to spending hours at the office inspired the word *workaholic*.

Neptune in Libra

Birth Dates:
   October 3, 1942–April 17, 1943
   August 2, 1943–December 24, 1955
   March 12, 1956–October 19, 1956
   June 15, 1957–August 6, 1957
   This was the time of World War II, and the immediate postwar period, when the world regained balance and returned to relative stability. Neptune in Libra was the romantic generation who would later be concerned with relating. As this generation matured, there was a new trend toward marriage and commitment. Racial and sexual equality became important issues, as they redesigned traditional roles to suit modern times.

Neptune in Scorpio

Birth Dates:
   December 24, 1955–March 12, 1956
   October 19, 1956–June 15, 1957
   August 6, 1957–January 4, 1970

May 3, 1970–November 6, 1970

Neptune in Scorpio brought in a generation that would become interested in transformative power. Born in an era that glamorized sex, drugs, rock and roll, and Eastern religion, they matured in a more sobering time of AIDS, cocaine abuse, and New Age spirituality. As they evolve, they will become active in healing the planet from the results of the abuse of power.

Neptune in Sagittarius

Birth Dates:
    January 4, 1970–May 3, 1970
    November 6, 1970–January 19, 1984
    June 23, 1984–November 21, 1984

Neptune in Sagittarius was the time when space travel became a reality. The Neptune influence glamorized new approaches to mysticism, religion, and mind expansion. This generation will take a new approach to spiritual life, with emphasis on visions, mysticism, and clairvoyance.

Neptune in Capricorn

Birth Dates:
    January 19, 1984–June 23, 1984
    November 21, 1984–January 29, 1998

Neptune in Capricorn brought a time when delusions about material power were glamorized in the mideighties and nineties. There was a boom in the stock market, and the Internet era spawned young tycoons who later lost all their wealth. It was also a time when the psychic and occult worlds spawned a new category of business enterprise, and sold services on television.

Neptune in Aquarius

Birth Dates:
    January 29, 1998–April 4, 2011

This should continue to be a time of breakthroughs. Here the creative influence of Neptune reaches a universal audience. This is a time of dissolving barriers and globalization—when we truly become one world. During this transit of high-tech Aquarius, new kinds of entertainment media reach across cultural differences. However, the transit of Neptune has also raised boundary issues between cultures, especially in Middle Eastern countries with Neptune-ruled oil fields. As Neptune raises issues of social and political structures not being as solid as they seem, this could continue to produce rebellion and chaos in the environment. However, by using imagination (Neptune) in partnership with a global view (Aquarius), we could reach creative solutions.

Those born with this placement should be true citizens of the world, with a remarkable creative ability to transcend social and cultural barriers.

Pluto Can Transform You

Though Pluto is a tiny, mysterious body in space, its influence is great. When Pluto zaps a strategic point in your horoscope, your life changes dramatically.

Little Pluto is the power behind the scenes; it affects you at deep levels of consciousness, causing events to come to the surface that will transform you and your generation. Nothing escapes, or is sacred, with this probing planet. Its purpose is to wipe out the past so something new can happen.

The Pluto place in your horoscope is where you have invisible power (Mars governs the visible power), where you can transform, heal, and affect the unconscious needs of the masses. Pluto tells lots about how your generation projects power and what makes it seem cool to others. And when Pluto changes signs, there is a whole new concept of what's cool. Pluto's strange elliptical orbit occasionally runs inside the orbit of neighboring Neptune. Because of its eccentric path, the length of time Pluto stays in any given sign can vary from thirteen to thirty-two years. It covered only seven signs in the last century.

Pluto in Gemini

Late 1800s–May 26, 1914

This was a time of mass suggestion and breakthroughs in communications, when many brilliant writers, such as Ernest Hemingway and F. Scott Fitzgerald, were born. Henry Miller, D. H. Lawrence, and James Joyce scandalized society by using explicit sexual images and language in their literature. "Muckraking" journalists exposed corruption. Pluto-ruled Scorpio president Theodore Roosevelt said, "Speak softly, but carry a big stick." This generation had an intense need to communicate and made major breakthroughs in knowledge. A compulsive restlessness and a thirst for a variety of experiences characterize many of this generation.

Pluto in Cancer

Birth Dates:

May 26, 1914–June 14, 1939

Dictators and mass media arose to wield emotional power over the masses. Women's rights were a popular issue. Deep sentimental feelings, acquisitiveness, and possessiveness characterized these times and people. Most of the great stars of the Hollywood era who embodied the American image were born during this period: Grace Kelly, Esther Williams, Frank Sinatra, and Lana Turner, to name a few.

Pluto in Leo

Birth Dates:

June 14, 1939–August 19, 1957

The performing arts played on the emotions of the masses. Mick Jagger, John Lennon, and rock and roll were born at this time. So were baby boomers like Bill and Hillary Clinton. Those born here tend to be self-centered, powerful, and boisterous. This generation does its own thing, for better or for worse. They are quick to embrace self-transformation in the form of antiaging and plastic surgery techniques, to stay forever young and stay relevant in society.

Pluto in Virgo

Birth Dates:
  August 19, 1957–October 5, 1971
  April 17, 1972–July 30, 1972

This is the yuppie generation that sparked a mass movement toward fitness, health, and career. It is a much more sober, serious, and driven generation than the fun-loving Pluto in Leo. During this time, machines were invented to process detail work efficiently. Inventions took a practical turn with answering machines, fax machines, car phones, and home-office equipment—all making the workplace far more efficient.

Pluto in Libra

Birth Dates:
  October 5, 1971–April 17, 1972
  July 30, 1972–November 5, 1983
  May 18, 1984–August 27, 1984

A mellower generation, people born at this time are concerned with partnerships, working together, and finding diplomatic solutions to problems. Marriage is important to this generation, and they will define it by combining traditional values with equal partnership. This was a time of women's liberation, gay rights, the ERA, and legal battles over abortion—all of which transformed our ideas about relationships.

Pluto in Scorpio

Birth Dates:
  November 5, 1983–May 18, 1984
  August 27, 1984–January 17, 1995

Pluto was in its ruling sign for a comparatively short period of time. However, this was a time of record achievements, destructive sexually transmitted diseases, nuclear power controversies, and explosive political issues. Pluto destroys in order to create new understanding—the phoenix rising from the ashes—which should be some consolation for those of you who felt Pluto's force before 1995. Sexual shockers were par for the course during these intense years, when black clothing, transvestites, body piercing, tattoos, and sexually explicit advertising pushed the boundaries of good taste.

Pluto in Sagittarius

Birth Dates:
>   January 17, 1995–April 20, 1995
>   November 10, 1995–January 27, 2008
>   June 13, 2008–November 26, 2008

During the most recent Pluto transit, we were pushed to expand our horizons and find deeper spiritual meaning in life.

Pluto's opposition with Saturn in 2001 brought an enormous conflict between traditional societies and the forces of change. It signaled a time when religious convictions exerted power in our political life as well.

Since Sagittarius is associated with travel, Pluto, the planet of extremes, made space travel a reality for wealthy adventurers, who paid for the privilege of travel on space shuttles. Globalization transformed business and traditional societies as outsourcing became the norm.

New dimensions in electronic publishing, concern with animal rights and the environment, and an increasing emphasis on extreme forms of religion were other signs of Pluto in Sagittarius. Charismatic religious leaders asserted themselves and questions of the boundaries between church and state arose. There were also sexual scandals associated with the church, which transformed the religious power structure.

Pluto in Capricorn

Birth Dates:
>   January 25, 2008–June 13, 2008
>   November 26, 2008–January 20, 2024

As Pluto in Jupiter-ruled Sagittarius signaled a time of expansion and globalization, Pluto's entry into Saturn-ruled Capricorn in 2008 signaled a time of adjustment, of facing reality and limitations, then finding pragmatic solutions. It will be a time when a new structure is imposed, when we become concerned with what actually works.

As Capricorn is associated with corporations and also with

responsibility and duty, look for dramatic changes in business practices, hopefully with more attention paid to ethical and social responsibility as well as the bottom line. Big business will have enormous power during this transit, perhaps handling what governments have been unable to accomplish. There will be an emphasis on trimming down, perhaps a new belt-tightening regime. And, since Capricorn is the sign of Father Time, there will be a new emphasis on the aging of the population. The generation born now is sure to be a more practical and realistic one than that of their older Pluto in Sagittarius siblings.

VENUS SIGNS 1901–2010

	Aries	Taurus	Gemini	Cancer	Leo	Virgo
1901	3/29–4/22	4/22–5/17	5/17–6/10	6/10–7/5	7/5–7/29	7/29–8/23
1902	5/7–6/3	6/3–6/30	6/30–7/25	7/25–8/19	8/19–9/13	9/13–10/7
1903	2/28–3/24	3/24–4/18	4/18–5/13	5/13–6/9	6/9–7/7	7/7–8/17
						9/6–11/8
1904	3/13–5/7	5/7–6/1	6/1–6/25	6/25–7/19	7/19–8/13	8/13–9/6
1905	2/3–3/6	3/6–4/9	7/8–8/6	8/6–9/1	9/1–9/27	9/27–10/21
	4/9–5/28	5/28–7/8				
1906	3/1–4/7	4/7–5/2	5/2–5/26	5/26–6/20	6/20–7/16	7/16–8/11
1907	4/27–5/22	5/22–6/16	6/16–7/11	7/11–8/4	8/4–8/29	8/29–9/22
1908	2/14–3/10	3/10–4/5	4/5–5/5	5/5–9/8	9/8–10/8	10/8–11/3
1909	3/29–4/22	4/22–5/16	5/16–6/10	6/10–7/4	7/4–7/29	7/29–8/23
1910	5/7–6/3	6/4–6/29	6/30–7/24	7/25–8/18	8/19–9/12	9/13–10/6
1911	2/28–3/23	3/24–4/17	4/18–5/12	5/13–6/8	6/9–7/7	7/8–11/18
1912	4/13–5/6	5/7–5/31	6/1–6/24	6/24–7/18	7/19–8/12	8/13–9/5
1913	2/3–3/6	3/7–5/1	7/8–8/5	8/6–8/31	9/1–9/26	9/27–10/20
	5/2–5/30	5/31–7/7				
1914	3/14–4/6	4/7–5/1	5/2–5/25	5/26–6/19	6/20–7/15	7/16–8/10
1915	4/27–5/21	5/22–6/15	6/16–7/10	7/11–8/3	8/4–8/28	8/29–9/21
1916	2/14–3/9	3/10–4/5	4/6–5/5	5/6–9/8	9/9–10/7	10/8–11/2
1917	3/29–4/21	4/22–5/15	5/16–6/9	6/10–7/3	7/4–7/28	7/29–8/21
1918	5/7–6/2	6/3–6/28	6/29–7/24	7/25–8/18	8/19–9/11	9/12–10/5
1919	2/27–3/22	3/23–4/16	4/17–5/12	5/13–6/7	6/8–7/7	7/8–11/8
1920	4/12–5/6	5/7–5/30	5/31–6/23	6/24–7/18	7/19–8/11	8/12–9/4
1921	2/3–3/6	3/7–4/25	7/8–8/5	8/6–8/31	9/1–9/25	9/26–10/20
	4/26–6/1	6/2–7/7				
1922	3/13–4/6	4/7–4/30	5/1–5/25	5/26–6/19	6/20–7/14	7/15–8/9
1923	4/27–5/21	5/22–6/14	6/15–7/9	7/10–8/3	8/4–8/27	8/28–9/20
1924	2/13–3/8	3/9–4/4	4/5–5/5	5/6–9/8	9/9–10/7	10/8–11/12
1925	3/28–4/20	4/21–5/15	5/16–6/8	6/9–7/3	7/4–7/27	7/28–8/21
1926	5/7–6/2	6/3–6/28	6/29–7/23	7/24–8/17	8/18–9/11	9/12–10/5
1927	2/27–3/22	3/23–4/16	4/17–5/11	5/12–6/7	6/8–7/7	7/8–11/9

74

Libra	Scorpio	Sagittarius	Capricorn	Aquarius	Pisces
8/23–9/17	9/17–10/12	10/12–1/16	1/16–2/9 11/7–12/5	2/9–3/5 12/5–1/11	3/5–3/29
10/7–10/31	10/31–11/24	11/24–12/18	12/18–1/11	2/6–4/4	1/11–2/6 4/4–5/7
8/17–9/6 11/8–12/9	12/9–1/5			1/11–2/4	2/4–2/28
9/6–9/30	9/30–10/25	1/5–1/30 10/25–11/18	1/30–2/24 11/18–12/13	2/24–3/19 12/13–1/7	3/19–4/13
10/21–11/14	11/14–12/8	12/8–1/1/06			1/7–2/3
8/11–9/7	9/7–10/9 12/15–12/25	10/9–12/15 12/25–2/6	1/1–1/25	1/25–2/18	2/18–3/14
9/22–10/16	10/16–11/9	11/9–12/3	2/6–3/6 12/3–12/27	3/6–4/2 12/27–1/20	4/2–4/27
11/3–11/28	11/28–12/22	12/22–1/15			1/20–2/4
8/23–9/17	9/17–10/12	10/12–11/17	1/15–2/9 11/17–12/5	2/9–3/5 12/5–1/15	3/5–3/29
10/7–10/30	10/31–11/23	11/24–12/17	12/18–12/31	1/1–1/15 1/29–4/4	1/16–1/28 4/5–5/6
11/19–12/8	12/9–12/31		1/1–1/10	1/11–2/2	2/3–2/27
9/6–9/30	1/1–1/4 10/1–10/24	1/5–1/29 10/25–11/17	1/30–2/23 11/18–12/12	2/24–3/18 12/13–12/31	3/19–4/12
10/21–11/13	11/14–12/7	12/8–12/31		1/1–1/6	1/7–2/2
8/11–9/6	9/7–10/9 12/6–12/30	10/10–12/5 12/31	1/1–1/24	1/25–2/17	2/18–3/13
9/22–10/15	10/16–11/8	1/1–2/6 11/9–12/2	2/7–3/6 12/3–12/26	3/7–4/1 12/27–12/31	4/2–4/26
11/3–11/27	11/28–12/21	12/22–12/31		1/1–1/19	1/20–2/13
8/22–9/16	9/17–10/11	1/1–1/14 10/12–11/6	1/15–2/7 11/7–12/5	2/8–3/4 12/6–12/31	3/5–3/28
10/6–10/29	10/30–11/22	11/23–12/16	12/17–12/31	1/1–1/5	4/6–5/6
11/9–12/8	12/9–12/31		1/1–1/9	1/10–2/2	2/3–2/26
9/5–9/30	1/1–1/3 9/31–10/23	1/4–1/28 10/24–11/17	1/29–2/22 11/18–12/11	2/23–3/18 12/12–12/31	3/19–4/11
10/21–11/13	11/14–12/7	12/8–12/31		1/1–1/6	1/7–2/2
8/10–9/6	9/7–10/10 11/29–12/31	10/11–11/28	1/1–1/24	1/25–2/16	2/17–3/12
9/21–10/14	1/1 10/15–11/7	1/2–2/6 11/8–12/1	2/7–3/5 12/2–12/25	3/6–3/31 12/26–12/31	4/1–4/26
11/13–11/26	11/27–12/21	12/22–12/31		1/1–1/19	1/20–2/12
8/22–9/15	9/16–10/11	1/1–1/14 10/12–11/6	1/15–2/7 11/7–12/5	2/8–3/3 12/6–12/31	3/4–3/27
10/6–10/29	10/30–11/22	11/23–12/16	12/17–12/31	1/1–4/5	4/6–5/6
11/10–12/8	12/9–12/31	1/1–1/7	1/8	1/9–2/1	2/2–2/26

VENUS SIGNS 1901–2010

	Aries	Taurus	Gemini	Cancer	Leo	Virgo
1928	4/12–5/5	5/6–5/29	5/30–6/23	6/24–7/17	7/18–8/11	8/12–9/4
1929	2/3–3/7 4/20–6/2	3/8–4/19 6/3–7/7	7/8–8/4	8/5–8/30	8/31–9/25	9/26–10/19
1930	3/13–4/5	4/6–4/30	5/1–5/24	5/25–6/18	6/19–7/14	7/15–8/9
1931	4/26–5/20	5/21–6/13	6/14–7/8	7/9–8/2	8/3–8/26	8/27–9/19
1932	2/12–3/8	3/9–4/3	4/4–5/5 7/13–7/27	5/6–7/12 7/28–9/8	9/9–10/6	10/7–11/1
1933	3/27–4/19	4/20–5/28	5/29–6/8	6/9–7/2	7/3–7/26	7/27–8/20
1934	5/6–6/1	6/2–6/27	6/28–7/22	7/23–8/16	8/17–9/10	9/11–10/4
1935	2/26–3/21	3/22–4/15	4/16–5/10	5/11–6/6	6/7–7/6	7/7–11/8
1936	4/11–5/4	5/5–5/28	5/29–6/22	6/23–7/16	7/17–8/10	8/11–9/4
1937	2/2–3/8 4/14–6/3	3/9–4/13 6/4–7/6	7/7–8/3	8/4–8/29	8/30–9/24	9/25–10/18
1938	3/12–4/4	4/5–4/28	4/29–5/23	5/24–6/18	6/19–7/13	7/14–8/8
1939	4/25–5/19	5/20–6/13	6/14–7/8	7/9–8/1	8/2–8/25	8/26–9/19
1940	2/12–3/7	3/8–4/3	4/4–5/5 7/5–7/31	5/6–7/4 8/1–9/8	9/9–10/5	10/6–10/31
1941	3/27–4/19	4/20–5/13	5/14–6/6	6/7–7/1	7/2–7/26	7/27–8/20
1942	5/6–6/1	6/2–6/26	6/27–7/22	7/23–8/16	8/17–9/9	9/10–10/3
1943	2/25–3/20	3/21–4/14	4/15–5/10	5/11–6/6	6/7–7/6	7/7–11/8
1944	4/10–5/3	5/4–5/28	5/29–6/21	6/22–7/16	7/17–8/9	8/10–9/2
1945	2/2–3/10 4/7–6/3	3/11–4/6 6/4–7/6	7/7–8/3	8/4–8/29	8/30–9/23	9/24–10/18
1946	3/11–4/4	4/5–4/28	4/29–5/23	5/24–6/17	6/18–7/12	7/13–8/8
1947	4/25–5/19	5/20–6/12	6/13–7/7	7/8–8/1	8/2–8/25	8/26–9/18
1948	2/11–3/7	3/8–4/3	4/4–5/6 6/29–8/2	5/7–6/28 8/3–9/7	9/8–10/5	10/6–10/31
1949	3/26–4/19	4/20–5/13	5/14–6/6	6/7–6/30	7/1–7/25	7/26–8/19
1950	5/5–5/31	6/1–6/26	6/27–7/21	7/22–8/15	8/16–9/9	9/10–10/3
1951	2/25–3/21	3/22–4/15	4/16–5/10	5/11–6/6	6/7–7/7	7/8–11/9
1952	4/10–5/4	5/5–5/28	5/29–6/21	6/22–7/16	7/17–8/9	8/10–9/3
1953	2/2–3/3 4/1–6/5	3/4–3/31 6/6–7/7	7/8–8/3	8/4–8/29	8/30–9/24	9/25–10/18

Libra	Scorpio	Sagittarius	Capricorn	Aquarius	Pisces
9/5–9/28	1/1–1/3	1/4–1/28	1/29–2/22	2/23–3/17	3/18–4/11
	9/29–10/23	10/24–11/16	11/17–12/11	12/12–12/31	
10/20–11/12	11/13–12/6	12/7–12/30	12/31	1/1–1/5	1/6–2/2
8/10–9/6	9/7–10/11	10/12–11/21	1/1–1/23	1/24–2/16	2/17–3/12
	11/22–12/31				
9/20–10/13	1/1–1/3	1/4–2/6	2/7–3/4	3/5–3/31	4/1–4/25
	10/14–11/6	11/7–11/30	12/1–12/24	12/25–12/31	
11/2–11/25	11/26–12/20	12/21–12/31		1/1–1/18	1/19–2/11
8/21–9/14	9/15–10/10	1/1–1/13	1/14–2/6	2/7–3/2	3/3–3/26
		10/11–11/5	11/6–12/4	12/5–12/31	
10/5–10/28	10/29–11/21	11/22–12/15	12/16–12/31	1/1–4/5	4/6–5/5
11/9–12/7	12/8–12/31		1/1–1/7	1/8–1/31	2/1–2/25
9/5–9/27	1/1–1/2	1/3–1/27	1/28–2/21	2/22–3/16	3/17–4/10
	9/28–10/22	10/23–11/15	11/16–12/10	12/11–12/31	
10/19–11/11	11/12–12/5	12/6–12/29	12/30–12/31	1/1–1/5	1/6–2/1
8/9–9/6	9/7–10/13	10/14–11/14	1/1–1/22	1/23–2/15	2/16–3/11
	11/15–12/31				
9/20–10/13	1/1–1/3	1/4–2/5	2/6–3/4	3/5–3/30	3/31–4/24
	10/14–11/6	11/7–11/30	12/1–12/24	12/25–12/31	
11/1–11/25	11/26–12/19	12/20–12/31		1/1–1/18	1/19–2/11
8/21–9/14	9/15–10/9	1/1–1/12	1/13–2/5	2/6–3/1	3/2–3/26
		10/10–11/5	11/6–12/4	12/5–12/31	
10/4–10/27	10/28–11/20	11/21–12/14	12/15–12/31	1/1–4/5	4/6–5/5
11/9–12/7	12/8–12/31		1/1–1/7	1/8–1/31	2/1–2/24
9/3–9/27	1/1–1/2	1/3–1/27	1/28–2/20	2/21–3/16	3/17–4/9
	9/28–10/21	10/22–11/15	11/16–12/10	12/11–12/31	
10/19–11/11	11/12–12/5	12/6–12/29	12/30–12/31	1/1–1/4	1/5–2/1
8/9–9/6	9/7–10/15	10/16–11/7	1/1–1/21	1/22–2/14	2/15–3/10
	11/8–12/31				
9/19–10/12	1/1–1/4	1/5–2/5	2/6–3/4	3/5–3/29	3/30–4/24
	10/13–11/5	11/6–11/29	11/30–12/23	12/24–12/31	
11/1–11/25	11/26–12/19	12/20–12/31		1/1–1/17	1/18–2/10
8/20–9/14	9/15–10/9	1/1–1/12	1/13–2/5	2/6–3/1	3/2–3/25
		10/10–11/5	11/6–12/5	12/6–12/31	
10/4–10/27	10/28–11/20	11/21–12/13	12/14–12/31	1/1–4/5	4/6–5/4
11/10–12/7	12/8–12/31		1/1–1/7	1/8–1/31	2/1–2/24
9/4–9/27	1/1–1/2	1/3–1/27	1/28–2/20	2/21–3/16	3/17–4/9
	9/28–10/21	10/22–11/15	11/16–12/10	12/11–12/31	
10/19–11/11	11/12–12/5	12/6–12/29	12/30–12/31	1/1–1/5	1/6–2/1

VENUS SIGNS 1901–2010

	Aries	Taurus	Gemini	Cancer	Leo	Virgo
1954	3/12–4/4	4/5–4/28	4/29–5/23	5/24–6/17	6/18–7/13	7/14–8/8
1955	4/25–5/19	5/20–6/13	6/14–7/7	7/8–8/1	8/2–8/25	8/26–9/18
1956	2/12–3/7	3/8–4/4	4/5–5/7 6/24–8/4	5/8–6/23 8/5–9/8	9/9–10/5	10/6–10/31
1957	3/26–4/19	4/20–5/13	5/14–6/6	6/7–7/1	7/2–7/26	7/27–8/19
1958	5/6–5/31	6/1–6/26	6/27–7/22	7/23–8/15	8/16–9/9	9/10–10/3
1959	2/25–3/20	3/21–4/14	4/15–5/10	5/11–6/6	6/7–7/8 9/21–9/24	7/9–9/20 9/25–11/9
1960	4/10–5/3	5/4–5/28	5/29–6/21	6/22–7/15	7/16–8/9	8/10–9/2
1961	2/3–6/5	6/6–7/7	7/8–8/3	8/4–8/29	8/30–9/23	9/24–10/17
1962	3/11–4/3	4/4–4/28	4/29–5/22	5/23–6/17	6/18–7/12	7/13–8/8
1963	4/24–5/18	5/19–6/12	6/13–7/7	7/8–7/31	8/1–8/25	8/26–9/18
1964	2/11–3/7	3/8–4/4	4/5–5/9 6/18–8/5	5/10–6/17 8/6–9/8	9/9–10/5	10/6–10/31
1965	3/26–4/18	4/19–5/12	5/13–6/6	6/7–6/30	7/1–7/25	7/26–8/19
1966	5/6–5/31	6/1–6/26	6/27–7/21	7/22–8/15	8/16–9/8	9/9–10/2
1967	2/24–3/20	3/21–4/14	4/15–5/10	5/11–6/6	6/7–7/8 9/10–10/1	7/9–9/9 10/2–11/9
1968	4/9–5/3	5/4–5/27	5/28–6/20	6/21–7/15	7/16–8/8	8/9–9/2
1969	2/3–6/6	6/7–7/6	7/7–8/3	8/4–8/28	8/29–9/22	9/23–10/17
1970	3/11–4/3	4/4–4/27	4/28–5/22	5/23–6/16	6/17–7/12	7/13–8/8
1971	4/24–5/18	5/19–6/12	6/13–7/6	7/7–7/31	8/1–8/24	8/25–9/17
1972	2/11–3/7	3/8–4/3	4/4–5/10 6/12–8/6	5/11–6/11 8/7–9/8	9/9–10/5	10/6–10/30
1973	3/25–4/18	4/18–5/12	5/13–6/5	6/6–6/29	7/1–7/25	7/26–8/19
1974	5/5–5/31	6/1–6/25	6/26–7/21	7/22–8/14	8/15–9/8	9/9–10/2
1975	2/24–3/20	3/21–4/13	4/14–5/9	5/10–6/6	6/7–7/9 9/3–10/4	7/10–9/2 10/5–11/9
1976	4/8–5/2	5/2–5/27	5/27–6/20	6/20–7/14	7/14–8/8	8/8–9/1
1977	2/2–6/6	6/6–7/6	7/6–8/2	8/2–8/28	8/28–9/22	9/22–10/17
1978	3/9–4/2	4/2–4/27	4/27–5/22	5/22–6/16	6/16–7/12	7/12–8/6
1979	4/23–5/18	5/18–6/11	6/11–7/6	7/6–7/30	7/30–8/24	8/24–9/17
1980	2/9–3/6	3/6–4/3	4/3–5/12 6/5–8/6	5/12–6/5 8/6–9/7	9/7–10/4	10/4–10/30
1981	3/24–4/17	4/17–5/11	5/11–6/5	6/5–6/29	6/29–7/24	7/24–8/18

Libra	Scorpio	Sagittarius	Capricorn	Aquarius	Pisces
8/9–9/6	9/7–10/22	10/23–10/27	1/1–1/22	1/23–2/15	2/16–3/11
	10/28–12/31				
9/19–10/13	1/1–1/6	1/7–2/5	2/6–3/4	3/5–3/30	3/31–4/24
	10/14–11/5	11/6–11/30	12/1–12/24	12/25–12/31	
11/1–11/25	11/26–12/19	12/20–12/31		1/1–1/17	1/18–2/11
8/20–9/14	9/15–10/9	1/1–1/12	1/13–2/5	2/6–3/1	3/2–3/25
		10/10–11/5	11/6–12/6	12/7–12/31	
10/4–10/27	10/28–11/20	11/21–12/14	12/15–12/31	1/1–4/6	4/7–5/5
11/10–12/7	12/8–12/31		1/1–1/7	1/8–1/31	2/1–2/24
9/3–9/26	1/1–1/2	1/3–1/27	1/28–2/20	2/21–3/15	3/16–4/9
	9/27–10/21	10/22–11/15	11/16–12/10	12/11–12/31	
10/18–11/11	11/12–12/4	12/5–12/28	12/29–12/31	1/1–1/5	1/6–2/2
8/9–9/6	9/7–12/31		1/1–1/21	1/22–2/14	2/15–3/10
9/19–10/12	1/1–1/6	1/7–2/5	2/6–3/4	3/5–3/29	3/30–4/23
	10/13–11/5	11/6–11/29	11/30–12/23	12/24–12/31	
11/1–11/24	11/25–12/19	12/20–12/31		1/1–1/16	1/17–2/10
8/20–9/13	9/14–10/9	1/1–1/12	1/13–2/5	2/6–3/1	3/2–3/25
		10/10–11/5	11/6–12/7	12/8–12/31	
10/3–10/26	10/27–11/19	11/20–12/13	2/7–2/25	1/1–2/6	4/7–5/5
			12/14–12/31	2/26–4/6	
11/10–12/7	12/8–12/31		1/1–1/6	1/7–1/30	1/31–2/23
9/3–9/26	1/1	1/2–1/26	1/27–2/20	2/21–3/15	3/16–4/8
	9/27–10/21	10/22–11/14	11/15–12/9	12/10–12/31	
10/18–11/10	11/11–12/4	12/5–12/28	12/29–12/31	1/1–1/4	1/5–2/2
8/9–9/7	9/8–12/31		1/1–1/21	1/22–2/14	2/15–3/10
9/18–10/11	1/1–1/7	1/8–2/5	2/6–3/4	3/5–3/29	3/30–4/23
	10/12–11/5	11/6–11/29	11/30–12/23	12/24–12/31	
10/31–11/24	11/25–12/18	12/19–12/31		1/1–1/16	1/17–2/10
8/20–9/13	9/14–10/8	1/1–1/12	1/13–2/4	2/5–2/28	3/1–3/24
		10/9–11/5	11/6–12/7	12/8–12/31	
10/3–10/26	10/27–11/19	11/20–12/13	12/14–12/31	3/1–4/6	4/7–5/4
			1/30–2/28	1/1–1/29	
11/10–12/7	12/8–12/31		1/1–1/6	1/7–1/30	1/31–2/23
9/1–9/26	9/26–10/20	1/1–1/26	1/26–2/19	2/19–3/15	3/15–4/8
10/17–11/10	11/10–12/4	12/4–12/27	12/27–1/20/78		1/4–2/2
8/6–9/7	9/7–1/7			1/20–2/13	2/13–3/9
9/17–10/11	10/11–11/4	1/7–2/5	2/5–3/3	3/3–3/29	3/29–4/23
		11/4–11/28	11/28–12/22	12/22–1/16/80	
10/30–11/24	11/24–12/18	12/18–1/11/81			1/16–2/9
8/18–9/12	9/12–10/9	10/9–11/5	1/11–2/4	2/4–2/28	2/28–3/24
			11/5–12/8	12/8–1/23/82	

VENUS SIGNS 1901–2010

	Aries	Taurus	Gemini	Cancer	Leo	Virgo
1982	5/4–5/30	5/30–6/25	6/25–7/20	7/20–8/14	8/14–9/7	9/7–10/2
1983	2/22–3/19	3/19–4/13	4/13–5/9	5/9–6/6	6/6–7/10	7/10–8/27
					8/27–10/5	10/5–11/9
1984	4/7–5/2	5/2–5/26	5/26–6/20	6/20–7/14	7/14–8/7	8/7–9/1
1985	2/2–6/6	6/7–7/6	7/6–8/2	8/2–8/28	8/28–9/22	9/22–10/16
1986	3/9–4/2	4/2–4/26	4/26–5/21	5/21–6/15	6/15–7/11	7/11–8/7
1987	4/22–5/17	5/17–6/11	6/11–7/5	7/5–7/30	7/30–8/23	8/23–9/16
1988	2/9–3/6	3/6–4/3	4/3–5/17	5/17–5/27	9/7–10/4	10/4–10/29
			5/27–8/6	8/28–9/22	9/22–10/16	
1989	3/23–4/16	4/16–5/11	5/11–6/4	6/4–6/29	6/29–7/24	7/24–8/18
1990	5/4–5/30	5/30–6/25	6/25–7/20	7/20–8/13	8/13–9/7	9/7–10/1
1991	2/22–3/18	3/18–4/13	4/13–5/9	5/9–6/6	6/6–7/11	7/11–8/21
					8/21–10/6	10/6–11/9
1992	4/7–5/1	5/1–5/26	5/26–6/19	6/19–7/13	7/13–8/7	8/7–8/31
1993	2/2–6/6	6/6–7/6	7/6–8/1	8/1–8/27	8/27–9/21	9/21–10/16
1994	3/8–4/1	4/1–4/26	4/26–5/21	5/21–6/15	6/15–7/11	7/11–8/7
1995	4/22–5/16	5/16–6/10	6/10–7/5	7/5–7/29	7/29–8/23	8/23–9/16
1996	2/9–3/6	3/6–4/3	4/3–8/7	8/7–9/7	9/7–10/4	10/4–10/29
1997	3/23–4/16	4/16–5/10	5/10–6/4	6/4–6/28	6/28–7/23	7/23–8/17
1998	5/3–5/29	5/29–6/24	6/24–7/19	7/19–8/13	8/13–9/6	9/6–9/30
1999	2/21–3/18	3/18–4/12	4/12–5/8	5/8–6/5	6/5–7/12	7/12–8/15
					8/15–10/7	10/7–11/9
2000	4/6–5/1	5/1–5/25	5/25–6/13	6/13–7/13	7/13–8/6	8/6–8/31
2001	2/2–6/6	6/6–7/5	7/5–8/1	8/1–8/26	8/26–9/20	9/20–10/15
2002	3/7–4/1	4/1–4/25	4/25–5/20	5/20–6/14	6/14–7/10	7/10–8/7
2003	4/21–5/16	5/16–6/9	6/9–7/4	7/4–7/29	7/29–8/22	8/22–9/15
2004	2/8–3/5	3/5–4/3	4/3–8/7	8/7–9/6	9/6–10/3	10/3–10/28
2005	3/22–4/15	4/15–5/10	5/10–6/3	6/3–6/28	6/28–7/23	7/23–8/17
2006	5/3–5/29	5/29–6/24	6/24–7/19	7/19–8/12	8/12–9/6	9/6–9/30
2007	2/21–3/16	3/17–4/10	4/11–5/7	5/8–6/4	6/5–7/13	7/14–8/7
					8/8–10/6	10/7–11/7
2008	4/6–4/30	5/1–5/24	5/25–6/17	6/18–7/11	7/12–8/4	8/5–8/29
2009	2/2–4/11	6/6–7/5	7/5–7/31	731/–8/26	8/26–9/20	9/20–10/14
	4/24–6/6					
2010	3/7–3/31	3/31–4/25	4/25–5/20	5/20–6/14	6/14–7/10	7/10–8/7

Libra	Scorpio	Sagittarius	Capricorn	Aquarius	Pisces
10/2–10/26	10/26–11/18	11/18–12/12	1/23–3/2	3/2–4/6	4/6–5/4
			12/12–1/5/83		
11/9–12/6	12/6–1/1/84			1/5–1/29	1/29–2/22
9/1–9/25	9/25–10/20	1/1–1/25	1/25–2/19	2/19–3/14	3/14–4/7
		10/20–11/13	11/13–12/9	12/10–1/4	
10/16–11/9	11/9–12/3	12/3–12/27	12/28–1/19		1/4–2/2
8/7–9/7	9/7–1/7			1/20–2/13	2/13–3/9
9/16–10/10	10/10–11/3	1/7–2/5	2/5–3/3	3/3–3/28	3/28–4/22
		11/3–11/28	11/28–12/22	12/22–1/15	
10/29–11/23	11/23–12/17	12/17–1/10			1/15–2/9
8/18–9/12	9/12–10/8	10/8–11/5	1/10–2/3	2/3–2/27	2/27–3/23
			11/5–12/10	12/10–1/16/90	
10/1–10/25	10/25–11/18	11/18–12/12	1/16–3/3	3/3–4/6	4/6–5/4
			12/12–1/5		
11/9–12/6	12/6–12/31	12/31–1/25/92		1/5–1/29	1/29–2/22
8/31–9/25	9/25–10/19	10/19–11/13	1/25–2/18	2/18–3/13	3/13–4/7
			11/13–12/8	12/8–1/3/93	
10/16–11/9	11/9–12/2	12/2–12/26	12/26–1/19		1/3–2/2
8/7–9/7	9/7–1/7			1/19–2/12	2/12–3/8
9/15–10/9	10/10–11/13	1/7–2/4	2/4–3/2	3/2–3/28	3/28–4/22
		11/3–11/27	11/27–12/21	12/21–1/15	
10/29–11/23	11/23–12/17	12/17–1/10/97			1/15–2/9
8/17–9/12	9/12–10/8	10/8–11/5	1/10–2/3	2/3–2/27	2/27–3/23
			11/5–12/12	12/12–1/9	
9/30–10/24	10/24–11/17	11/17–12/11	1/9–3/4	3/4–4/6	4/6–5/3
11/9–12/5	12/5–12/31	12/31–1/24		1/4–1/28	1/28–2/21
8/31–9/24	9/24–10/19	10/19–11/13	1/24–2/18	2/18–3/12	3/13–4/6
			11/13–12/8	12/8	
10/15–11/8	11/8–12/2	12/2–12/26	12/26/01–	12/8/00–1/3/01	1/3–2/2
			1/18/02		
8/7–9/7	9/7–1/7/03		12/26/01–1/18	1/18–2/11	2/11–3/7
9/15–10/9	10/9–11/2	1/7–2/4	2/4–3/2	3/2–3/27	3/27–4/21
		11/2–11/26	11/26–12/21	12/21–1/14/04	
10/28–11/22	11/22–12/16	12/16–1/9/05		1/1–1/14	1/14–2/8
8/17–9/11	9/11–10/8	10/8–11/15	1/9–2/2	2/2–2/26	2/26–3/22
			11/5–12/15	12/15–1/1/06	
9/30–10/24	10/24–11/17	11/17–12/11	1/1–3/5	3/5–4/6	4/6–5/3
11/8–12/4	12/5–12/29	12/30–1/24/08		1/3–1/26	1/27–2/20
8/6–9/7	9/7–1/7			1/20–2/13	2/13–3/9
8/30–9/22	9/23–10/17	10/18–11/11	1/24–2/16	2/17–3/11	3/12–4/5
			11/12–12/6	12/7–1/2/09	
10/14–11/7	11/7–12/1	12/1–12/25	12/25–1/18/10	12/7/08–	1/3–2/2
				1/31/09	4/11–4/24
8/7–9/8	9/8–11/8			1/18/10–	2/11–3/7
11/8–11/30	11/30–1/7/11			2/11/10	

How to Use the Mars, Jupiter, and Saturn Tables

Find the year of your birth on the left side of each column. The dates when the planet entered each sign are listed on the right side of each column. (Signs are abbreviated to three letters.) Your birthday should fall on or between each date listed, and your planetary placement should correspond to the earlier sign of that period.

All planet changes are calculated for the Greenwich Mean Time zone.

MARS SIGNS 1901–2010

1901	MAR	1	Leo
	MAY	11	Vir
	JUL	13	Lib
	AUG	31	Scp
	OCT	14	Sag
	NOV	24	Cap
1902	JAN	1	Aqu
	FEB	8	Pic
	MAR	19	Ari
	APR	27	Tau
	JUN	7	Gem
	JUL	20	Can
	SEP	4	Leo
	OCT	23	Vir
	DEC	20	Lib
1903	APR	19	Vir
	MAY	30	Lib
	AUG	6	Scp
	SEP	22	Sag
	NOV	3	Cap
	DEC	12	Aqu
1904	JAN	19	Pic
	FEB	27	Ari
	APR	6	Tau
	MAY	18	Gem
	JUN	30	Can
	AUG	15	Leo

	OCT	1	Vir
	NOV	20	Lib
1905	JAN	13	Scp
	AUG	21	Sag
	OCT	8	Cap
	NOV	18	Aqu
	DEC	27	Pic
1906	FEB	4	Ari
	MAR	17	Tau
	APR	28	Gem
	JUN	11	Can
	JUL	27	Leo
	SEP	12	Vir
	OCT	30	Lib
	DEC	17	Scp
1907	FEB	5	Sag
	APR	1	Cap
	OCT	13	Aqu
	NOV	29	Pic
1908	JAN	11	Ari
	FEB	23	Tau
	APR	7	Gem
	MAY	22	Can
	JUL	8	Leo
	AUG	24	Vir
	OCT	10	Lib
	NOV	25	Scp

1909	JAN	10	Sag		
	FEB	24	Cap		
	APR	9	Aqu		
	MAY	25	Pic		
	JUL	21	Ari		
	SEP	26	Pic		
	NOV	20	Ari		
1910	JAN	23	Tau		
	MAR	14	Gem		
	MAY	1	Can		
	JUN	19	Leo		
	AUG	6	Vir		
	SEP	22	Lib		
	NOV	6	Scp		
	DEC	20	Sag		
1911	JAN	31	Cap		
	MAR	14	Aqu		
	APR	23	Pic		
	JUN	2	Ari		
	JUL	15	Tau		
	SEP	5	Gem		
	NOV	30	Tau		
1912	JAN	30	Gem		
	APR	5	Can		
	MAY	28	Leo		
	JUL	17	Vir		
	SEP	2	Lib		
	OCT	18	Scp		
	NOV	30	Sag		
1913	JAN	10	Cap		
	FEB	19	Aqu		
	MAR	30	Pic		
	MAY	8	Ari		
	JUN	17	Tau		
	JUL	29	Gem		
	SEP	15	Can		
1914	MAY	1	Leo		
	JUN	26	Vir		
	AUG	14	Lib		
	SEP	29	Scp		
	NOV	11	Sag		
	DEC	22	Cap		
1915	JAN	30	Aqu		

	MAR	9	Pic
	APR	16	Ari
	MAY	26	Tau
	JUL	6	Gem
	AUG	19	Can
	OCT	7	Leo
1916	MAY	28	Vir
	JUL	23	Lib
	SEP	8	Scp
	OCT	22	Sag
	DEC	1	Cap
1917	JAN	9	Aqu
	FEB	16	Pic
	MAR	26	Ari
	MAY	4	Tau
	JUN	14	Gem
	JUL	28	Can
	SEP	12	Leo
	NOV	2	Vir
1918	JAN	11	Lib
	FEB	25	Vir
	JUN	23	Lib
	AUG	17	Scp
	OCT	1	Sag
	NOV	11	Cap
	DEC	20	Aqu
1919	JAN	27	Pic
	MAR	6	Ari
	APR	15	Tau
	MAY	26	Gem
	JUL	8	Can
	AUG	23	Leo
	OCT	10	Vir
	NOV	30	Lib
1920	JAN	31	Scp
	APR	23	Lib
	JUL	10	Scp
	SEP	4	Sag
	OCT	18	Cap
	NOV	27	Aqu
1921	JAN	5	Pic
	FEB	13	Ari
	MAR	25	Tau

	MAY	6	Gem	OCT	26	Scp
	JUN	18	Can	DEC	8	Sag
	AUG	3	Leo	1928 JAN	19	Cap
	SEP	19	Vir	FEB	28	Aqu
	NOV	6	Lib	APR	7	Pic
	DEC	26	Scp	MAY	16	Ari
1922	FEB	18	Sag	JUN	26	Tau
	SEP	13	Cap	AUG	9	Gem
	OCT	30	Aqu	OCT	3	Can
	DEC	11	Pic	DEC	20	Gem
1923	JAN	21	Ari	1929 MAR	10	Can
	MAR	4	Tau	MAY	13	Leo
	APR	16	Gem	JUL	4	Vir
	MAY	30	Can	AUG	21	Lib
	JUL	16	Leo	OCT	6	Scp
	SEP	1	Vir	NOV	18	Sag
	OCT	18	Lib	DEC	29	Cap
	DEC	4	Scp	1930 FEB	6	Aqu
1924	JAN	19	Sag	MAR	17	Pic
	MAR	6	Cap	APR	24	Ari
	APR	24	Aqu	JUN	3	Tau
	JUN	24	Pic	JUL	14	Gem
	AUG	24	Aqu	AUG	28	Can
	OCT	19	Pic	OCT	20	Leo
	DEC	19	Ari	1931 FEB	16	Can
1925	FEB	5	Tau	MAR	30	Leo
	MAR	24	Gem	JUN	10	Vir
	MAY	9	Can	AUG	1	Lib
	JUN	26	Leo	SEP	17	Scp
	AUG	12	Vir	OCT	30	Sag
	SEP	28	Lib	DEC	10	Cap
	NOV	13	Scp	1932 JAN	18	Aqu
	DEC	28	Sag	FEB	25	Pic
1926	FEB	9	Cap	APR	3	Ari
	MAR	23	Aqu	MAY	12	Tau
	MAY	3	Pic	JUN	22	Gem
	JUN	15	Ari	AUG	4	Can
	AUG	1	Tau	SEP	20	Leo
1927	FEB	22	Gem	NOV	13	Vir
	APR	17	Can	1933 JUL	6	Lib
	JUN	6	Leo	AUG	26	Scp
	JUL	25	Vir	OCT	9	Sag
	SEP	10	Lib	NOV	19	Cap

	DEC	28	Aqu		FEB	17	Tau
1934	FEB	4	Pic		APR	1	Gem
	MAR	14	Ari		MAY	17	Can
	APR	22	Tau		JUL	3	Leo
	JUN	2	Gem		AUG	19	Vir
	JUL	15	Can		OCT	5	Lib
	AUG	30	Leo		NOV	20	Scp
	OCT	18	Vir	1941	JAN	4	Sag
	DEC	11	Lib		FEB	17	Cap
1935	JUL	29	Scp		APR	2	Aqu
	SEP	16	Sag		MAY	16	Pic
	OCT	28	Cap		JUL	2	Ari
	DEC	7	Aqu	1942	JAN	11	Tau
1936	JAN	14	Pic		MAR	7	Gem
	FEB	22	Ari		APR	26	Can
	APR	1	Tau		JUN	14	Leo
	MAY	13	Gem		AUG	1	Vir
	JUN	25	Can		SEP	17	Lib
	AUG	10	Leo		NOV	1	Scp
	SEP	26	Vir		DEC	15	Sag
	NOV	14	Lib	1943	JAN	26	Cap
1937	JAN	5	Scp		MAR	8	Aqu
	MAR	13	Sag		APR	17	Pic
	MAY	14	Scp		MAY	27	Ari
	AUG	8	Sag		JUL	7	Tau
	SEP	30	Cap		AUG	23	Gem
	NOV	11	Aqu	1944	MAR	28	Can
	DEC	21	Pic		MAY	22	Leo
1938	JAN	30	Ari		JUL	12	Vir
	MAR	12	Tau		AUG	29	Lib
	APR	23	Gem		OCT	13	Scp
	JUN	7	Can		NOV	25	Sag
	JUL	22	Leo	1945	JAN	5	Cap
	SEP	7	Vir		FEB	14	Aqu
	OCT	25	Lib		MAR	25	Pic
	DEC	11	Scp		MAY	2	Ari
1939	JAN	29	Sag		JUN	11	Tau
	MAR	21	Cap		JUL	23	Gem
	MAY	25	Aqu		SEP	7	Can
	JUL	21	Cap		NOV	11	Leo
	SEP	24	Aqu		DEC	26	Can
	NOV	19	Pic	1946	APR	22	Leo
1940	JAN	4	Ari		JUN	20	Vir

85

	AUG	9	Lib	OCT	12	Cap
	SEP	24	Scp	NOV	21	Aqu
	NOV	6	Sag	DEC	30	Pic
	DEC	17	Cap	1953 FEB	8	Ari
1947	JAN	25	Aqu	MAR	20	Tau
	MAR	4	Pic	MAY	1	Gem
	APR	11	Ari	JUN	14	Can
	MAY	21	Tau	JUL	29	Leo
	JUL	1	Gem	SEP	14	Vir
	AUG	13	Can	NOV	1	Lib
	OCT	1	Leo	DEC	20	Scp
	DEC	1	Vir	1954 FEB	9	Sag
1948	FEB	12	Leo	APR	12	Cap
	MAY	18	Vir	JUL	3	Sag
	JUL	17	Lib	AUG	24	Cap
	SEP	3	Scp	OCT	21	Aqu
	OCT	17	Sag	DEC	4	Pic
	NOV	26	Cap	1955 JAN	15	Ari
1949	JAN	4	Aqu	FEB	26	Tau
	FEB	11	Pic	APR	10	Gem
	MAR	21	Ari	MAY	26	Can
	APR	30	Tau	JUL	11	Leo
	JUN	10	Gem	AUG	27	Vir
	JUL	23	Can	OCT	13	Lib
	SEP	7	Leo	NOV	29	Scp
	OCT	27	Vir	1956 JAN	14	Sag
	DEC	26	Lib	FEB	28	Cap
1950	MAR	28	Vir	APR	14	Aqu
	JUN	11	Lib	JUN	3	Pic
	AUG	10	Scp	DEC	6	Ari
	SEP	25	Sag	1957 JAN	28	Tau
	NOV	6	Cap	MAR	17	Gem
	DEC	15	Aqu	MAY	4	Can
1951	JAN	22	Pic	JUN	21	Leo
	MAR	1	Ari	AUG	8	Vir
	APR	10	Tau	SEP	24	Lib
	MAY	21	Gem	NOV	8	Scp
	JUL	3	Can	DEC	23	Sag
	AUG	18	Leo	1958 FEB	3	Cap
	OCT	5	Vir	MAR	17	Aqu
	NOV	24	Lib	APR	27	Pic
1952	JAN	20	Scp	JUN	7	Ari
	AUG	27	Sag	JUL	21	Tau

	SEP	21	Gem		NOV	6	Vir
	OCT	29	Tau	1965	JUN	29	Lib
1959	FEB	10	Gem		AUG	20	Scp
	APR	10	Can		OCT	4	Sag
	JUN	1	Leo		NOV	14	Cap
	JUL	20	Vir		DEC	23	Aqu
	SEP	5	Lib	1966	JAN	30	Pic
	OCT	21	Scp		MAR	9	Ari
	DEC	3	Sag		APR	17	Tau
1960	JAN	14	Cap		MAY	28	Gem
	FEB	23	Aqu		JUL	11	Can
	APR	2	Pic		AUG	25	Leo
	MAY	11	Ari		OCT	12	Vir
	JUN	20	Tau		DEC	4	Lib
	AUG	2	Gem	1967	FEB	12	Scp
	SEP	21	Can		MAR	31	Lib
1961	FEB	5	Gem		JUL	19	Scp
	FEB	7	Can		SEP	10	Sag
	MAY	6	Leo		OCT	23	Cap
	JUN	28	Vir		DEC	1	Aqu
	AUG	17	Lib	1968	JAN	9	Pic
	OCT	1	Scp		FEB	17	Ari
	NOV	13	Sag		MAR	27	Tau
	DEC	24	Cap		MAY	8	Gem
1962	FEB	1	Aqu		JUN	21	Can
	MAR	12	Pic		AUG	5	Leo
	APR	19	Ari		SEP	21	Vir
	MAY	28	Tau		NOV	9	Lib
	JUL	9	Gem		DEC	29	Scp
	AUG	22	Can	1969	FEB	25	Sag
	OCT	11	Leo		SEP	21	Cap
1963	JUN	3	Vir		NOV	4	Aqu
	JUL	27	Lib		DEC	15	Pic
	SEP	12	Scp	1970	JAN	24	Ari
	OCT	25	Sag		MAR	7	Tau
	DEC	5	Cap		APR	18	Gem
1964	JAN	13	Aqu		JUN	2	Can
	FEB	20	Pic		JUL	18	Leo
	MAR	29	Ari		SEP	3	Vir
	MAY	7	Tau		OCT	20	Lib
	JUN	17	Gem		DEC	6	Scp
	JUL	30	Can	1971	JAN	23	Sag
	SEP	15	Leo		MAR	12	Cap

	MAY	3	Aqu		JUN	6	Tau
	NOV	6	Pic		JUL	17	Gem
	DEC	26	Ari		SEP	1	Can
1972	FEB	10	Tau		OCT	26	Leo
	MAR	27	Gem	1978	JAN	26	Can
	MAY	12	Can		APR	10	Leo
	JUN	28	Leo		JUN	14	Vir
	AUG	15	Vir		AUG	4	Lib
	SEP	30	Lib		SEP	19	Scp
	NOV	15	Scp		NOV	2	Sag
	DEC	30	Sag		DEC	12	Cap
1973	FEB	12	Cap	1979	JAN	20	Aqu
	MAR	26	Aqu		FEB	27	Pic
	MAY	8	Pic		APR	7	Ari
	JUN	20	Ari		MAY	16	Tau
	AUG	12	Tau		JUN	26	Gem
	OCT	29	Ari		AUG	8	Can
	DEC	24	Tau		SEP	24	Leo
1974	FEB	27	Gem		NOV	19	Vir
	APR	20	Can	1980	MAR	11	Leo
	JUN	9	Leo		MAY	4	Vir
	JUL	27	Vir		JUL	10	Lib
	SEP	12	Lib		AUG	29	Scp
	OCT	28	Scp		OCT	12	Sag
	DEC	10	Sag		NOV	22	Cap
1975	JAN	21	Cap		DEC	30	Aqu
	MAR	3	Aqu	1981	FEB	6	Pic
	APR	11	Pic		MAR	17	Ari
	MAY	21	Ari		APR	25	Tau
	JUL	1	Tau		JUN	5	Gem
	AUG	14	Gem		JUL	18	Can
	OCT	17	Can		SEP	2	Leo
	NOV	25	Gem		OCT	21	Vir
1976	MAR	18	Can		DEC	16	Lib
	MAY	16	Leo	1982	AUG	3	Scp
	JUL	6	Vir		SEP	20	Sag
	AUG	24	Lib		OCT	31	Cap
	OCT	8	Scp		DEC	10	Aqu
	NOV	20	Sag	1983	JAN	17	Pic
1977	JAN	1	Cap		FEB	25	Ari
	FEB	9	Aqu		APR	5	Tau
	MAR	20	Pic		MAY	16	Gem
	APR	27	Ari		JUN	29	Can

	AUG	13	Leo		1990	JAN	29	Cap
	SEP	30	Vir			MAR	11	Aqu
	NOV	18	Lib			APR	20	Pic
1984	JAN	11	Scp			MAY	31	Ari
	AUG	17	Sag			JUL	12	Tau
	OCT	5	Cap			AUG	31	Gem
	NOV	15	Aqu			DEC	14	Tau
	DEC	25	Pic		1991	JAN	21	Gem
1985	FEB	2	Ari			APR	3	Can
	MAR	15	Tau			MAY	26	Leo
	APR	26	Gem			JUL	15	Vir
	JUN	9	Can			SEP	1	Lib
	JUL	25	Leo			OCT	16	Scp
	SEP	10	Vir			NOV	29	Sag
	OCT	27	Lib		1992	JAN	9	Cap
	DEC	14	Scp			FEB	18	Aqu
1986	FEB	2	Sag			MAR	28	Pic
	MAR	28	Cap			MAY	5	Ari
	OCT	9	Aqu			JUN	14	Tau
	NOV	26	Pic			JUL	26	Gem
1987	JAN	8	Ari			SEP	12	Can
	FEB	20	Tau		1993	APR	27	Leo
	APR	5	Gem			JUN	23	Vir
	MAY	21	Can			AUG	12	Lib
	JUL	6	Leo			SEP	27	Scp
	AUG	22	Vir			NOV	9	Sag
	OCT	8	Lib			DEC	20	Cap
	NOV	24	Scp		1994	JAN	28	Aqu
1988	JAN	8	Sag			MAR	7	Pic
	FEB	22	Cap			APR	14	Ari
	APR	6	Aqu			MAY	23	Tau
	MAY	22	Pic			JUL	3	Gem
	JUL	13	Ari			AUG	16	Can
	OCT	23	Pic			OCT	4	Leo
	NOV	1	Ari			DEC	12	Vir
1989	JAN	19	Tau		1995	JAN	22	Leo
	MAR	11	Gem			MAY	25	Vir
	APR	29	Can			JUL	21	Lib
	JUN	16	Leo			SEP	7	Scp
	AUG	3	Vir			OCT	20	Sag
	SEP	19	Lib			NOV	30	Cap
	NOV	4	Scp		1996	JAN	8	Aqu
	DEC	18	Sag			FEB	15	Pic

	MAR	24	Ari
	MAY	2	Tau
	JUN	12	Gem
	JUL	25	Can
	SEP	9	Leo
	OCT	30	Vir
1997	JAN	3	Lib
	MAR	8	Vir
	JUN	19	Lib
	AUG	14	Scp
	SEP	28	Sag
	NOV	9	Cap
	DEC	18	Aqu
1998	JAN	25	Pic
	MAR	4	Ari
	APR	13	Tau
	MAY	24	Gem
	JUL	6	Can
	AUG	20	Leo
	OCT	7	Vir
	NOV	27	Lib
1999	JAN	26	Scp
	MAY	5	Lib
	JUL	5	Scp
	SEP	2	Sag
	OCT	17	Cap
	NOV	26	Aqu
2000	JAN	4	Pic
	FEB	12	Ari
	MAR	23	Tau
	MAY	3	Gem
	JUN	16	Can
	AUG	1	Leo
	SEP	17	Vir
	NOV	4	Lib
	DEC	23	Scp
2001	FEB	14	Sag
	SEP	8	Cap
	OCT	27	Aqu
	DEC	8	Pic
2002	JAN	18	Ari
	MAR	1	Tau
	APR	13	Gem
	MAY	28	Can
	JUL	13	Leo
	AUG	29	Vir
	OCT	15	Lib
	DEC	1	Scp
2003	JAN	17	Sag
	MAR	4	Cap
	APR	21	Aqu
	JUN	17	Pic
	DEC	16	Ari
2004	FEB	3	Tau
	MAR	21	Gem
	MAY	7	Can
	JUN	23	Leo
	AUG	10	Vir
	SEP	26	Lib
	NOV	11	Sep
	DEC	25	Sag
2005	FEB	6	Cap
	MAR	20	Aqu
	MAY	1	Pic
	JUN	12	Ari
	JUL	28	Tau
2006	FEB	17	Gem
	APR	14	Can
	JUN	3	Leo
	JUL	22	Vir
	SEP	8	Lib
	OCT	23	Scp
	DEC	6	Sag
2007	JAN	16	Cap
	FEB	25	Aqu
	APR	6	Pic
	MAY	15	Ari
	JUNE	24	Tau
	AUG	7	Gem
	SEP	28	Can
	DEC	31	Gem*
2008	MAR	4	Can
	MAY	9	Leo
	JUL	1	Vir
	AUG	19	Lib
	OCT	3	Scp

	NOV	16	Sag		AUG	25	Can
	DEC	27	Cap		OCT	16	Leo
2009	FEB	4	Aqu	2010	JUN	7	Vir
	MAR	14	Pic		JUL	29	Lib
	APR	22	Ari		SEP	14	Scp
	MAY	31	Tau		OCT	28	Sag
	JUL	11	Gem		DEC	7	Cap

JUPITER SIGNS 1901–2010

1901	JAN	19	Cap	1927	JAN	18	Pic
1902	FEB	6	Aqu		JUN	6	Ari
1903	FEB	20	Pic		SEP	11	Pic
1904	MAR	1	Ari	1928	JAN	23	Ari
	AUG	8	Tau		JUN	4	Tau
	AUG	31	Ari	1929	JUN	12	Gem
1905	MAR	7	Tau	1930	JUN	26	Can
	JUL	21	Gem	1931	JUL	17	Leo
	DEC	4	Tau	1932	AUG	11	Vir
1906	MAR	9	Gem	1933	SEP	10	Lib
	JUL	30	Can	1934	OCT	11	Scp
1907	AUG	18	Leo	1935	NOV	9	Sag
1908	SEP	12	Vir	1936	DEC	2	Cap
1909	OCT	11	Lib	1937	DEC	20	Aqu
1910	NOV	11	Scp	1938	MAY	14	Pic
1911	DEC	10	Sag		JUL	30	Aqu
1913	JAN	2	Cap		DEC	29	Pic
1914	JAN	21	Aqu	1939	MAY	11	Ari
1915	FEB	4	Pic		OCT	30	Pic
1916	FEB	12	Ari		DEC	20	Ari
	JUN	26	Tau	1940	MAY	16	Tau
	OCT	26	Ari	1941	MAY	26	Gem
1917	FEB	12	Tau	1942	JUN	10	Can
	JUN	29	Gem	1943	JUN	30	Leo
1918	JUL	13	Can	1944	JUL	26	Vir
1919	AUG	2	Leo	1945	AUG	25	Lib
1920	AUG	27	Vir	1946	SEP	25	Scp
1921	SEP	25	Lib	1947	OCT	24	Sag
1922	OCT	26	Scp	1948	NOV	15	Cap
1923	NOV	24	Sag	1949	APR	12	Aqu
1924	DEC	18	Cap		JUN	27	Cap
1926	JAN	6	Aqu		NOV	30	Aqu

Year				Year		
1950	APR	15	Pic	1970	APR 30	Lib
	SEP	15	Aqu		AUG 15	Scp
	DEC	1	Pic	1971	JAN 14	Sag
1951	APR	21	Ari		JUN 5	Scp
1952	APR	28	Tau		SEP 11	Sag
1953	MAY	9	Gem	1972	FEB 6	Cap
1954	MAY	24	Can		JUL 24	Sag
1955	JUN	13	Leo		SEP 25	Cap
	NOV	17	Vir	1973	FEB 23	Aqu
1956	JAN	18	Leo	1974	MAR 8	Pic
	JUL	7	Vir	1975	MAR 18	Ari
	DEC	13	Lib	1976	MAR 26	Tau
1957	FEB	19	Vir		AUG 23	Gem
	AUG	7	Lib		OCT 16	Tau
1958	JAN	13	Scp	1977	APR 3	Gem
	MAR	20	Lib		AUG 20	Can
	SEP	7	Scp		DEC 30	Gem
1959	FEB	10	Sag	1978	APR 12	Can
	APR	24	Scp		SEP 5	Leo
	OCT	5	Sag	1979	FEB 28	Can
1960	MAR	1	Cap		APR 20	Leo
	JUN	10	Sag		SEP 29	Vir
	OCT	26	Cap	1980	OCT 27	Lib
1961	MAR	15	Aqu	1981	NOV 27	Scp
	AUG	12	Cap	1982	DEC 26	Sag
	NOV	4	Aqu	1984	JAN 19	Cap
1962	MAR	25	Pic	1985	FEB 6	Aqu
1963	APR	4	Ari	1986	FEB 20	Pic
1964	APR	12	Tau	1987	MAR 2	Ari
1965	APR	22	Gem	1988	MAR 8	Tau
	SEP	21	Can		JUL 22	Gem
	NOV	17	Gem		NOV 30	Tau
1966	MAY	5	Can	1989	MAR 11	Gem
	SEP	27	Leo		JUL 30	Can
1967	JAN	16	Can	1990	AUG 18	Leo
	MAY	23	Leo	1991	SEP 12	Vir
	OCT	19	Vir	1992	OCT 10	Lib
1968	FEB	27	Leo	1993	NOV 10	Scp
	JUN	15	Vir	1994	DEC 9	Sag
	NOV	15	Lib	1996	JAN 3	Cap
1969	MAR	30	Vir	1997	JAN 21	Aqu
	JUL	15	Lib	1998	FEB 4	Pic
	DEC	16	Scp	1999	FEB 13	Ari

	JUN	28	Tau				
	OCT	23	Ari	2005	OCT	26	Scp
2000	FEB	14	Tau	2006	NOV	24	Sag
	JUN	30	Gem	2007	DEC	17	Cap
2001	JUL	14	Can	2009	JAN	5	Aqu
2002	AUG	1	Leo	2010	JAN	18	Pis
2003	AUG	27	Vir		JUN	6	Ari
2004	SEP	24	Lib		SEP	9	Pis

SATURN SIGNS 1903–2010

1903	JAN	19	Aqu		OCT	18	Pic
1905	APR	13	Pic	1938	JAN	14	Ari
	AUG	17	Aqu	1939	JUL	6	Tau
1906	JAN	8	Pic		SEP	22	Ari
1908	MAR	19	Ari	1940	MAR	20	Tau
1910	MAY	17	Tau	1942	MAY	8	Gem
	DEC	14	Ari	1944	JUN	20	Can
1911	JAN	20	Tau	1946	AUG	2	Leo
1912	JUL	7	Gem	1948	SEP	19	Vir
	NOV	30	Tau	1949	APR	3	Leo
1913	MAR	26	Gem		MAY	29	Vir
1914	AUG	24	Can	1950	NOV	20	Lib
	DEC	7	Gem	1951	MAR	7	Vir
1915	MAY	11	Can		AUG	13	Lib
1916	OCT	17	Leo	1953	OCT	22	Scp
	DEC	7	Can	1956	JAN	12	Sag
1917	JUN	24	Leo		MAY	14	Scp
1919	AUG	12	Vir		OCT	10	Sag
1921	OCT	7	Lib	1959	JAN	5	Cap
1923	DEC	20	Scp	1962	JAN	3	Aqu
1924	APR	6	Lib	1964	MAR	24	Pic
	SEP	13	Scp		SEP	16	Aqu
1926	DEC	2	Sag		DEC	16	Pic
1929	MAR	15	Cap	1967	MAR	3	Ari
	MAY	5	Sag	1969	APR	29	Tau
	NOV	30	Cap	1971	JUN	18	Gem
1932	FEB	24	Aqu	1972	JAN	10	Tau
	AUG	13	Cap		FEB	21	Gem
	NOV	20	Aqu	1973	AUG	1	Can
1935	FEB	14	Pic	1974	JAN	7	Gem
1937	APR	25	Ari		APR	18	Can

1975	SEP	17	Leo
1976	JAN	14	Can
	JUN	5	Leo
1977	NOV	17	Vir
1978	JAN	5	Leo
	JUL	26	Vir
1980	SEP	21	Lib
1982	NOV	29	Scp
1983	MAY	6	Lib
	AUG	24	Scp
1985	NOV	17	Sag
1988	FEB	13	Cap
	JUN	10	Sag
	NOV	12	Cap
1991	FEB	6	Aqu
1993	MAY	21	Pic

	JUN	30	Aqu
1994	JAN	28	Pic
1996	APR	7	Ari
1998	JUN	9	Tau
	OCT	25	Ari
1999	MAR	1	Tau
2000	AUG	10	Gem
	OCT	16	Tau
2001	APR	21	Gem
2003	JUN	3	Can
2005	JUL	16	Leo
2007	SEP	2	Vir
2009	OCT	29	Lib
2010	APR	7	Vir
	JUL	21	Lib

CHAPTER 6

Where It All Happens: Your Rising Sign

To find out what's happening in a horoscope, you first have to look east. The degree of the zodiac ascending over the eastern horizon at the time you were born, which is called the rising sign or ascendant, marks the beginning of the first house, one of twelve divisions of the horoscope, each of which represents a different area of life. These "houses" contain the planets, the doers in a chart. After the rising sign, the other houses parade around the chart in sequence, with the following sign on the next house cusp. Therefore, the setup of the chart—*what* happens *where*—depends on the rising sign.

Though you can learn much about a person by the signs and interactions of the sun, moon, and planets in the horoscope, without a valid rising sign, the collection of planets has no "homes." One would have no idea which area of life could be influenced by a particular planet. For example, you might know that a person has Mars in Aries, which will describe that person's dynamic fiery energy. But if you also know that the person has a Capricorn rising sign, this Mars will fall in the fourth house of home and family, so you know where that energy will operate.

Due to the earth's rotation, the rising sign changes every two hours, which means that babies born later or earlier on the same day in the same hospital will have most planets in the same signs, but may not have the same rising sign. Therefore, their planets may fall in different houses in the chart. For instance, if Mars is in Gemini and your rising sign is Taurus,

Mars will most likely be active in the second or financial house of your chart. Someone born later in the same day when the rising sign is Virgo would have Mars positioned at the top of the chart, energizing the tenth house of career.

Most astrologers insist on knowing the exact time of a client's birth before they analyze a chart. The more accurate your birth time, the more accurately an astrologer can position the planets in your chart by determining the correct rising sign.

How Your Rising Sign Can Influence Your Sun Sign

Your rising sign has an important relationship with your sun sign. Some will complement the sun sign; others hide it under a totally different mask, as if playing an entirely different role, making it difficult to guess the person's sun sign from outer appearances. This may be the reason why you might not look or act like your sun sign's archetype. For example, a Leo with a conservative Capricorn ascendant would come across as much more serious than a Leo with a fiery Aries or Sagittarius ascendant.

Though the rising sign usually creates the first impression you make, there are exceptions. When the sun sign is reinforced by other planets in the same sign, this might overpower the impression of the rising sign. For instance, a Leo sun plus a Leo Venus and Leo Jupiter would counteract the more conservative image that would otherwise be conveyed by the person's Capricorn ascendant.

Those born early in the morning when the sun was on the horizon will be most likely to project the image of their sun sign. These people are often called a "double Aries" or a "double Virgo" because the same sun sign and ascendant reinforce each other.

Find Your Rising Sign

Look up your rising sign on the chart at the end of this chapter. Since rising signs change every two hours, it is important to know your birth time as close to the minute as possible. Even a few minutes' difference could change the rising sign and therefore the setup of your chart. If you are unsure about the exact time, but know within a few hours, check the following descriptions to see which is most like the personality you project.

Aries Rising: Alpha Energy

You are the most aggressive version of your sun sign, with boundless energy that can be used productively if it's channeled in the right direction. Watch a tendency to overreact emotionally and blow your top. You come across as openly competitive, a positive asset in business or sports. Be on guard against impatience, which could lead to head injuries. Your walk and bearing could have the telltale head-forward Aries posture. You may wear more bright colors, especially red, than others of your sign, or be a redhead. You may also have a tendency to drive your car faster.

Can you see the alpha Aries tendency in Barbra Streisand (a sun sign Taurus) and Bette Midler (a sun sign Sagittarius)?

Taurus Rising: Down-to-Earth

You're slow-moving, with a beautiful (or distinctive) speaking or singing voice. You probably surround yourself with comfort, good food, luxurious surroundings, and other sensual pleasures. You prefer welcoming others into your home to gadding about. You may have a talent for business, especially in trading, appraising, and real estate. A Taurus ascendant gives a well-padded physique that gains weight easily, like Liza Minnelli. This ascendant can also endow females with a curvaceous beauty.

Gemini Rising: A Way with Words

You're naturally sociable, with lighter, more ethereal mannerisms than others of your sign, especially if you're female. You love to communicate with people, and express your ideas easily, like former British prime minister Tony Blair. You may have a talent for writing or public speaking. You thrive on variety, a constantly changing scene, and a lively social life. However, you may relate to others at a deeper level than might be suspected. And you will be far more sympathetic and caring than you project. You will probably travel widely, changing partners and jobs several times (or juggle two at once). Physically, your nerves are quite sensitive. Occasionally, you would benefit from a calm, tranquil atmosphere away from your usual social scene.

Cancer Rising: Nurturing Instincts

You are naturally acquisitive, possessive, private, a moneymaker like Bill Gates or Michael Bloomberg. You easily pick up others' needs and feelings—a great gift in business, the arts, and personal relationships. But you must guard against overreacting or taking things too personally, especially during full-moon periods. Find creative outlets for your natural nurturing gifts, such as helping the less fortunate, particularly children. Your insights would be helpful in psychology. Your desire to feed and care for others would be useful in the restaurant, hotel, or child-care industries. You may be especially fond of wearing romantic old clothes, collecting antiques, and dining on exquisite food. Since your body may retain fluids, pay attention to your diet. To relax, escape to places near water.

Leo Rising: Diva Dazzle

You may come across as more poised than you really feel. However, you play it to the hilt, projecting a proud royal presence. A Leo ascendant gives you a natural flair for drama, like Marilyn Monroe, and you might be accused of stealing the spotlight. You'll also project a much more outgoing, optimistic, and sunny personality than others of your sign. You take care to please your public by always projecting star quality, probably tossing a luxuriant mane of hair, sporting a striking hairstyle, or dressing to impress. Females often dazzle with colorful clothing or spectacular jewelry. Since you may have a strong parental nature, you could well become a family matriarch or patriarch, like George H. W. Bush.

Virgo Rising: High Standards

Virgo rising endows you with a practical, analytical outer image. You seem neat, orderly, and more particular than others of your sign. Others in your life may feel they must live up to your high standards. Though at times you may be openly critical, this masks a well-meaning desire to have only the best for loved ones. Your sharp eye for details could be used in the financial world, or your literary skills could draw you to teaching or publishing. The healing arts, health care, and service-oriented professions attract many with a Virgo ascendant. You're likely to take good care of yourself, with great attention to health, diet, and exercise, like Madonna. You might even show some hypochondriac tendencies, like Woody Allen. Physically, you may have a very sensitive digestive system.

Libra Rising: The Charmer

Libra rising gives you a charming, social, and public persona, like John F. Kennedy and Bill Clinton. You tend to avoid confrontations in relationships, preferring to smooth the way or negotiate diplomatically rather than give in to an emotional reaction. Because you are interested in all aspects of a situation, you may be slow to reach decisions. Physically, you'll have good proportions and physical symmetry. You will move with natural grace and balance. You're likely to have pleasing, if not beautiful, facial features, with a winning smile, like Cary Grant. You'll show natural good taste and harmony in your clothes and home decor. Legal, diplomatic, or public relations professions could draw your interest.

Scorpio Rising: Air of Mystery

You project an intriguing air of mystery with this ascendant, as the Scorpio secretiveness and sense of underlying power combine with your sun sign. Like Jacqueline Kennedy Onassis, you convey that there's more to you than meets the eye. You seem like someone who is always in control and who can move comfortably in the world of power. Your physical look comes across as intense. Many of you have remarkable eyes, with a direct, penetrating gaze. But you'll never reveal your private agenda, and you tend to keep your true feelings under wraps (watch a tendency toward paranoia). You may have an interesting romantic history with secret love affairs, like Grace Kelly. Many of you heighten your air of mystery by wearing black. You're happiest near water; you should provide yourself with a seaside retreat.

Sagittarius Rising: The Explorer

You travel with this ascendant. You may also be a more outdoor, sportive type, with an athletic, casual, and outgoing air. Your moods are camouflaged with cheerful optimism or a philosophical attitude. Though you don't hesitate to speak your mind—like Ted Turner, who was called the Mouth of the South—you can also laugh at your troubles or crack a joke more easily than others of your sign. A Sagittarius ascendant can also draw you to the field of higher education or to spiritual life. You'll seem to have less attachment to things and people, and you may explore the globe. Your strong, fast legs are a physical bonus.

Capricorn Rising: Serious Business

This rising sign makes you come across as serious, goal-oriented, disciplined, and careful with cash. You are not one of the zodiac's big spenders, though you might splurge occasionally on items with good investment value. You're the conservative type in dress and environment, and you might come across as quite formal and businesslike, like Rupert Murdoch. You'll function well in a structured or corporate environment where you can climb to the top. (You are always aware of who's the boss.) In your personal life, you could be a loner or a single parent who is father and mother to your children.

Aquarius Rising: One of a Kind

You come across as less concerned about what others think and could even be a bit eccentric. Your appearance is sure to be unique and memorable. You're more at ease with groups of people than others in your sign, and you may be attracted to public life, like Jay Leno. Your appearance may be unique, either unconventional or unimportant to you. Those of you whose sun is in a water sign (Cancer, Scorpio, or Pisces) may exercise your nurturing qualities with a large group, an extended family, or a day-care or community center.

Pisces Rising: Romantic Roles

Your creative, nurturing talents are heightened and so is your ability to project emotional drama. And, like Antonio Banderas, your dreamy eyes and poetic air bring out the protective instinct in others. You could be attracted to the arts, especially theater, dance, film, and photography, or to psychology, spiritual practice, and charity work. You are happiest when you are using your creative ability to help others. Since you are vulnerable to mood swings, it is important for you to find interesting, creative work where you can express your talents and heighten your self-esteem. Accentuate the positive. Be wary of escapist tendencies, particularly involving alcohol or drugs to which you are supersensitive, like Whitney Houston.

RISING SIGNS—A.M. BIRTHS

	1 AM	2 AM	3 AM	4 AM	5 AM	6 AM	7 AM	8 AM	9 AM	10 AM	11 AM	12 NOON
Jan 1	Lib	Sc	Sc	Sc	Sag	Sag	Cap	Cap	Aq	Aq	Pis	Ar
Jan 9	Lib	Sc	Sc	Sag	Sag	Sag	Cap	Cap	Aq	Pis	Ar	Tau
Jan 17	Sc	Sc	Sc	Sag	Sag	Cap	Cap	Aq	Aq	Pis	Ar	Tau
Jan 25	Sc	Sc	Sag	Sag	Sag	Cap	Cap	Aq	Pis	Ar	Tau	Tau
Feb 2	Sc	Sc	Sag	Sag	Cap	Cap	Aq	Pis	Pis	Ar	Tau	Gem
Feb 10	Sc	Sag	Sag	Sag	Cap	Cap	Aq	Pis	Ar	Tau	Tau	Gem
Feb 18	Sc	Sag	Sag	Cap	Cap	Aq	Pis	Pis	Ar	Tau	Gem	Gem
Feb 26	Sag	Sag	Sag	Cap	Aq	Aq	Pis	Ar	Tau	Tau	Gem	Gem
Mar 6	Sag	Sag	Cap	Cap	Aq	Pis	Pis	Ar	Tau	Gem	Gem	Can
Mar 14	Sag	Cap	Cap	Aq	Aq	Pis	Ar	Tau	Tau	Gem	Gem	Can
Mar 22	Sag	Cap	Cap	Aq	Pis	Ar	Ar	Tau	Gem	Gem	Can	Can
Mar 30	Cap	Cap	Aq	Pis	Pis	Ar	Tau	Tau	Gem	Can	Can	Can
Apr 7	Cap	Cap	Aq	Pis	Ar	Ar	Tau	Gem	Gem	Can	Can	Leo
Apr 14	Cap	Aq	Aq	Pis	Ar	Tau	Tau	Gem	Gem	Can	Can	Leo
Apr 22	Cap	Aq	Pis	Ar	Ar	Tau	Gem	Gem	Can	Can	Leo	Leo
Apr 30	Aq	Aq	Pis	Ar	Tau	Tau	Gem	Can	Can	Can	Leo	Leo
May 8	Aq	Pis	Ar	Ar	Tau	Gem	Gem	Can	Can	Leo	Leo	Leo
May 16	Aq	Pis	Ar	Tau	Gem	Gem	Can	Can	Can	Leo	Leo	Vir
May 24	Pis	Ar	Ar	Tau	Gem	Gem	Can	Can	Leo	Leo	Leo	Vir
June 1	Pis	Ar	Tau	Gem	Gem	Can	Can	Can	Leo	Leo	Vir	Vir
June 9	Ar	Ar	Tau	Gem	Gem	Can	Can	Leo	Leo	Leo	Vir	Vir
June 17	Ar	Tau	Gem	Gem	Can	Can	Can	Leo	Leo	Vir	Vir	Vir
June 25	Tau	Tau	Gem	Gem	Can	Can	Leo	Leo	Leo	Vir	Vir	Lib
July 3	Tau	Gem	Gem	Can	Can	Can	Leo	Leo	Vir	Vir	Vir	Lib
July 11	Tau	Gem	Gem	Can	Can	Leo	Leo	Leo	Vir	Vir	Lib	Lib
July 18	Gem	Gem	Can	Can	Can	Leo	Leo	Vir	Vir	Vir	Lib	Lib
July 26	Gem	Gem	Can	Can	Leo	Leo	Vir	Vir	Vir	Lib	Lib	Lib
Aug 3	Gem	Can	Can	Can	Leo	Leo	Vir	Vir	Vir	Lib	Lib	Sc
Aug 11	Gem	Can	Can	Leo	Leo	Leo	Vir	Vir	Lib	Lib	Lib	Sc
Aug 18	Can	Can	Can	Leo	Leo	Vir	Vir	Vir	Lib	Lib	Sc	Sc
Aug 27	Can	Can	Leo	Leo	Leo	Vir	Vir	Lib	Lib	Lib	Sc	Sc
Sept 4	Can	Can	Leo	Leo	Leo	Vir	Vir	Vir	Lib	Lib	Sc	Sc
Sept 12	Can	Leo	Leo	Leo	Vir	Vir	Lib	Lib	Lib	Sc	Sc	Sag
Sept 20	Leo	Leo	Leo	Vir	Vir	Vir	Lib	Lib	Sc	Sc	Sc	Sag
Sept 28	Leo	Leo	Leo	Vir	Vir	Lib	Lib	Lib	Sc	Sc	Sag	Sag
Oct 6	Leo	Leo	Vir	Vir	Vir	Lib	Lib	Sc	Sc	Sc	Sag	Sag
Oct 14	Leo	Vir	Vir	Vir	Lib	Lib	Lib	Sc	Sc	Sag	Sag	Cap
Oct 22	Leo	Vir	Vir	Lib	Lib	Lib	Sc	Sc	Sc	Sag	Sag	Cap
Oct 30	Vir	Vir	Vir	Lib	Lib	Sc	Sc	Sc	Sag	Sag	Cap	Cap
Nov 7	Vir	Vir	Lib	Lib	Lib	Sc	Sc	Sc	Sag	Sag	Cap	Cap
Nov 15	Vir	Vir	Lib	Lib	Sc	Sc	Sc	Sag	Sag	Cap	Cap	Aq
Nov 23	Vir	Lib	Lib	Lib	Sc	Sc	Sag	Sag	Sag	Cap	Cap	Aq
Dec 1	Vir	Lib	Lib	Sc	Sc	Sc	Sag	Sag	Cap	Cap	Aq	Aq
Dec 9	Lib	Lib	Lib	Sc	Sc	Sag	Sag	Sag	Cap	Cap	Aq	Pis
Dec 18	Lib	Lib	Sc	Sc	Sc	Sag	Sag	Cap	Cap	Aq	Aq	Pis
Dec 28	Lib	Lib	Sc	Sc	Sag	Sag	Sag	Cap	Aq	Aq	Pis	Ar

RISING SIGNS—P.M. BIRTHS

	1 PM	2 PM	3 PM	4 PM	5 PM	6 PM	7 PM	8 PM	9 PM	10 PM	11 PM	12 MID-NIGHT
Jan 1	Tau	Gem	Gem	Can	Can	Can	Leo	Leo	Vir	Vir	Vir	Lib
Jan 9	Tau	Gem	Gem	Can	Can	Leo	Leo	Leo	Vir	Vir	Vir	Lib
Jan 17	Gem	Gem	Can	Can	Can	Leo	Leo	Vir	Vir	Vir	Lib	Lib
Jan 25	Gem	Gem	Can	Can	Leo	Leo	Leo	Vir	Vir	Lib	Lib	Lib
Feb 2	Gem	Can	Can	Can	Leo	Leo	Vir	Vir	Vir	Lib	Lib	Sc
Feb 10	Gem	Can	Can	Leo	Leo	Leo	Vir	Vir	Lib	Lib	Lib	Sc
Feb 18	Can	Can	Can	Leo	Leo	Vir	Vir	Vir	Lib	Lib	Sc	Sc
Feb 26	Can	Can	Leo	Leo	Leo	Vir	Vir	Lib	Lib	Lib	Sc	Sc
Mar 6	Can	Leo	Leo	Leo	Vir	Vir	Vir	Lib	Lib	Sc	Sc	Sc
Mar 14	Can	Leo	Leo	Vir	Vir	Vir	Lib	Lib	Lib	Sc	Sc	Sag
Mar 22	Leo	Leo	Leo	Vir	Vir	Lib	Lib	Lib	Sc	Sc	Sc	Sag
Mar 30	Leo	Leo	Vir	Vir	Vir	Lib	Lib	Sc	Sc	Sc	Sag	Sag
Apr 7	Leo	Leo	Vir	Vir	Lib	Lib	Lib	Sc	Sc	Sc	Sag	Sag
Apr 14	Leo	Vir	Vir	Vir	Lib	Lib	Sc	Sc	Sc	Sag	Sag	Cap
Apr 22	Leo	Vir	Vir	Lib	Lib	Sc	Sc	Sc	Sc	Sag	Sag	Cap
Apr 30	Vir	Vir	Vir	Lib	Lib	Sc	Sc	Sc	Sag	Sag	Cap	Cap
May 8	Vir	Vir	Lib	Lib	Lib	Sc	Sc	Sag	Sag	Sag	Cap	Cap
May 16	Vir	Vir	Lib	Lib	Sc	Sc	Sc	Sag	Sag	Cap	Cap	Aq
May 24	Vir	Lib	Lib	Lib	Sc	Sc	Sag	Sag	Sag	Cap	Cap	Aq
June 1	Vir	Lib	Lib	Sc	Sc	Sc	Sag	Sag	Cap	Cap	Aq	Aq
June 9	Lib	Lib	Lib	Sc	Sc	Sag	Sag	Sag	Cap	Cap	Aq	Pis
June 17	Lib	Lib	Sc	Sc	Sc	Sag	Sag	Cap	Cap	Aq	Aq	Pis
June 25	Lib	Lib	Sc	Sc	Sag	Sag	Sag	Cap	Cap	Aq	Pis	Ar
July 3	Lib	Sc	Sc	Sc	Sag	Sag	Cap	Cap	Aq	Aq	Pis	Ar
July 11	Lib	Sc	Sc	Sag	Sag	Sag	Cap	Cap	Aq	Pis	Ar	Tau
July 18	Sc	Sc	Sc	Sag	Sag	Cap	Cap	Aq	Aq	Pis	Ar	Tau
July 26	Sc	Sc	Sag	Sag	Sag	Cap	Cap	Aq	Pis	Ar	Tau	Tau
Aug 3	Sc	Sc	Sag	Sag	Cap	Cap	Aq	Aq	Pis	Ar	Tau	Gem
Aug 11	Sc	Sag	Sag	Sag	Cap	Cap	Aq	Pis	Ar	Tau	Tau	Gem
Aug 18	Sc	Sag	Sag	Cap	Cap	Aq	Pis	Pis	Ar	Tau	Gem	Gem
Aug 27	Sag	Sag	Sag	Cap	Cap	Aq	Pis	Ar	Tau	Tau	Gem	Gem
Sept 4	Sag	Sag	Cap	Cap	Aq	Pis	Pis	Ar	Tau	Gem	Gem	Can
Sept 12	Sag	Sag	Cap	Cap	Aq	Aq	Pis	Ar	Tau	Tau	Gem	Can
Sept 20	Sag	Cap	Cap	Aq	Pis	Pis	Ar	Tau	Gem	Gem	Can	Can
Sept 28	Cap	Cap	Aq	Aq	Pis	Ar	Tau	Tau	Gem	Gem	Can	Can
Oct 6	Cap	Cap	Aq	Pis	Ar	Ar	Tau	Gem	Gem	Can	Can	Leo
Oct 14	Cap	Aq	Aq	Pis	Ar	Tau	Tau	Gem	Gem	Can	Can	Leo
Oct 22	Cap	Aq	Pis	Ar	Ar	Tau	Gem	Gem	Can	Can	Leo	Leo
Oct 30	Aq	Aq	Pis	Ar	Tau	Tau	Gem	Can	Can	Can	Leo	Leo
Nov 7	Aq	Aq	Pis	Ar	Tau	Tau	Gem	Can	Can	Leo	Leo	Leo
Nov 15	Aq	Pis	Ar	Tau	Gem	Gem	Can	Can	Can	Leo	Leo	Vir
Nov 23	Pis	Ar	Ar	Tau	Gem	Gem	Can	Can	Leo	Leo	Leo	Vir
Dec 1	Pis	Ar	Tau	Gem	Gem	Can	Can	Can	Leo	Leo	Vir	Vir
Dec 9	Ar	Tau	Tau	Gem	Gem	Can	Can	Leo	Leo	Leo	Vir	Vir
Dec 18	Ar	Tau	Gem	Gem	Can	Can	Can	Leo	Leo	Vir	Vir	Vir
Dec 28	Tau	Tau	Gem	Gem	Can	Can	Leo	Leo	Vir	Vir	Vir	Lib

CHAPTER 7

The Keys to Reading Your Horoscope: The Glyphs

Are you ready to take your astrology knowledge to the next level and read your first horoscope chart? If so, you'll encounter a new language of symbols, because horoscope charts are written in glyphs, a centuries-old pictographic language. These little "pictures" are a type of shorthand used by astrologers around the world to indicate the planets and the signs.

There's no way to avoid learning the glyphs, if you want to get deeper into astrology. Whether you download your chart from one of the many Internet sites that offer free charts or you buy one of the many interesting astrology programs, you'll find charts are always written in glyph language. Some software makes it easier for beginners by listing the planets and their signs in English alongside the chart and other programs will pop up an English interpretation as your roll your mouse over the glyph. However, in the long run, it's much easier—and more fun—to learn the glyphs yourself.

There's an extra bonus to learning the glyphs: They contain a kind of visual code, with built-in clues that will tell you not only which sign or planet each represents, but what the symbol means in a deeper, more esoteric sense. Actually the physical act of writing the symbol is a mystical experience in itself, a way to invoke the deeper meaning of the sign or planet through age-old visual elements that have been with us since time began.

Since there are only twelve signs and ten planets (not counting a few asteroids and other space objects some astrologers use), it's a lot easier than learning to read a foreign language. Here's a code cracker for the glyphs, beginning with the glyphs for the planets. To those who already know their glyphs, don't just skim over the chapter. These familiar graphics have hidden meanings you will discover!

The Glyphs for the Planets

The glyphs for the planets are easy to learn. They're simple combinations of the most basic visual elements: the circle, the semicircle or arc, and the cross. However, each component of a glyph has a special meaning in relation to the other parts of the symbol.

The circle, which has no beginning or end, is one of the oldest symbols of spirit or spiritual forces. Early diagrams of the heavens—spiritual territory—are shown in circular form. The never-ending line of the circle is the perfect symbol for eternity. The semicircle or arc is an incomplete circle, symbolizing the receptive, finite soul, which contains spiritual potential in the curving line.

The vertical line of the cross symbolizes movement from heaven to earth. The horizontal line describes temporal movement, here and now, in time and space. Combined in a cross, the vertical and horizontal planes symbolize manifestation in the material world.

The Sun Glyph ☉

The sun is always shown by this powerful solar symbol, a circle with a point in the center. The center point is you, your spiritual center, and the symbol represents your infinite personality incarnating (the point) into the finite cycles of birth and death.

The sun has been represented by a circle or disk since ancient Egyptian times when the solar disk represented the sun god, Ra. Some archaeologists believe the great stone circles found in England were centers of sun worship. This particular version of the symbol was brought into common use in the sixteenth century after German occultist and scholar Cornelius Agrippa (1486–1535) wrote a book called *Die Occulta Philosophia,* which became accepted as the authority in the field. Agrippa collected many of the medieval astrological and magical symbols in this book, which have been used by astrologers since then.

The Moon Glyph ☽

The moon glyph is the most recognizable symbol on a chart, a left-facing arc stylized into the crescent moon. As part of a circle, the arc symbolizes the potential fulfillment of the entire circle, the life force that is still incomplete. Therefore, it is the ideal representation of the reactive, receptive, emotional nature of the moon.

The Mercury Glyph ☿

Mercury contains all three elemental symbols: the crescent, the circle, and the cross in vertical order. This is the "Venus with a hat" glyph (compare with the symbol of Venus). With another stretch of the imagination, can't you see the winged cap of Mercury the messenger? Think of the upturned crescent as antennae that tune in and transmit messages from the sun, reminding you that Mercury is the way you communicate, the way your mind works. The upturned arc is receiving energy into the spirit or solar circle, which will later be translated into action on the material plane, symbolized by the cross. All the elements are equally sized because Mercury is neutral; it doesn't play favorites! This planet symbolizes objective, detached, unemotional thinking.

The Venus Glyph ♀

Here the relationship is between two components: the circle of spirit and the cross of matter. Spirit is elevated over matter, pulling it upward. Venus asks, "What is beautiful? What do you like best? What do you love to have done to you?" Consequently, Venus determines both your ideal of beauty and what feels good sensually. It governs your own allure and power to attract, as well as what attracts and pleases you.

The Mars Glyph ♂

In this glyph, the cross of matter is stylized into an arrowhead pointed up and outward, propelled by the circle of spirit. With a little imagination, you can visualize it as the shield and spear of Mars, the ancient god of war. You can deduce that Mars embodies your spiritual energy projected into the outer world. It's your assertiveness, your initiative, your aggressive drive, what you like to do to others, your temper. If you know someone's Mars, you know whether they'll blow up when angry or do a slow burn. Your task is to use your outgoing Mars energy wisely and well.

The Jupiter Glyph ♃

Jupiter is the basic cross of matter, with a large stylized crescent perched on the left side of the horizontal, temporal plane. You might think of the crescent as an open hand, because one meaning of Jupiter is "luck," what's handed to you. You don't have to work for what you get from Jupiter; it comes to you, if you're open to it.

The Jupiter glyph might also remind you of a jumbo jet plane, with a huge tail fin, about to take off. This is the planet of travel, mental and spiritual, of expanding your horizons via new ideas, new spiritual dimensions, and new places. Jupiter embodies the optimism and enthusiasm of the traveler about to embark on an exciting adventure.

The Saturn Glyph ♄

Flip Jupiter over, and you've got Saturn. This might not be immediately apparent because Saturn is usually stylized into an "h" form like the one shown here. The principle it expresses is the opposite of Jupiter's expansive tendencies. Saturn pulls you back to earth: the receptive arc is pushed down underneath the cross of matter. Before there are any rewards or expansion, the duties and obligations of the material world must be considered. Saturn says, "Stop, wait, finish your chores before you take off!"

Saturn's glyph also resembles the sickle of old "Father Time."

Saturn was first known as Chronos, the Greek god of time, for time brings all matter to an end. When it was the most distant planet (before the discovery of Uranus), Saturn was believed to be the place where time stopped. After the soul departed from earth, it journeyed back to the outer reaches of the universe and finally stopped at Saturn, or at "the end of time."

The Uranus Glyph ♅

The glyph for Uranus is often stylized to form a capital *H* after Sir William Herschel, who discovered the planet. But the more esoteric version curves the two pillars of the H into crescent antennae, or "ears," like satellite disks receiving signals from space. These are perched on the horizontal material line of the cross of matter and pushed from below by the circle of the spirit. To many sci-fi fans, Uranus looks like an orbiting satellite.

Uranus channels the highest energy of all, the white electrical light of the universal spiritual force that holds the cosmos together. This pure electrical energy is gathered from all over the universe. Because Uranus energy doesn't follow any ordinary celestial drumbeat, it can't be controlled or predicted (which is also true of those who are strongly influenced by this eccentric planet). In the symbol, this energy is manifested through the balance of polarities (the two opposite arms of the glyph) like the two polarized wires of a lightbulb.

The Neptune Glyph ♆

Neptune's glyph is usually stylized to look like a trident, the weapon of the Roman god Neptune. However, on a more esoteric level, it shows the large upturned crescent of the soul pierced through by the cross of matter. Neptune nails down, or materializes, soul energy, bringing impulses from the soul level into manifestation. That is why Neptune is associated with imagination or "imagining in," making an image of the soul. Neptune works through feelings, sensitivity, and the mystical capacity to bring the divine into the earthly realm.

The Pluto Glyph ♇

Pluto is written two ways. One is a composite of the letters *PL,* the first two letters of the word Pluto and coincidentally the initials of Percival Lowell, one of the planet's discoverers. The other, more esoteric symbol is a small circle above a large open crescent that surmounts the cross of matter. This depicts Pluto's power to regenerate. Imagine a new little spirit emerging from the sheltering cup of the soul. Pluto rules the forces of life and death. After this planet has passed a sensitive point in your chart, you are transformed, reborn in some way.

Sci-fi fans might visualize this glyph as a small satellite (the circle) being launched. It was shortly after Pluto's discovery that we learned how to harness the nuclear forces that made space exploration possible. Pluto rules the transformative power of atomic energy, which totally changed our lives and from which there is no turning back.

The Glyphs for the Signs

On an astrology chart, the glyph for the sign will appear after that of the planet. For example, when you see the moon glyph followed first by a number and then by another glyph representing the sign, this means that the moon was passing over a certain degree of that astrological sign at the time of the chart. On the dividing lines between the houses on your chart, you'll find the symbol for the sign that rules the house.

Because sun sign symbols do not contain the same basic geometric components of the planetary glyphs, we must look elsewhere for clues to their meanings. Many have been passed down from ancient Egyptian and Chaldean civilizations with few modifications. Others have been adapted over the centuries.

In deciphering many of the glyphs, you'll often find that the symbols reveal a dual nature of the sign, which is not always apparent in the usual sun sign descriptions. For instance, the Gemini glyph is similar to the Roman numeral for two, and reveals this sign's longing to discover a twin soul. The Cancer glyph may be interpreted as resembling either the nurturing breasts or the self-protective claws of a crab, both symbols associated with the contrasting qualities of this sign. Libra's glyph embodies the duality of the spirit balanced with material reality. The Sagittarius glyph shows that the aspirant must also carry along the earthly animal nature in his quest. The Capricorn sea goat is another symbol with dual emphasis. The goat climbs high, yet is always pulled back by the deep waters of the unconscious. Aquarius embodies the double waves of mental detachment, balanced by the desire for connection with others, in a friendly way. Finally, the two fishes of Pisces, which are forever tied together, show the duality of the soul and the spirit that must be reconciled.

The Aries Glyph ♈

Since the symbol for Aries is the Ram, this glyph is obviously associated with a ram's horns, which characterize one aspect of the Aries personality—an aggressive, me-first, leaping-headfirst attitude. But the symbol can be interpreted in other ways as well. Some astrologers liken it to a fountain of energy, which Aries people also embody. The first sign of the zodiac bursts on the scene eagerly, ready to go. Another analogy is to the eyebrows and nose of the human head, which Aries rules, and the thinking power that is initiated by the brain.

One theory of this symbol links it to the Egyptian god Amun, represented by a ram in ancient times. As Amun-Ra, this god was believed to embody the creator of the universe, the leader of all the other gods. This relates easily to the position of Aries as the leader (or first sign) of the zodiac, which begins at the spring equinox, a time of the year when nature is renewed.

The Taurus Glyph ♉

This is another easy glyph to draw and identify. It takes little imagination to decipher the bull's head with long curving horns. Like its symbol the Bull, the archetypal Taurus is slow to anger but ferocious when provoked, as well as stubborn, steady, and sensual. Another association is the larynx (and thyroid) of the throat area (ruled by Taurus) and the eustachian tubes running up to the ears, which coincides with the relationship of Taurus to the voice, song, and music. Many famous singers, musicians, and composers have prominent Taurus influences.

Many ancient religions involved a bull as the central figure in fertility rites or initiations, usually symbolizing the victory of man over his animal nature. Another possible origin is in the sacred bull of Egypt, who embodied the incarnate form of Osiris, god of death and resurrection. In early Christian imagery, the Taurus Bull represented St. Luke.

The Gemini Glyph ♊

The standard glyph immediately calls to mind the Roman numeral for two (II) and the Twins symbol, as it is called, for Gemini. In almost all drawings and images used for this sign, the relationship between two persons is emphasized. Usually one twin will be touching the other, which signifies communication, human contact, the desire to share.

The top line of the Gemini glyph indicates mental communication, while the bottom line indicates shared physical space.

The most famous Gemini legend is that of the twin sons Castor and Pollux, one of whom had a mortal father while the other was the son of Zeus, king of the gods. When it came time for the mortal twin to die, his grief-stricken brother pleaded with Zeus, who agreed to let them spend half the year on earth in mortal form and half in immortal life, with the gods on Mount Olympus. This reflects a basic duality of humankind, which possesses an immortal soul yet is also subject to the limits of mortality.

The Cancer Glyph ♋

Two convenient images relate to the Cancer glyph. It is easiest to decode the curving claws of the Cancer symbol, the Crab. Like the crab's, Cancer's element is water. This sensitive sign also has a hard protective shell to protect its tender interior. The crab must be wily to escape predators, scampering sideways and hiding under rocks. The crab also responds to the cycles of the moon, as do all shellfish. The other image is that of two female breasts, which Cancer rules, showing that this is a sign that nurtures and protects others as well as itself.

In ancient Egypt, Cancer was also represented by the scarab beetle, a symbol of regeneration and eternal life.

The Leo Glyph ♌

Notice that the Leo glyph seems to be an extension of Cancer's glyph, with a significant difference. In the Cancer glyph, the lines curve inward protectively. The Leo glyph expresses energy outwardly. And there is no duality in the symbol, the Lion, or in Leo, the sign.

Lions have belonged to the sign of Leo since earliest times. It is not difficult to imagine the king of beasts with his sweeping mane and curling tail from this glyph. The upward sweep of the glyph easily describes the positive energy of Leo: the flourishing tail, the flamboyant qualities. Another analogy, perhaps a stretch of the imagination, is that of a heart leaping up with joy and enthusiasm, also very typical of Leo, which also rules the heart. In early Christian imagery, the Leo Lion represented St. Mark.

The Virgo Glyph ♍

You can read much into this mysterious glyph. For instance, it could represent the initials of "Mary Virgin," or a young woman holding a staff of wheat, or stylized female genitalia, all common interpretations. The M shape might also remind you that Virgo is ruled by Mercury. The cross beneath the symbol reveals the grounded, practical nature of this earth sign.

The earliest zodiacs link Virgo with the Egyptian goddess Isis, who gave birth to the god Horus after her husband Osiris had been killed, in the archetype of a miraculous conception. There are many ancient statues of Isis nursing her baby son, which are reminiscent of medieval Virgin and Child motifs. This sign has also been associated with the image of the Holy Grail, when the Virgo symbol was substituted with a chalice.

The Libra Glyph ♎

It is not difficult to read the standard image for Libra, the Scales, into this glyph. There is another meaning, however, that is equally relevant: the setting sun as it descends over the horizon. Libra's natural position on the zodiac wheel is the descendant, or sunset position (as the Aries natural position is the ascendant, or rising sign). Both images relate to Libra's personality. Libra is always weighing pros and cons for a balanced decision. In the sunset image, the sun (male) hovers over the horizontal earth (female) before setting. Libra is the space between these lines, harmonizing yin and yang, spiritual and material, male and female, ideal and real worlds. The glyph has also been linked to the kidneys, which are associated with Libra.

The Scorpio Glyph ♏

With its barbed tail, this glyph is easy to identify as the Scorpion for the sign of Scorpio. It also represents the male sexual parts, over which the sign rules. From the arrowhead, you can draw the conclusion that Mars was once its ruler. Some earlier Egyptian glyphs for Scorpio represent it as an erect serpent, so the Serpent is an alternate symbol.

Another symbol for Scorpio, which is not identifiable in this glyph, is the Eagle. Scorpios can go to extremes, either in soaring like the eagle or self-destructing like the scorpion. In early Christian imagery, which often used zodiacal symbols, the Scorpio Eagle was chosen to symbolize the intense apostle St. John the Evangelist.

The Sagittarius Glyph ♐

This is one of the easiest to spot and draw: an upward pointing arrow lifting up a cross. The arrow is pointing skyward, while the cross represents the four elements of the material world, which the arrow must convey. Elevating materiality into spirituality is an important Sagittarius quality, which explains why this sign is associated with higher learning, religion, philosophy, travel—the aspiring professions. Sagittarius can also send barbed arrows of frankness in the pursuit of truth, so the Archer symbol for Sagittarius is apt. (Sagittarius is also the sign of the supersalesman.)

Sagittarius is symbolically represented by the centaur, a mythological creature who is half man, half horse, aiming his arrow toward the skies. Though Sagittarius is motivated by spiritual aspiration, it also must balance the powerful appetites of the animal nature. The centaur Chiron, a figure in Greek mythology, became a wise teacher who, after many adventures and world travels, was killed by a poisoned arrow.

The Capricorn Glyph ♑

One of the most difficult symbols to draw, this glyph may take some practice. It is a representation of the sea goat: a mythical animal that is a goat with a curving fish's tail. The goat part of Capricorn wants to leave the waters of the emotions and climb to the elevated areas of life. But the fish tail is the unconscious, the deep chaotic psychic level that draws the goat back. Capricorn is often trying to escape the deep, feeling part of life by submerging himself in work, steadily ascending to the top. To some people, the glyph represents a seated figure with a bent knee, a reminder that Capricorn governs the knee area of the body.

An interesting aspect of this glyph is the contrast of the sharp pointed horns—which represent the penetrating, shrewd, conscious side of Capricorn—with the swishing tail—which represents its serpentine, unconscious, emotional force. One Capricorn legend, which dates from Roman times, tells of the earthy fertility god, Pan, who tried to save himself from uncontrollable sexual desires by jumping into the Nile. His upper body then turned into a goat, while the lower part became a fish. Later, Jupiter gave him a safe haven as a constellation in the skies.

The Aquarius Glyph ♒

This ancient water symbol can be traced back to an Egyptian hieroglyph representing streams of life force. Symbolized by the Water Bearer, Aquarius is distributor of the waters of life—the magic liquid of regeneration. The two waves can also be linked to the positive and negative charges of the electrical energy that Aquarius rules, a sort of universal wavelength. Aquarius is tuned in intuitively to higher forces via this electrical force. The duality of the glyph could also refer to the dual nature of Aquarius, a sign that runs hot and cold and that is friendly but also detached in the mental world of air signs.

In Greek legends, Aquarius is represented by Ganymede, who was carried to heaven by an eagle in order to become the cupbearer of Zeus and to supervise the annual flooding of the Nile. The sign later became associated with aviation and notions of flight. Like the other fixed signs (Taurus, Scorpio, and Leo), Aquarius is associated with an apostle, in this case St. Matthew.

The Pisces Glyph ♓

Here is an abstraction of the familiar image of Pisces, two Fishes swimming in opposite directions yet bound together by a cord. The Fishes represent the spirit—which yearns for the freedom of heaven—and the soul—which remains attached to the desires of the temporal world. During life on earth, the spirit and the soul are bound together. When they complement each other, instead of pulling in opposite directions, they facilitate the Pisces creativity. The ancient version of this glyph, taken from the Egyptians, had no connecting line, which was added in the fourteenth century.

In another interpretation, it is said that the left fish indicates the direction of involution or the beginning of a cycle, while the right fish signifies the direction of evolution, the way to completion of a cycle. It's an appropriate grand finale for Pisces, the last sign of the zodiac.

CHAPTER 8

Join the Astrology Community

Astrology fans love to share their knowledge and socialize. So why not join the community of astrologers online or at a conference? You might be surprised to find an astrology club in your local area. Connecting with other astrology fans and learning more about this fascinating subject has never been easier. In fact the many options available with just a click of your computer are mind-boggling.

You need only type the word *astrology* into any Internet search engine and watch hundreds of listings of astrology-related sites pop up. There are local meetings and international conferences where you can meet and study with other astrologers, and books and tapes to help you learn at home. You could even combine your vacation with an astrological workshop in an exotic locale, such as Bali or Mexico.

To help you sort out the variety of options available, here are our top picks of the Internet and the astrological community at large.

National Council for Geocosmic Research (NCGR)

Whether you'd like to know more about such specialties as financial astrology or techniques for timing events, or if you'd prefer the psychological or mythological approach, you'll meet the top astrologers at conferences sponsored by the National Council for Geocosmic Research. NCGR is dedicated to providing quality education, bringing astrologers and astrology fans together at conferences, and promoting fellowship. Their course structure provides a systematized study of the many facets of astrology. The organization sponsors educational workshops, taped lectures, conferences, and a directory of professional astrologers.

For an annual membership fee, you get their excellent publications and newsletters, plus the opportunity to network with other astrology buffs at local chapter events. At this writing there are chapters in twenty-six states and four countries.

To join NCGR and for the latest information on upcoming events and chapters in your city, consult their Web site: www.geocosmic.org.

American Federation of Astrologers (AFA)

Established in 1938, this is one of the oldest astrological organizations in the United States. AFA offers conferences, conventions, and a correspondence course. If you are looking for a reading, their interesting Web site will refer you to an accredited AFA astrologer.

6535 South Rural Road
Tempe, AZ 85283
Phone: (888) 301-7630 or (480) 838-1751
Fax: (480) 838-8293
Web site: www.astrologers.com

Association for Astrological Networking (AFAN)

Did you know that astrologers are still being harassed for practicing astrology? AFAN provides support and legal information, and works toward improving the public image of astrology. AFAN's network of local astrologers links with the international astrological community. Here are the people who will go to bat for astrology when it is attacked in the media. Everyone who cares about astrology should join!

8306 Wilshire Boulevard
PMB 537
Beverly Hills, CA 90211
Phone: (800) 578-2326
E-mail: info@afan.org
Web site: www.afan.org

International Society for Astrology Research (ISAR)

An international organization of professional astrologers dedicated to encouraging the highest standards of quality in the field of astrology with an emphasis on research. Among ISAR's benefits are quarterly journals, a weekly e-mail newsletter, and a free membership directory.

P.O. Box 38613
Los Angeles, CA 90038
Fax: (805) 933-0301
Web site: www.isarastrology.com

Astrology Magazines

In addition to articles by top astrologers, most have listings of astrology conferences, events, and local happenings.

Horoscope Guide
Kappa Publishing Group
6198 Butler Pike
Suite 200
Blue Bell, PA 19422-2600
Web site: www.kappapublishing.com/astrology

Dell Horoscope
Their Web site features a listing of local astrological meetings.

Customer Service
6 Prowitt Street
Norwalk, CT 06855
Phone: (800) 220-7443
Web site: www.dellhoroscope.com

The Mountain Astrologer
A favorite magazine of astrology fans, *The Mountain Astrologer* also has an interesting Web site featuring the latest news from an astrological point of view, plus feature articles from the magazine.

P.O. Box 970
Cedar Ridge, CA 95924
Web site: www.mountainastrologer.com

Astrology College

Kepler College of Astrological Arts and Sciences

A degree-granting college, which is also a center of astrology, has long been the dream of the astrological community and is a giant step forward in providing credibility to the profession. Therefore, the opening of Kepler College in 2000 was a historical event for astrology. It is the only college in the United States authorized to issue BA and MA degrees in astrological studies. Here is where to study with the best scholars, teachers, and communicators in the field. A long-distance study program is available for those interested.

Kepler College also offers online noncredit courses that anyone can take via the Kepler Community Learning Center. Classes range from two days to ten weeks in length, and the cost will vary depending upon the class taken. Students can access an online Web site to enroll in specific classes and interact with other students and instructors.

For more information, contact:

4630 200th Street SW
Suite P
Lynnwood, WA 98036
Phone: (425) 673-4292
Fax: (425) 673-4983
Web site: www.kepler.edu

Our Favorite Web sites

Of the thousands of astrological Web sites that come and go on the Internet, these have stood the test of time and are likely to still be operating when this book is published.

Astrodienst (www.astro.com)

Don't miss this fabulous international site, which has long been one of the best astrology resources on the Internet. It's a great place to view your own astrology chart. The world atlas on this site will give you the accurate longitude and latitude of your birthplace for setting up your horoscope. Then you can print out your free chart in a range of easy-to-read formats. Other attractions: a list of famous people born on your birth date, a feature that helps you choose the best vacation spot, and articles by world-famous astrologers.

AstroDatabank (www.astrodatabank.com)

When the news is breaking, you can bet this site will be the first to get accurate birthdays of the headliners. The late astrologer Lois Rodden was a stickler for factual information and her meticulous research is being continued, much to the benefit of the astrological community. The Web site specializes in charts of current newsmakers, political figures, and international celebrities. You can also participate in discussions and analysis of the charts and see what some of the world's best astrologers have to say about them. Their AstroDatabank program, which you can purchase at the site, provides thousands of birthdays sorted into categories. It's an excellent research tool.

StarIQ (www.stariq.com)

Find out how top astrologers view the latest headlines at the must-see StarIQ site. Many of the best minds in astrology comment on the latest news, stock market ups and downs, and political contenders. You can sign up to receive e-mail forecasts at the most important times keyed to your individual chart. (This is one of the best of the online forecasts.)

Astro-Noetics (www.astro-noetics.com)

For those who are ready to explore astrology's interface with politics, popular culture, and current events, here is a sophisticated site with in-depth articles and personality profiles. Lots of depth and content here for the astrology-savvy surfer.

Astrology Books (www.astroamerica.com)

The Astrology Center of America sells a wide selection of books on all aspects of astrology, from the basics to the most advanced, at this online bookstore. Also available are many hard-to-find and used books.

Astrology Scholars' Sites

See what Robert Hand, one of astrology's great teachers, has to offer on his site at www.robhand.com. A leading expert on the history of astrology, he's on the cutting edge of the latest research.

The Project Hindsight group of astrologers is devoted to restoring the astrology of the Hellenistic period, the primary source for all later Western astrology. There are fascinating articles for astrology fans on this site at www.projecthindsight. com.

Financial Astrology Sites

Financial astrology is a hot specialty, with many tipsters, players, and theorists. There are online columns, newsletters, specialized financial astrology software, and mutual funds run by astrology seers. One of the more respected financial astrologers is Ray Merriman, whose market comments on www.mmacycles.com are a must for those following the bulls and bears.

Explore Your Relationships (www.topsynergy.com)

Ever wondered how you'd get along with Brad Pitt, Halle Berry, or another famous hottie? TopSynergy offers a clever tool called a relationship analyst that will help you use astrology to analyze past, present, or possible future relationships. There's a database of celebrity horoscopes for you to partner with your own as well. It's free for unlimited use.

How to Zoom Around the Sky

If you haven't already discovered the wonders of Google Earth (www.earth.google.com), then you've been missing close-up aerial views of anyplace on the planet from your old hometown to the beaches of Hawaii. Even more fascinating for astrology buffs is the newest feature called Google Sky, a marvel of computer technology that lets you view the sky overhead from anyplace you choose. Want to see the stars over Paris at the moment? A few clicks of your mouse will take you there. Then you can follow the tracks of the sun, moon, and planets or check astronomical information and beautiful Hubble images. Go to the Google Web site to download this free program. Then get ready to take a cosmic tour around the earth and sky.

Listen to the Sounds of Your Sign

Astrology Weekly (www.astrologyweekly.com) is a Web site from Romania, with lots to offer astro surfers. Here you can check all the planetary placements for the week, get free charts, join an international discussion group, and check out charts for countries and world leaders. Of special interest is the chart generator, an easy-to-use feature that will create a natal chart. Just click on *new chart* and enter the year, month, day, time, longitude, and latitude of your birth place. Select the Placidus or Koch house system and click on *show it*. Your chart should come right up on the screen. You can then copy the link to your astrology chart, store it, and later share your chart with friends. If you don't have astrology software, this is a good way to view charts instantly. This site also has some fun ways to pass the time, such as listening to music especially chosen for your sun sign.

Stellar Gifts

If you've ever wondered what to give your astrology buddies, here's the place to find foolproof gifts. How about a mug, mouse pad, or plaque decorated with someone's chart? Would a special person like a pendant personalized with their planets? Check out www.milestonegifts.co.uk for some great ideas for putting those astrology charts to decorative use.

CHAPTER 9

The Best Astrology Software: Take Your Knowledge to the Next Level

Are you ready to begin looking at charts of friends and family? Would you like to call up your favorite celebrity's chart or check the aspects every day on your BlackBerry? Perhaps you'd like to study astrology in depth and would prefer a more comprehensive program that adapts to your needs as you learn. If you haven't discovered the wonders of astrology software, you're missing out!

Astrology technology has advanced to the point where even a computerphobe can call up a Web site on a BlackBerry browser and put a chart on the screen in seconds. It does help to have some basic knowledge of the signs, houses, planets, and especially the glyphs for the planets and the signs. Then you can practice reading charts and relating the planets to the lives of friends, relatives, and daily events, the ideal way to get more involved with astrology.

There's a program for every level of interest at all price points—starting with free. For the dabbler, there are the affordable Winstar Express, Know, and Time Passages. For the serious student, there are Astrology (free), Solar Fire, Kepler, Winstar Plus—software that does every technique on the planet and gives you beautiful chart printouts. If you're a MAC user, you'll be satisfied with the wonderful IO and Time Passages software.

However, since all the programs use the astrology symbols, or glyphs, for planets and signs, rather than written words, you should learn the glyphs before you purchase your software. Chapter 7 will help you do just that. Here are some software options for you to explore.

Easy for Beginners

Time Passages

Designed for either a Macintosh or Windows computer, Time Passages is straightforward and easy to use. It allows you to generate charts and interpretation reports for yourself or friends and loved ones at the touch of a button. If you haven't yet learned the astrology symbols, this might be the program for you. Just roll your mouse over any symbols of the planets, signs, or house cusps, and you'll be shown a description in plain English below the chart. Then click on the planet, sign, or house cusp and up pops a detailed interpretation. Couldn't be easier. A new Basic Edition, under fifty dollars at this writing, is bargain priced and ideal for beginners.

Time Passages
(866) 772-7876 (866-77-ASTRO)
Web site: www.astrograph.com

The "Know Thru Astrology" Series

This new series is designed especially for the nonastrologer. There are four programs in the series: KNOW Your Self, KNOW Your Future, KNOW Your Lover, and KNOW Your Child, each priced at an affordable $49.95 (at this writing). Though it is billed as beginner software, the KNOW series offers many sophisticated options, such as a calendar to let you navigate future or past influences, detailed chart interpretations, built-in pop-ups to show you what everything means. You'll need a PC running current Windows versions starting with Windows 98 SE, with 512 Mb RAM, and a hard drive with 170–300 Mb free space.

Matrix Software
126 South Michigan Avenue
Big Rapids, MI 49307
(800) 752-6387
Web site: www.astrologysoftware.com

Growth Opportunities

Astrolabe

Astrolabe is one of the top astrology software resources.
Check out the latest version of their powerful Solar Fire software for Windows. It's a breeze to use and will grow with your
increasing knowledge of astrology to the most sophisticated
levels. This company also markets a variety of programs for all
levels of expertise and a wide selection of computer-generated
astrology readings. This is a good resource for innovative software as well as applications for older computers.

The Astrolabe Web site is a great place to start your astrology tour of the Internet. Visitors to the site are greeted with a
chart of the time you log on. And you can get your chart calculated, also free, with a mini interpretation e-mailed to you.

Astrolabe
Box 1750-R
Brewster, MA 02631
Phone: (800) 843-6682
Web site: www.alabe.com

Matrix Software

You'll find a wide variety of software at student and advanced
levels in all price ranges, demo disks, lots of interesting readings. Check out Winstar Express, a powerful but reasonably
priced program suitable for all skill levels. The Matrix Web
site offers lots of fun activities for Web surfers, such as free
readings from the I Ching, the runes, and the tarot. There are
many free desktop backgrounds with astrology themes.

Matrix Software
126 South Michigan Avenue
Big Rapids, MI 49307
Phone: (800) 752-6387
Web site: www.astrologysoftware.com

Astro Computing Services (ACS)

Books, software, individual charts, and telephone readings are offered by this company. Their freebies include astrology greeting cards and new moon reports. Find technical astrology materials here such as *The American Ephemeris* and PC atlases. ACS will calculate and send charts to you, a valuable service if you do not have a computer.

Starcrafts Publishing
334 Calef Hwy.
Epping, NH 03042
Phone: (866) 953-8458
Web site: www.astrocom.com

Air Software

Here you'll find powerful, creative astrology software, plus current stock market analysis. Financial astrology programs for stock market traders are a specialty. There are some interesting freebees at this site. Check out the maps of eclipse paths for any year and a free astrology clock program.

Air Software
115 Caya Avenue
West Hartford, CT 06110
Phone: (800) 659-1247
Web site: www.alphee.com

Kepler: State of the Art

Here's a program that's got everything. Gorgeous graphic images, audio-visual effects, and myriad sophisticated chart options are built into this fascinating software. It's even got an astrological encyclopedia, plus diagrams and images to help you understand advanced concepts. This program is pricey, but if you're serious about learning astrology, it's an investment that will grow with you! Check out its features at www.astrosoftware.com.

Timecycles Research: For Mac Users

Here's where Mac users can find astrology software that's as sophisticated as it gets. If you have a Mac, you'll love their beautiful graphic IO Series programs.

Time Cycles Research
P.O. Box 797
Waterford, CT 06385
(800) 827-2240
Web site: www.timecycles.com

Shareware and Freeware: The Price Is Right!

Halloran Software: A Super Shareware Program

Check out Halloran Software's Web site, which offers several levels of Windows astrology software. Beginners should consider their Astrology for Windows shareware program, which is available in unregistered demo form as a free download and in registered form for a very reasonable price.

Halloran Software
P.O. Box 75713
Los Angeles, CA 90075
(800) 732-4628
Web site: www.halloran.com

ASTROLOG

If you're computer-savvy, you can't go wrong with Walter Pullen's amazingly complete Astrology program, which is offered absolutely free at the site. The Web address is www.astrolog. org/astrolog.htm.

Astrolog is an ultrasophisticated program with all the features of much more expensive programs. It comes in versions for all formats: DOS, Windows, Mac, and UNIX. It has some cool features, such as a revolving globe and a constellation map. If you are looking for astrology software with all the bells and whistles that doesn't cost big bucks, this program has it all!

Buying a Computer with Astrology in Mind?

The good news is that astrology software is becoming more sophisticated and fun to use. However, if you've inherited an old computer, don't despair. You don't need the fastest processor and all the newest bells and whistles to run perfectly adequate astrology software. It is still possible to find programs for elder systems, including many new exciting programs.

To take full advantage of all the options, it is best to have a system that runs versions of Windows starting with Windows 98 SE. If you're buying a new computer, invest in one with as much RAM as possible, at least 1 GB. A CD drive will be necessary to load programs or an Internet connection, if you prefer to download programs online.

Mac fans who want to run Windows astrology software should invest in dual boot computers that will operate both the Mac and the Windows XP and Vista platforms.

CHAPTER 10

Ask the Expert: A Personal Reading Could Help

In these changing times, preparing ourselves for challenges ahead becomes a top priority as new issues surface in our lives. This could be the ideal time to add an astrologer to your dream team of advisers. Horoscopes can offer general advice to all members of your sign, but a personal reading can deal with what matters most to you. It can help you sort out a problem, find and use the strengths in your horoscope, set you on a more fulfilling career path, give you insight into your romantic life, or help you decide where to relocate. Many people consult astrologers to find the optimum time to schedule an important event, such as a wedding or business meeting.

Another good reason for a reading is to refine your knowledge of astrology by consulting with someone who has years of experience analyzing charts. You might choose an astrologer with a specialty that intrigues you. Armed with the knowledge of your chart that you have acquired so far, you can then learn to interpret subtle nuances or gain insight into your talents and abilities.

How do you choose when there are so many different kinds of readings available, especially since the Internet has brought astrology into the mainstream? Besides individual one-on-one readings with a professional astrologer, there are personal readings by mail, telephone, Internet, and tape. Well-advertised computer-generated reports and celebrity-sponsored readings are sure to attract your attention on commercial Web sites and in magazines. You can even purchase a reading that is incorporated into an expensive handmade fine art book. Then there are astrologers who specialize in specific areas such as finance or medical astrology. And unfortunately, there are many questionable practitioners who range from streetwise Gypsy fortune-tellers to unscrupulous scam artists.

The following basic guidelines can help you sort out your options to find the reading that's right for you.

One-on-One Consultations with a Professional Astrologer

Nothing compares to a one-on-one consultation with a professional astrologer who has analyzed thousands of charts and can pinpoint the potential in yours. During your reading, you can get your specific questions answered and discuss possible paths you might take. There are many astrologers who now combine their skills with training in psychology and are well-suited to help you examine your alternatives.

To give you an accurate reading, an astrologer needs certain information from you: the date, time, and place where you were born. (A horoscope can be cast about anyone or anything that has a specific time and place.) Most astrologers will then enter this information into a computer, which will calculate a chart in seconds, and interpret the resulting chart.

If you don't know your exact birth time, you can usually locate it at the Bureau of Vital Statistics at the city hall of the town or the county seat in the state where you were born. If you still have no success in getting your time of birth, some astrologers can estimate an approximate birth time by using past events in your life to determine the chart. This technique is called rectification.

How to Find an Astrologer

Choose your astrologer with the same care as you would any trusted adviser, such as a doctor, lawyer, or banker. Unfortunately, anyone can claim to be an astrologer—to date, there is no licensing of astrologers or universally established professional criteria. However, there are nationwide organizations of serious, committed astrologers that can help you in your search.

Good places to start your investigation are organizations such as the American Federation of Astrologers (AFA) or the National Council for Geocosmic Research (NCGR), which offer a program of study and certification. If you live near a major city, there is sure to be an active NCGR chapter or astrology club in your area; many are listed in astrology magazines available at your local newsstand. In response to many requests for referrals, both the AFA and the NCGR have directories of professional astrologers listed on their Web sites; these directories include a glossary of terms and an explanation of specialties within the astrological field. Contact the NCGR and AFA headquarters for information. (See also Chapter 8.)

What Happens in a Reading

As a potentially lucrative freelance business, astrology has always attracted self-styled experts who may not have the knowledge or the counseling experience to give a helpful reading. These astrologers can range from the well-meaning amateur to the charlatan or street-corner Gypsy who has for many years given astrology a bad name. Be very wary of astrologers who claim to have occult powers or who make pretentious claims of celebrated clients or miraculous achievements. You can often tell from the initial phone conversation if the astrologer is legitimate. He or she should ask for your birthday time and place and then conduct the conversation in a professional manner. Any astrologer who gives a reading based only on your sun sign is highly suspect.

When you arrive at the reading, the astrologer should be prepared. The consultation should be conducted in a private, quiet place. The astrologer should be interested in your problems of the moment. A good reading is interactive and involves feedback on your part, so if the reading is not relating to your concerns, you should let the astrologer know. You should feel free to ask questions and get clarifications of any technical terms. The more you actively participate, rather than expecting the astrologer to carry the reading or come forth with oracular predictions, the more meaningful your experience will be. An astrologer should help you validate your current experience and be frank about possible negative happenings, but also suggest a positive course of action.

In their approach to a reading, some astrologers may be more literal and others more intuitive. Those who have had counseling training may take a more psychological approach. Though some astrologers may seem to have an almost psychic ability, extrasensory perception or any other parapsychological talent is not essential. A very accurate picture can be drawn from the data in your horoscope chart.

An astrologer may do several charts for each client, including one for the time of birth and a progressed chart, showing the evolution from birth to the present time. According to your individual needs, there are many other possibilities, such as a chart for a different location if you are contemplating a change of place. Relationships between any two people, things, or events can be interpreted with a chart that compares one partner's horoscope with the other's. A composite chart, which uses the midpoint between planets in two individual charts to describe the relationship, is another commonly used device.

An astrologer will be particularly interested in transits, those times when cycling planets activate the planets or sensitive points in your birth chart. These indicate important events in your life.

Many astrologers offer readings recorded on tape or CD, which is another option to consider, especially if the astrologer you choose lives at a distance from you. In this case, you'll be mailed a recorded reading based on your birth chart. This type of reading is more personal than a computer printout and can give you valuable insights, though it is not equivalent to a live dialogue with the astrologer when you can discuss your specific interest and issues of the moment.

The Telephone Reading

Telephone readings come in two varieties: a dial-in taped reading, usually recorded in advance by an astrologer, or a live consultation with an "astrologer" on the other end of the line. The recorded readings are general daily or weekly forecasts, applied to all members of your sign and charged by the minute. The quality depends on the astrologer. Be aware that these readings can run up quite a telephone bill, especially if you get into the habit of calling every day. Be sure that you are aware of the per-minute cost of each call beforehand.

Live telephone readings also vary with the expertise of the astrologer. Ideally, the astrologer at the other end of the line enters your birth data into a computer, which then quickly calculates your chart. This chart will be referred to during the consultation. The advantage of a live telephone reading is that your individual chart is used and you can ask about a specific problem. However, before you invest in any reading, be sure that your astrologer is qualified and that you fully understand in advance how much you will be charged. There should be no unpleasant financial surprises later. The best astrologer is one who is recommended to you by a friend or family member.

Computer-Generated Reports

Companies that offer computer programs (such as ACS, Matrix, and Astrolabe) also offer a variety of computer-generated horoscope readings. These can be quite comprehensive, offering a beautiful printout of the chart plus many pages of detailed information about each planet and aspect of the chart. You can then study it at your convenience. Of course, the interpretations will be general, since there is no personal input from you, and might not cover your immediate concerns. Since computer-generated horoscopes are much lower in cost than live consultations, you might consider them as either a supplement or a preparation for an eventual live reading. You'll then be more familiar with your chart and able to plan specific questions in advance. They also make a terrific gift for astrology fans. In chapter 9, there are listed several companies that offer computerized readings prepared by reputable astrologers.

Whichever option you decide to pursue, may your reading be an empowering one!

CHAPTER 11

Loving Every Sign in the Zodiac

In times of change, we crave the comfort of a loving partner more than ever. If we don't have love, we want to know how and where to find it; and if we already have a loving relationship, we want to know how to make it last forever. You can use astrology to find a lover, understand the one you have, or add excitement to your current relationship. Here are sun-sign seduction tips for romancing every sign in the zodiac.

Aries: Play Hard to Get

This highly physical sign is walking dynamite with a brief attention span. Don't be too easy to get, ladies. A little challenge, a lively debate, and a merry chase only heat them up. They want to see what you're made of. Once you've lured them into your lair, be a challenge and a bit of a daredevil. Pull out your X-rated tricks. Don't give your all—let them know there's more where that came from. Make it exciting; show you're up for adventure. Wear bright red somewhere interesting. Since Aries rules the head and face, be sure to focus on these areas in your lovemaking. Use your lips, tongue, breath, and even your eyelashes to the max. Practice scalp massages and deep kissing techniques. Aries won't wait, so when you make your move, be sure you're ready to follow through. No head games or teasing!

To keep you happy, you've got to voice your *own* needs, because this lover will be focused on *his*. Teach him how to please, or this could be a one-sided adventure.

Taurus: Appeal to All Their Senses

Taurus wins as the most sensual sign, with the most sexual stamina. This man is earthy and lusty in bed; he can go on all night. This is not a sign to tease. Like a bull, he'll see red, not bed. So make him comfortable, and then bombard all his senses. Good food gets Taurus in the mood. So do the right music, fragrance, revealing clothes, and luxurious bedlinens. Give him a massage with delicious-smelling and -tasting oils; focus on the neck area.

Don't forget to turn off the phone! Taurus hates interruptions. Since they can be very vocal lovers, choose a setting where you won't be disturbed. And don't ever rush; enjoy a long, slow, delicious encounter.

Gemini: Be a Playmate

Playful Gemini loves games, so make your seduction fun. Be their lost twin soul or confidante. Good communication is essential, so share deep secrets and live out fantasies. This sign adores variety. Nothing bores Gemini more than making love the same way all the time, or bringing on the heavy emotions. So trot out all the roles you've been longing to play. Here's the perfect partner. But remember to keep it light and fun. Gemini's turn-on zone is the hands, and this sign gives the best massages. Gadgets that can be activated with a touch amuse Gemini. This sign is great at doing two things at once, like making love while watching an erotic film. Turn the cell phone off unless you want company. On the other hand, Gemini is your sign for superhot phone sex.

Gemini loves a change of scene. So experiment on the floor, in the shower, or on the kitchen table. Borrow a friend's apartment or rent a hotel room for variety.

Cancer: Use the Moon

The key to Cancer is to get this moon child in the mood. Consult the moon—a full moon is best. Wining, dining, old-fashioned courtship, and breakfast in bed are turn-ons. Whatever makes your Cancer feel secure will promote shedding inhibitions in the sack. (Don't try any of your Aries daredevil techniques here!) Cancer prefers familiar, comfortable, homey surroundings. Cancer's turn-on zone is the breasts. Cancer women often have naturally inflated chests. Cancer men may fantasize about a well-endowed playmate. If your breasts are enhanced, show them off. Cancer will want to know all your deepest secrets, so invent a few good ones. But lots of luck delving into *their* innermost thoughts!

Take your Cancer near water. The sight and sound of the sea can be their aphrodisiac. A moonlit beach, a deserted swimming pool, a Jacuzzi, or a bubble bath are good seduction spots. Listen to the rain patter on the roof in a mountain cabin.

Leo: Offer the Royal Treatment

Leo must be the best and hear it from you often. In return, they'll perform for you, telling you just what you want to hear (true or not). They like a lover with style and endurance, and to be swept off their feet and into bed. Leos like to go first-class all the way, so build them up with lots of attention, wining and dining, and special gifts.

Never mention other lovers or make them feel second-best. A sure signal for Leo to look elsewhere is a competitive spouse. Leos take great pride in their bodies, so you should pour on the admiration. A few well-placed mirrors could inspire them. So would a striptease with beautiful lingerie, expensive fragrance on the sheets, and, if female, an occasional luxury hotel room, with champagne and caviar delivered by room service. Leo's erogenous zone is the lower back, so a massage with expensive oils would make your lion purr with pleasure.

Virgo: Let Them Be the Teacher

Virgo's standards are so sky-high that you may feel intimidated at first. The key to pleasing fussy Virgo lovers is to look for the hot fantasy beneath their cool surface. They're really looking for someone to make over. So let Virgo play teacher, and you play the willing student; the doctor-patient routine works as well. Be Eliza Doolittle to his Henry Higgins.

Let Virgo help you improve your life, quit smoking, learn French, and diet. Read an erotic book together, and then practice the techniques. Or study esoteric, erotic exercises from the Far East.

The Virgo erogenous zone is the tummy area, which should be your base of operations. Virgo likes things pristine and clean. Fall onto crisp, immaculate white sheets. Wear a sheer virginal white nightie. Smell shower-fresh with no heavy perfume. Be sure your surroundings pass the hospital test. A shower together afterward (with great-smelling soap) could get the ball rolling again.

Libra: Look Your Best

Libra must be turned on aesthetically. Make sure you look as beautiful as possible, and wear something stylishly seductive but never vulgar. Have a mental affair first, as you flirt and flatter this sign. Then proceed to the physical. Approach Libra like a dance partner, ready to waltz or tango.

Libra must be in the mood for love; otherwise, forget it. Any kind of ugliness is a turnoff. Provide an elegant and harmonious atmosphere, with no loud noise, clashing colors, or uncomfortable beds. Libra is not an especially spontaneous lover, so it is best to spend time warming them up. Libra's back is his erogenous zone, your cue to provide back rubs with scented potions. Once in bed, you can be a bit aggressive sexually. Libra loves strong, decisive moves. Set the scene, know what you want, and let Libra be happy to provide it.

Scorpio: Be an All-or-Nothing Lover

Scorpio is legendary in bed, often called the sex sign of the zodiac. But seducing them is often a power game. Scorpio likes to be in control, even the quiet, unassuming ones. Scorpio loves a mystery, so don't tell all. Keep them guessing about you, offering tantalizing hints along the way. The hint of danger often turns Scorpio on, so you'll find members of this sign experimenting with the exotic and highly erotic forms of sex. Sadomasochism, bondage, or anything that tests the limits of power could be a turn-on for Scorpio.

Invest in some sexy black leather and some powerful music. Clothes that lace, buckle, or zip tempt Scorpio to untie you. Present yourself as a mysterious package just waiting to be unwrapped.

Once in bed, there are no holds barred with Scorpio. They'll find your most pleasurable pressure points, and touch you as you've never been touched before. They are quickly aroused (the genital area belongs to this sign) and are willing to try anything. But they can be possessive. Don't expect your Scorpio to share you with anyone. It's all or nothing for them.

Sagittarius: Be a Happy Wanderer

Sagittarius men are the Don Juans of the zodiac—love-'em-and-leave-'em types who are difficult to pin down. Your seduction strategy is to join them in their many pursuits, and then hook them with love on the road. Sagittarius enjoys sex in venues that suggest movement; planes, SUVs, or boats. But a favorite turn-on place is outdoors, in nature. A deserted hiking path, a field of tall grass, or a remote woodland glade—all give the centaur sexy ideas. Athletic Sagittarius might go for some personal training in an empty gym. Join your Sagittarius for amorous aerobics, meditate together, and explore the tantric forms of sex. Lovemaking after hiking and skiing would be healthy fun.

Sagittarius enjoys lovers from exotic ethnic backgrounds, or lovers met in spiritual pursuits or on college campuses. Sagittarius are great cheerleaders and motivators, and will enjoy feeling that they have inspired you to be all that you can be.

There may be a canine or feline companion sharing your Sagittarius lover's bed with you, so check your allergies. And bring Fido or Felix a toy to keep them occupied.

Capricorn: Take Their Mind off Business

The great news about Capricorn lovers is that they improve with age. They are probably the sexiest seniors. So stick around, if you have a young one. They're lusty in bed (it's not the sign of the goat for nothing), and can be quite raunchy and turned on by X-rated words and deeds. If this is not your thing, let them know. The Capricorn erogenous zone is the knees. Some discreet fondling in public places could be your opener. Capricorn tends to think of sex as part of a game plan for the future. They are well-organized, and might regard lovemaking as relaxation after a long day's work. This sign often combines business with pleasure. So look for a Capricorn where there's a convention, trade show, or work-related conference.

Getting Capricorn's mind off his agenda and onto yours could take some doing. Separate him from his buddies by whispering sexy secrets in his ear. Then convince him you're an asset to his image and a boon to his health. Though he may seem uptight at first, you'll soon discover he's a love animal who makes a wonderful and permanent pet.

Aquarius: Give Them Enough Space

This sign really does not want an all-consuming passion or an all-or-nothing relationship. Aquarius needs space. But once they feel free to experiment with a spontaneous and exciting partner, Aquarius can give you a far-out sexual adventure.

Passion begins in the mind, so a good mental buildup is key. Aquarius is an inventive sign who believes love is a playground without rules. Plan surprise, unpredictable encounters in unusual places. Find ways to make love transcendental, an extraordinary and unique experience. Be ready to try anything Aquarius suggests, if only once. Calves and ankles are the special Aquarius erogenous zone, so perfect your legwork.

Be careful not to be too possessive. Your Aquarius needs lots of space and tolerance for friends (including old lovers) and their many outside interests.

Pisces: Live Their Fantasies

Pisces is the sign of fantasy and imagination. This sign has great theatrical talent. Pisces looks for lovers who will take care of them. Pisces will return the favor! Here is someone who can psych out your deepest desires without mentioning them. Pisces falls for sob stories and is always ready to empathize. It wouldn't hurt to have a small problem for Pisces to help you overcome. It might help if you cry on his shoulder, for this sign needs to be needed. Use your imagination when setting the scene for love. A dramatic setting brings out Pisces theatrical talents. Or creatively use the element of water. Rain on the roof, waterfalls, showers, beach houses, water beds, and Jacuzzis could turn up the heat. Experiment with pulsating jets of water. Take midnight skinny-dips in deserted pools.

The Pisces erogenous zone is the feet. This is your cue to give a sensuous foot massage using scented lotions. Let him paint your toes. Beautiful toenails in sexy sandals are a special turn-on.

Your Hottest Love Match

Here's a tip for finding your hottest love match. If your lover's Mars sign makes favorable aspects to your Venus, is in the same element (earth, air, fire, water), or is in the same sign, your lover will do what you want done! Mars influences how we act when we make love, while Venus shows what we like done to us. Sometimes fighting and making up is the sexiest fun of all. If you're the type who needs a spark to keep lust alive (you know who you are!), then look for Mars and Venus in different signs of the same quality (fixed or cardinal or mutable). For instance, a fixed sign (Taurus, Leo, Scorpio, Aquarius) paired with another fixed sign can have a sexy tug-of-war before you finally surrender. Two cardinal signs (Aries, Cancer, Libra, Capricorn) set off passionate fireworks when they clash. Mutable signs (Gemini, Virgo, Sagittarius, Pisces) play a fascinating game of cat and mouse, never quite catching each other.

Your Most Seductive Time

The best time for love is when Venus is in your sign, making you the most desirable sign in the zodiac. This only lasts about three weeks (unless Venus is retrograde) so don't waste time! And find out the time this year when Venus is in your sign by consulting the Venus chart at the end of chapter 5.

What's the Sexiest Sign?

It depends on what sign you are. Astrology has traditionally given this honor to Scorpio, the sign associated with the sex organs. However, we are all a combination of different signs (and turn-ons). Gemini's communicating ability and manual dexterity could deliver the magic touch. Cancer's tenderness and understanding could bring out your passion more than regal Leo.

Which Is the Most Faithful Sign?

The earth signs of Capricorn, Taurus, and Virgo are usually the most faithful. They tend to be more home- and family-oriented, and they are usually choosy about their mates. It's impractical, inconvenient, and probably expensive to play around, or so they think.

Who'll Play Around?

The mutable signs of Gemini, Pisces, and Sagittarius win the playboy or playgirl sweepstakes. These signs tend to be changeable, fickle, and easily bored. But they're so much fun!

CHAPTER 12

Financial Tips from the Stars

Getting the most bang from our buck will be our personal challenge this year, as we continue to learn to live within our means and balance our budgets. One of the advantages of astrology is that we can know the natural direction of the cosmic forces in advance and make financial plans accordingly.

Over the past few years, we've experienced a dramatic shift from the expansive risk taking of Pluto in Sagittarius to the conservative, thrift-promoting Pluto in Capricorn. This influence should continue for several years. Financially savvy astrologers also look to the movement of Jupiter, the planet of luck and expansion, for growth opportunities. Jupiter gives an extra boost to the sign it is passing through. Jupiter moves through Pisces, a sign that Jupiter especially favors, so Pisces and fellow water signs, Cancer and Scorpio, receive extra-lucky rays. Most of us could benefit from using some Pisces-inspired creativity, insight, and imagination especially in the area of our horoscope where Jupiter will be giving us growth opportunities. Pisces will give us the imaginative ideas; then Jupiter enters Aries briefly over the summer and for a lengthy stay next year, which should give us the courage and pioneering spirit to pursue them.

Aries

You've got a taste for fast money, quick turnover, and edgy investments, with no patience for gradual, long-term gains.

You're an impulse buyer with the nerve for risky tactics that could backfire. On the other hand, you're a pioneer who can see into the future, who dares to take a gamble on a new idea or product that could change the world ... like Sam Walton of the Wal-Mart stores, who changed the way we shop. You need a backup plan in case one of your big ideas burns out. To protect your money, get a backup plan you can follow without thinking about it. Have a percentage of your income automatically put into a savings or retirement account. Then give yourself some extra funds to play with. Your weak point is your impatience; so you're not one to wait out a slow market or watch savings slowly accumulate. When Jupiter moves into Aries temporarily this summer, you'll want to move full steam ahead. However, you may have to reevaluate your goals in the fall. Save your big moves for next year, when Jupiter reenters Aries and you can make real progress.

Taurus

You're a saver who loves to see your cash, as well as your possessions, accumulate. You have no qualms about steadily increasing your fortune. You're a savvy trader and a shrewd investor, in there for long-term gains. You have low toleration for risk; you hate to lose anything. But you do enjoy luxuries, and may need to reward yourself frequently. You might pass up an opportunity because it seems too risky, but you should take a chance once in a while. Since you're inspired by Jupiter in Pisces and Aries this year, it's time to support your long-range goals and ideals by exploring socially conscious investments, especially in the clean-energy field and the creative arts. You're especially lucky in real estate or any occupation that requires appraising and trading, as well as earth-centered businesses like organic farming and conservation.

Gemini

With Gemini, the cash can flow in and then out just as quickly. You naturally multi-task, and you are sure to have several projects going at once, as well as several credit cards, which can easily get out of hand. Saving is not one of your strong points—too boring. You fall in and out of love with different ideas; you have probably tried a round of savings techniques. Diversification is your best strategy. Have several different kinds of investments—at least one should be a long-term plan. Set savings goals and then regularly deposit small amounts into your accounts. Follow the lead of Gemini financial adviser Suze Orman and get a good relationship going with your money! With lucky Jupiter accenting your public image, there should be new career opportunities this year. Investigate careers in communications and the media.

Cancer

You can be a natural moneymaker with your peerless intuition. You can spot a winner that everyone else misses. Consider Cancer success stories like those of cosmetics queen Estee Lauder and Roxanne Quimby, of Burt's Bees, who turned her friend's stash of beeswax into a thriving cosmetics business. Who knew? So trust your intuition. You are a saver who always has a backup plan, just in case. Remember to treat and nurture yourself as well as others. Investments in the food industry, restaurants, hotels, shipping, and water-related industries are Cancer territory. You're one of the luckiest signs this year, so keep your antennae tuned for new investment opportunities.

Leo

You love the first-class lifestyle, but may not always have the resources to support it. Finding a way to fund your extravagant tastes is the Leo challenge. Some courses in money management or an expert financial coach could set you on the right track. However, you're also a terrific salesperson, and you're fabulous in high-profile jobs that pay a lot. You're the community tastemaker; you satisfy your appetite for "the best" by working for a quality company that sells luxury goods, splendid real estate, dream vacations, and first-class travel—that way you'll have access to the lifestyle without having to pay for it. This year, Jupiter brings luck through fortunate partnerships and travel.

Virgo

Your sign is a stickler for details, which includes your money management. You like to follow your spending and saving closely; you enjoy planning, budgeting, and price comparison. Your sign usually has no problem sticking to a savings or investment plan. You have a critical eye for quality, and you like to bargain and to shop to get the best value. In fact, Warren Buffet, a Virgo billionaire, is known for value investing. You buy cheap and sell at a profit. Investing in health care, organic products, and food could be profitable for you. With Jupiter in Pisces accenting partnerships, you might want to team up for investing purposes this year.

Libra

Oh, do you ever love to shop! And you often have an irresistible urge to acquire an exquisite object or a designer dress you can't really afford or to splurge on the perfect antique armoire. You don't like to settle for second-rate or bargain buys. Learning to prioritize your spending is especially difficult for your sign, so try to find a good money manager to do it for you. Following a strictly balanced budget is your key to financial success. With Libra's keen eye for quality and good taste, you are a savvy picker at auctions and antiques fairs, so you might be able to turn around your purchase for a profit. With Jupiter accenting the care and maintenance part of your life, this is an excellent year to put your finances in order and balance the budget.

Scorpio

Scorpios prefer to stay in control of their finances at all times. You're sure to have a financial-tracking program on your computer. You're not an impulse buyer, unless you see something that immediately turns you on. Rely on your instincts! Scorpio is the sign of credit cards, taxes, and loans, so you are able to use these tools cleverly. Investing for Scorpio is rarely casual. You'll do extensive research and track your investments by reading the financial pages, annual reports, and profit-loss statements. Investigate the arts, media, and oil and water projects for Jupiter-favored investments this year.

Sagittarius

Sagittarius is a natural gambler, with a high tolerance for risk. It's important for you to learn when to hold 'em, and when to fold 'em, as the song goes, by setting limits on your risk taking and covering your assets. You enjoy the thrill of playing the stock market, where you could win big and lose big. Money itself is rarely the object for Sagittarius—it's the game that counts. Since your sign rarely saves for a rainy day, your best strategy might be a savings plan that transfers a certain amount into a savings account. Regular bill-paying plans are another strategy to keep you on track. Jupiter favors investing in home improvements and family-related businesses this year.

Capricorn

You're one of the strongest money managers in the zodiac, which should serve you well this year when Jupiter, the planet of luck and expansion, is blessing your house of finance. You're a born bargain hunter and clever negotiator—a saver rather than a spender. You are the sign of self-discipline, which works well when it comes to sticking with a budget and living frugally while waiting for resources to accumulate. You are likely to plan carefully for your elder years, profiting from long-term investments. You have a keen sense of value, and you will pick up a bargain and then turn it around at a nice profit. Jupiter favors the communications industry and opportunities in your local area this year.

Aquarius

There should be many chances to speculate on forward-looking ventures this year. The Aquarius trait of unpredictability extends to your financial life, where you surprise us all with your ability to turn something totally unique into a money spinner. Consider your wealthy sign mates Oprah Winfrey and Michael Bloomberg, who have been able to intuit what the public will buy at a given moment. Some of your ideas might sound far-out, but they turn out to be right on the money. Investing in high-tech companies that are on the cutting edge of their field is good for Aquarius. You'll probably intuit which ones will stay the course. You'll feel good about investing in companies that improve the environment, such as new types of fuel, or ones that are related to your favorite cause.

Pisces

Luck is with you this year! The typical Pisces is probably the sign least interested in money management. However, there are many billionaires born under your sign, such as Michael Dell, David Geffen, and Steve Jobs. Generally they have made money from innovative ideas and left the details to others. That might work for you. Find a Scorpio, Capricorn, or Virgo to help you set a profitable course and systematically save (which is not in your nature). Sign up for automatic bill paying so you won't have to think about it. If you keep in mind how much less stressful life will be and how much more you can do when you're not worried about paying bills, you might be motivated enough to stick to a sensible budget. Investment-wise, consider anything to do with water—off-shore drilling, water conservation and purifying, shipping, and seafood. Petroleum is also ruled by your sign, as are institutions related to hospitals.

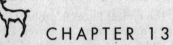

CHAPTER 13

Children of 2010

Parents of several children may see a marked difference between children born in 2010 and those born more than two years ago, because the cosmic atmosphere has changed, which should imprint the personalities of this year's children.

Astrologers look to the slow-moving outer planets—Uranus, Neptune, and Pluto—to describe a generation. When an outer planet changes signs, this indicates a significant shift in energy, which is the case in 2010. In the first half of the year, Uranus and Jupiter in Pisces continue the visionary and creative influence of that sign, which will be reflected in the children born then. However, Uranus moves briefly into fiery Aries in June, which will be accompanied by Jupiter, the planet of expansion, indicating a very astrologically active summer of 2010. Children born during the warm months will reflect this with more drive and energy. After Uranus retrogrades back into Pisces in mid-August for the remainder of the year, the atmosphere becomes somewhat calmer. Neptune still passing through Aquarius and Pluto in Capricorn should add vision and practicality to the personality of this year's children. This generation will be focused on saving the planet and on making things work in order to clear the path for the future. Saturn in Libra will enter the mixture, teaching them diplomacy in getting along with others.

Astrology can be an especially helpful tool when used to design an environment that enhances and encourages each child's positive qualities. Some parents start before conception, planning the birth of their child as far as possible to harmonize with the signs of other family members. However, each baby has its own schedule, so if yours arrives a week early or late, or elects a different sign than you'd planned, recognize that the new sign may be more in line with the mission your child is here to accomplish. In other words, if you were hoping for a Libra child and he arrives during Virgo, that Virgo energy may be just what is needed to stimulate or complement your family. Remember that there are many astrological elements besides the sun sign that indicate strong family ties. Usually each child will share a particular planetary placement, an emphasis on a particular sign or house, or a certain chart configuration with his parents and other family members. Often there is a significant planetary angle that will define the parent-child relationship, such as family sun signs that form a T-square or a triangle.

One important thing you can do is to be sure the exact moment of birth is recorded. This will be essential in calculating an accurate astrological chart. The following descriptions can be applied to the sun or moon sign (if known) of a child—the sun sign will describe basic personality and the moon sign indicates the child's emotional needs.

The Aries Child

Baby Aries is quite a handful. This energetic child will walk—and run—as soon as possible, and perform daring feats of exploration. Caregivers should be vigilant. Little Aries seems to know no fear (and is especially vulnerable to head injuries). Many Aries children, in their rush to get on with life, seem hyperactive, and they are easily frustrated when they can't get their own way. Violent temper tantrums and dramatic physical displays are par for the course with this child, requiring a time-out mat or naughty chair.

The very young Aries should be monitored carefully, since he is prone to take risks and may injure himself. Aries love to take things apart and may break toys easily, but with encouragement, the child will develop formidable coordination. Aries's bossy tendencies should be molded into leadership qualities, rather than bullying, which should be easy to do with this year's babies. Encourage these children to take out aggressions and frustrations in active, competitive sports, where they usually excel. When young Aries learns to focus energies long enough to master a subject and learns consideration for others, the indomitable Aries spirit will rise to the head of the class.

Aries born in 2010 will be a more subdued version of this sign, but still loaded with energy. The Capricorn effect should make little Aries easier to discipline and more focused on achievement. A natural leader!

The Taurus Child

This is a cuddly, affectionate child who eagerly explores the world of the senses, especially the senses of taste and touch. The Taurus child can be a big eater and will put on weight easily if not encouraged to exercise. Since this child likes comfort and gravitates to beauty, try coaxing little Taurus to exercise to music, or take him or her out of doors, with hikes or long walks. Though Taurus may be a slow learner, this sign has an excellent retentive memory and generally masters a subject thoroughly. Taurus is interested in results and will see each project patiently through to completion, continuing long after others have given up. This year's earth sign planets will give him a wonderful sense of support and accomplishment.

Choose Taurus toys carefully to help develop innate talents. Construction toys, such as blocks or erector sets, appeal to their love of building. Paints or crayons develop their sense of color. Many Taurus have musical talent and love to sing, which is apparent at a young age.

This year's Taurus will want a pet or two, and a few plants of his own. Give little Taurus a small garden, and watch the natural green thumb develop. This child has a strong sense of acquisition and an early grasp of material value. After filling a piggy bank, Taurus graduates to a savings account, before other children have started to learn the value of money.

Little Taurus gets a bonanza of good luck from Jupiter in compatible Pisces, supported by Pluto in Capricorn and Saturn retrograding back into Virgo, a compatible earth sign. These should give little Taurus an especially easygoing disposition and provide many opportunities to live up to his sign's potential.

The Gemini Child

Little Gemini will talk as soon as possible, filling the air with questions and chatter. This is a friendly child who enjoys social contact, seems to require company, and adapts quickly to different surroundings. Geminis have quick minds that easily grasp the use of words, books, and telephones, and will probably learn to talk and read at an earlier age than most. Though they are fast learners, Gemini may have a short attention span, darting from subject to subject. Projects and games that help focus the mind could be used to help them concentrate. Musical instruments, typewriters, and computers help older Gemini children combine mental with manual dexterity. Geminis should be encouraged to finish what they start before they go on to another project. Otherwise, they can become jack-of-all-trade types who have trouble completing anything they do. Their disposition is usually cheerful and witty, making these children popular with their peers and delightful company at home.

This year's Gemini baby is impulsive and full of energy, with a strong Aries influence in his life. He will be highly independent and original, a go-getter. When he grows up, Gemini may change jobs several times before he finds a position that satisfies his need for stimulation and variety.

The Cancer Child

This emotional, sensitive child is especially influenced by patterns set in early life. Young Cancers cling to their first memories as well as their childhood possessions. They thrive in calm emotional waters, with a loving, protective mother, and usually remain close to her (even if their relationship with her was difficult) throughout their lives. Divorce and death—anything that disturbs the safe family unit—are devastating to Cancers, who may need extra support and reassurance during a family crisis.

They sometimes need a firm hand to push the positive, creative side of their personality and discourage them from getting swept away by emotional moods or resorting to emotional manipulation to get their way. If this child is praised and encouraged to find creative expression, Cancers will be able to express their positive side consistently, on a firm, secure foundation.

This year's Cancer baby may run against type, thanks to a meeting of Jupiter and Uranus in hyperactive Aries, which might make him much more outgoing and energetic than usual. He should have natural leadership tendencies, which should be encouraged, and the parents' challenge will be to find positive outlets for his energy.

The Leo Child

Leo children love the limelight and will plot to get the lion's share of attention. These children assert themselves with flair and drama, and can behave like tiny tyrants to get their way. But in general, they have a sunny, positive disposition and are rarely subject to blue moods.

At school, they're the types voted most popular, head cheerleader, or homecoming queen. Leo is sure to be noticed for personality, if not for stunning looks or academic work; the homely Leo will be a class clown, and the unhappy Leo can be the class bully.

Above all, a Leo child cannot tolerate being ignored for long. Drama or performing-arts classes, sports, and school politics are healthy ways for Leo to be a star. But Leos must learn to take lesser roles occasionally, or they will have some painful putdowns in store. Usually, their popularity is well earned; they are hard workers who try to measure up to their own high standards—and usually succeed.

This year's Leo should be a highly active version of the sign, with Saturn in Libra teaching lessons of balance and diplomacy in relationships, while Jupiter and Uranus in Aries amp up the energy level and Pluto in Capricorn demands focus and results. Good use of this energy could produce pioneers, fearless natural leaders who could change the world for the better.

The Virgo Child

The young Virgo can be a quiet, rather serious child, with a quick, intelligent mind. Early on, little Virgo shows far more attention to detail and concern with small things than other children. Little Virgo has a built-in sense of order and a fascination with how things work. It is important for these children to have a place of their own, which they can order as they wish and where they can read or busy themselves with crafts and hobbies. This child's personality can be very sensitive. Little Virgo may get hyper and overreact to seemingly small irritations, which can take the form of stomach upsets or delicate digestive systems. But this child will flourish where there is mental stimulation and a sense of order. Virgos thrive in school, especially in writing or language skills, and they seem truly happy when buried in books. Chances are, young Virgo will learn to read ahead of classmates. Hobbies that involve detail work or that develop fine craftsmanship are especially suited to young Virgos.

Baby Virgo of 2010 is likely to be an early talker, and will show concern for the welfare of others. This child should be a natural communicator and may show an interest in the arts or the legal profession.

The Libra Child

The Libra child learns early about the power of charm and appearance. This is often a very physically appealing child with an enchanting dimpled smile, who is naturally sociable and enjoys the company of both children and adults. It is a rare Libra child who is a discipline problem, but when their behavior is unacceptable, they respond better to calm discussion than displays of emotion, especially if the discussion revolves around fairness. Because young Libras without a strong direction tend to drift with the mood of the group, these children should be encouraged to develop their unique talents and powers of discrimination, so they can later stand on their own.

In school, this child is usually popular and will often have to choose between social invitations and studies. In the teen years, social pressures mount as the young Libra begins to look for a partner. This is the sign of best friends, so Libra's choice of companions can have a strong effect on his future direction. Beautiful Libra girls may be tempted to go steady or have an unwise early marriage. Chances are, both sexes will fall in and out of love several times in their search for the ideal partner.

Little Libra of 2010 is an especially creative, expressive child, who may have strong artistic talents. This child is endowed with much imagination, as well as social skills.

The Scorpio Child

The Scorpio child may seem quiet and shy, but will surprise others with intense feelings and formidable willpower. Scorpio children are single-minded when they want something and intensely passionate about whatever they do. One of a caregiver's tasks is to teach this child to balance activities and emotions, yet at the same time to make the most of his great concentration and intense commitment.

Since young Scorpios do not show their depth of feelings easily, parents will have to learn to read almost imperceptible signs that troubles are brewing beneath the surface. Both Scorpio boys and girls enjoy games of power and control on or off the playground. Scorpio girls may take an early interest in the opposite sex, masquerading as tomboys, while Scorpio boys may be intensely competitive and loners. When her powerful energies are directed into work, sports, or challenging studies, Scorpio is a superachiever, focused on a goal. With trusted friends, young Scorpio is devoted and caring—the proverbial friend through thick and thin, loyal for life.

Scorpio 2010 has a strong emphasis on achievement and success. Uranus and lucky Jupiter in Pisces in their house of creativity should put them on the cutting edge of whichever field they choose.

The Sagittarius Child

This restless, athletic child will be out of the playpen and off on explorative adventures as soon as possible. Little Sagittarius is remarkably well-coordinated, attempting daredevil feats on any wheeled vehicle from scooters to skateboards. These natural athletes need little encouragement to channel their energies into sports. Their cheerful friendly dispositions earn them popularity in school, and once they have found a subject where their talent and imagination can soar, they will do well academically. They love animals, especially horses, and will be sure to have a pet or two, if not a home zoo. When they are old enough to take care of themselves, they'll clamor to be off on adventures of their own, away from home, if possible.

This is a child who loves to travel, who will not get homesick at summer camp, and who may sign up to be a foreign-exchange student or spend summers abroad. Outdoor adventure appeals to little Sagittarius, especially if it involves an active sport, such as skiing, cycling or mountain climbing. Give them enough space and encouragement, and their fiery spirit will propel them to achieve high goals.

Baby Sagittarius of 2010 has a natural generosity of spirit and an optimistic, social nature. Home and family will be especially important to him, though he may have an unconventional family life. He'll have an ability to look past the surface of things to seek out what has lasting value.

The Capricorn Child

These purposeful, goal-oriented children will work to capacity if they feel this will bring results. They're not ones who enjoy work for its own sake—there must be a goal in sight. Authority figures can do much to motivate these children, but once set on an upward path, young Capricorn will mobilize his energy and talent and work harder, and with more perseverance, than any other sign. Capricorn has built-in self-discipline that can achieve remarkable results, even if lacking the flashy personality, quick brainpower, or penetrating insight of others. Once involved, young Capricorn will stick to a task until it is mastered. This child also knows how to use others to his advantage and may well become the team captain or class president.

A wise parent will set realistic goals for the Capricorn child, paving the way for the early thrill of achievement. Youngsters should be encouraged to express their caring, feeling side to others, as well as their natural aptitude for leadership. Capricorn children may be especially fond of grandparents and older relatives, and will enjoy spending time with them and learning from them. It is not uncommon for young Capricorns to have an older mentor or teacher who guides them. With their great respect for authority, Capricorn children will take this influence very much to heart.

The Capricorn born in 2010 should be a good talker, with sharp mental abilities. He is likely to be social and outgoing, with lots of friends and closeness to brothers and sisters.

The Aquarius Child

The Aquarius child has a well-focused, innovative mind that often streaks so far ahead of peers that this child seems like an oddball. Routine studies never hold the restless youngster for long; he or she will look for another, more experimental place to try out his ideas and develop his inventions. Life is a laboratory to the inquiring Aquarius mind. School politics, sports, science, and the arts offer scope for their talents. But if there is no room for expression within approved social limits, Aquarius is sure to rebel. Questioning institutions and religions comes naturally, so these children may find an outlet elsewhere, becoming rebels with a cause. It is better not to force these children to conform, but rather to channel forward-thinking young minds into constructive group activities.

This year's Aquarius will have special financial talent. Luck and talent are his and fame could be in the stars!

The Pisces Child

Give young Pisces praise, applause, and a gentle, but firm, push in the right direction. Lovable Pisces children may be abundantly talented, but may be hesitant to express themselves, because they are quite sensitive and easily hurt. It is a parent's challenge to help them gain self-esteem and self-confidence. However, this same sensitivity makes them trusted friends who'll have many confidants as they develop socially. It also endows many Pisces with spectacular creative talent.

Pisces adores drama and theatrics of all sorts; therefore, encourage them to channel their creativity into art forms rather than indulging in emotional dramas. Understand that they may need more solitude than other children may as they develop their creative ideas. But though daydreaming can be creative, it is important that these natural dreamers not dwell too long in the world of fantasy. Teach them practical coping skills for the real world.

Since Pisces are sensitive physically, parents should help them build strong bodies with proper diet and regular exercise. Young Pisces may gravitate to more individual sports, such as swimming, sailing, and skiing, rather than to team sports. Or they may prefer more artistic physical activities, like dance or ice-skating.

Born givers, these children are often drawn to the underdog (they quickly fall for sob stories) and attract those who might take advantage of their empathic nature. Teach them to choose friends wisely, to set boundaries in relationships, and to protect their emotional vulnerability—invaluable lessons in later life.

With the planet Uranus now in Pisces along with lucky Jupiter, the 2010 baby belongs to a generation of Pisces movers and shakers. This child may have a rebellious streak that rattles the status quo. But this generation also has a visionary nature, which will be much concerned with the welfare of the world at large.

CHAPTER 14

Give the Perfect Gift
to Every Sign

So often we're in a quandary about what to give a loved one, someone who has everything, that hard-to-please friend, or a fascinating new person in your life, or about the right present for a wedding, birthday, or hostess gift. Why not let astrology help you make the perfect choice by appealing to each sun sign's personality. When you're giving a gift, you're also making a memory, so it should be a special occasion. The gift that's most appreciated is one that touches the heart, reminds you both of a shared experience, or shows that the giver has really cared enough to consider the recipient's personality.

In general, the water signs (Cancer, Pisces, Scorpio) enjoy romantic, sentimental, and imaginative gifts given in a very personal way. Write your loved one a poem or a song to express your feelings. Assemble an album of photos or mementos of all the good times you've shared. Appeal to their sense of fantasy. Scorpio Richard Burton had the right idea when he gave Pisces Elizabeth Taylor a diamond bracelet hidden in lavender roses (her favorite color).

Fire signs (Aries, Leo, Sagittarius) appreciate a gift presented with lots of flair. Pull out the drama, like the actor who dazzled his Aries sweetheart by presenting her with trash cans overflowing with daisies.

Air signs (Gemini, Libra, Aquarius) love to be surprised with unusual gifts. The Duke of Windsor gave his elegant Gemini duchess, Wallis Windsor, fabulous jewels engraved with love notes and secret messages in their own special code.

Earth signs (Taurus, Virgo, Capricorn) value solid, tangible gifts or ones that appeal to all the senses. Delicious gourmet treats, scented body lotions, the newest CDs, the gift of a massage, or stocks and bonds are sure winners! Capricorn Elvis Presley once received a gold-plated piano from his wife.

Here are some specific ideas for each sign:

Aries

These are the trendsetters of the zodiac, who appreciate the latest thing! For Aries, it's the excitement that counts, so present your gift in a way that will knock their socks off. Aries is associated with the head, so a jaunty hat, hair ornaments, chandelier earrings, sunglasses, and hair-taming devices are good possibilities. Aries love games of any kind that offer a real challenge, like war video games, military themes, or rousing music with a beat. Anything red is a good bet: red flowers, red gems, and red accessories. How about giving Aries a way to let off steam with a gym membership or aerobic-dancing classes? Monogram a robe with a nickname in red.

Taurus

These are touchy-feely people who love things that appeal to all their senses. Find something that sounds, tastes, smells, feels, or looks good. And don't stint on quality or comfort. Taurus know the value of everything and will be aware of the price tag. Taurus foodies will appreciate chef-worthy kitchen gadgets, the latest cookbook, and gourmet treats. Taurus is a great collector. Find out what their passion is and present them with a rare item or a beautiful storage container such as an antique jewelry box. Green-thumb Taurus would love some special plants or flowers, garden tools, beautiful plant containers. Appeal to their sense of touch with fine fabrics—high-thread-count sheets, cashmere, satin, and mohair. One of the animal-loving signs, Taurus might appreciate a retractable leash or soft bed for the dog or cat. Get them a fine wallet or checkbook cover. They'll use it often.

Gemini

Mercury-ruled Gemini appreciates gifts that appeal to their mind. The latest book or novel, a talked-about film, a CD from a hot new singer, or a high-tech gadget might appeal. A beautiful diary or a tape recorder would record their adventures. Since Geminis often do two things at once, a telephone gadget that leaves their hands free would be appreciated. In fact, a new telephone device or superphone would appeal to these great communicators. Gloves, rings, and bracelets accent their expressive hands. Clothes from an interesting new designer appeal to their sense of style. You might try giving Gemini a variety of little gifts in a beautiful box or a Christmas stocking. A tranquil massage at a local spa would calm Gemini's sensitive nerves. Find an interesting way to wrap your gift. Nothing boring, please!

Cancer

Cancer is associated with home and family, so anything to do with food, entertaining at home, and family life is a good bet. Beautiful dishes or serving platters, silver items, fine crystal and linen, gourmet cookware, cooking classes or the latest DVD from a cooking teacher might be appreciated. Cancer designers Vera Wang and Giorgio Armani have perfected the Cancer style and have many home products available, as well as their elegant designer clothing. Naturally, anything to do with the sea is a possibility: pearls, coral, or shell jewelry. Boat and water-sports equipment might work. Consider cruise wear for traveling Cancers. Sentimental Cancer loves antiques and silver frames for family photos. Cancer people are often good photographers, so consider frames, albums, and projectors to showcase their work. Present your gift in a personal way with a special note.

Leo

Think big with Leo and appeal to this sign's sense of drama. Go for the gold (Leo's color) with gold jewelry, designer clothing, or big attention-getting accessories. Follow their signature style, which could be superelegant, like Jacqueline Onassis, or superstar, like Madonna or Jennifer Lopez. This sign is always ready for the red carpet and stays beautifully groomed, so stay within these guidelines when choosing your gift. Feline motifs and animal prints are usually a hit. The latest grooming aids, high-ticket cosmetics, and mirrors reflect their best image. Beautiful hairbrushes tame their manes. Think champagne, high-thread-count linens, and luxurious loungewear or lingerie. Make Leo feel special with a custom portrait or photo shoot with your local star photographer. Be sure to go for spectacular wrapping, with beautiful paper and ribbons. Present your gift with a flourish!

Virgo

Virgo usually has a special subject of interest and would appreciate relevant books, films, lectures, or classes. Choose health-oriented things: gifts to do with fitness and self-improvement. Virgo enjoys brainteasers, crossword puzzles, computer programs, organizers, and digital planners. Fluffy robes, bath products, and special soaps appeal to Virgo's sense of cleanliness. Virgo loves examples of good, practical design: efficient telephones, beautiful briefcases, computer cases, desk accessories. Choose natural fibers and quiet colors when choosing clothes for Virgo. Virgo has high standards, so go for quality when choosing a gift.

Libra

Whatever you give this romantic sign, go for beauty and romance. Libra loves accessories, decorative objects, whatever makes him or his surroundings more aesthetically pleasing. Beautiful flowers in pastel colors are always welcome. Libras are great hosts and hostesses, who might appreciate a gift related to fine dining: serving pieces, linens, glassware, flower vases. Evening or party clothes please since Libra has a gadabout social life. Interesting books, objets d'art, memberships to museums, and tickets to cultural events are good ideas. Fashion or home-decorating magazine subscriptions usually please Libra women. Steer away from anything loud, garish, or extreme. Think pink, one of their special colors, when giving Libra jewelry, clothing, or accessories. It's a very romantic sign, so be sure to remember birthdays, holidays, and anniversaries with a token of affection.

Scorpio

Scorpios love mystery, so bear that in mind when you buy these folks a present. You could take this literally and buy them a good thriller DVD, novel, or video game. Scorpios are power players, so a book about one of their sign might please. Bill Gates, Jack Welch, Condoleezza Rice, and Hillary Clinton are hot Scorpio subjects. Scorpios love black leather, suede, fur, anything to do with the sea, power tools, tiny spy tape recorders, and items with secret compartments or intricate locks. When buying a handbag for Scorpio, go for simple shapes with lots of interior pockets. Sensuous Scorpios appreciate hot lingerie, sexy linens, body lotions, and perfumed candles. Black is the favored color for Scorpio clothing—go for sexy textures like cashmere and satin in simple shapes by designers like Calvin Klein. This sign is fascinated with the occult, so give them an astrology or tarot-card reading, beautiful crystals, or an astrology program for the computer.

Sagittarius

For these outdoor people, consider adventure trips, designer sportswear, gear for their favorite sports. A funny gift or something for their pets pleases Sagittarius. For clothing and accessories, the fashionista of this sign tends to like bright colors and dramatic innovative styles. Otherwise, casual sportswear is a good idea. These travelers usually have a favorite getaway place; give them a travel guide, DVD, novel, or history book that would make their trip more interesting. Luggage is also a good bet. Sleek carry-ons, travel wallets, ticket holders, business-card cases, and wheeled computer bags might please these wanderers. Anything that makes travel more comfortable and pleasant is good for Sagittarius, including a good book to read en route. This sign is the great gambler of the zodiac, so gifts related to their favorite gambling venue would be appreciated.

Capricorn

For this quality-conscious sign, go for a status label from the best store in town. Get Capricorns something good for their image and career. They could be fond of things Spanish, like flamenco or tango music, or of country-and-western music and motifs. In the bookstore, go for biographies of the rich and famous, or advice books to help Capricorn get to the top. Capricorns take their gifts seriously, so steer away from anything too frivolous. Garnet, onyx, or malachite jewelry, Carolina Herrera fragrance and clothing, and beautiful briefcases and wallets are good ideas. Glamorous status tote bags carry business gear in style. Capricorns like golf, tennis, and sports that involve climbing, cycling, or hiking, so presents could be geared to their outdoor interests. Elegant evening accessories would be fine for this sign, which often entertains for business.

Aquarius

Give Aquarius a surprise gift. This sign is never impressed with things that are too predictable. So use your imagination to present the gift in an unusual way or at an unexpected time. With Aquarius, originality counts. When in doubt, give them something to think about, a new electronic gadget, perhaps a small robot, or an advanced computer game. Or something New Age, like an amethyst-crystal cluster. Aquarius like innovative materials with a space-age look. They are the ones with the wraparound glasses, the titanium computer cases. This air sign loves to fly—an airplane ticket always pleases. Books should be on innovative subjects, politics, or adventures of the mind. Aquarius goes for unusual color combinations—especially electric blue or hot pink—and abstract patterns. They like the newest, coolest looks on the cutting edge of fashion and are not afraid to experiment. Think of Paris Hilton's constantly changing looks. Look for an Aquarius gift in an out-of-the-way boutique or local hipster hangout. They'd be touched if you find out Aquarius's special worthy cause and make a donation. Spirit them off to hear their favorite guru.

Pisces

Pisces respond to gifts that have a touch of fantasy, magic, and romance. Look for mystical gifts with a touch of the occult. Romantic music (a customized CD of favorite love songs) and love stories appeal to Pisces sentimentalists. Pisces is associated with perfume and fragrant oils, so help this sign indulge with their favorite scent in many forms. Anything to do with the ocean, fish, and water sports appeals to Pisces. How about a whirlpool, a water-therapy spa treatment, or a sea salt rub. Appeal to this sign with treats for the feet: foot massages, pedicures, ballet tickets, and dance lessons. Cashmere socks and metallic evening sandals are other Pisces pleasers. A romantic dinner overlooking the water is Pisces paradise. A case of fine wine or another favorite liquid is always appreciated. Write a love poem and enclose it with your gift.

CHAPTER 15

Your Pet-Scope for 2010: How to Choose Your Best Friend for Life

With Jupiter, the planet of luck and expansion, in compassionate Pisces, this is a great time to bring joy into your life by adopting an animal friend. At this writing, 63 percent of all American households have at least one pet, according to a recent survey by the American Pet Product Manufacturers Association. And we spend billions of dollars on the care and feeding of our beloved pets. Our pets are counted as part of the family, often sharing our beds and accompanying us on trips.

Whether you choose to adopt an animal from a local shelter or buy a Thoroughbred from a breeder, try for an optimal time of adoption and sun sign of your new friend. If you're rescuing an animal, however, it's difficult to know the sun sign of the animal, but you can adopt on a day when the moon is compatible with yours, which should bless the emotional relationship. Using the moon signs listed in the daily forecasts in this book, choose a day when the moon is in your sign, a sign of the same element, or a compatible element. This means fire and air signs should go for a day when the moon is in fire signs Aries, Leo, Sagittarius or air signs Gemini, Libra, or Aquarius. Water and earth signs should choose a day when the moon is in water signs Cancer, Scorpio, or Pisces or earth signs Taurus, Virgo, or Capricorn. If possible, aim for a new moon, good for beginning a new relationship.

Here are some sign-specific tips for adopting an animal that will be your best friend for life.

Aries: The Rescuer

Aries gets special pleasure from rescuing animals in distress and rehabbing them, so do check your local shelters if you're thinking of adopting an animal. As an active fire sign, you'd be happiest with a lively animal that can accompany you, and you might do well with a rescue animal such as a German shepherd or Labrador retriever. You'd also enjoy training such an animal. Otherwise look for intelligence, alertness, playfulness and obedience in your friend. Since Aries tend to have an active life, look for a sleek, low maintenance coat on your dog or cat. Cat lovers would enjoy the more active breeds such as the Siamese or Abyssinian.

An Aries sun-sign dog or cat would be ideal. Aries animals have a brave, energetic, rather combative nature. They can be mischievous, so the kittens and puppies should be monitored for safety. They'll dare to jump higher, run faster, and chase more animals than their peers. They may require stronger words and more obedience training than other signs. Give them plenty of toys and play active games with them often.

Taurus: The Toucher

Taurus is a touchy-feely sign, and this extends to your animal relationships. Look for a dog or cat that enjoys being petted and groomed, is affectionate, and adapts well to family life. As one of the great animal-loving signs, Taurus is likely to have several pets, so it is important that they all get along together. Give each one its own special safe space to minimize turf wars.

Taurus animals are calm and even tempered, but do not like being teased and could retaliate, so be sure to instruct children in the proper way to handle and play with their pet. Since this sign has strong appetites and tends to put on weight easily, be careful not to overindulge them in caloric treats and table snacks. Sticking to a regular feeding schedule could help eliminate between-meal snacking.

Taurus female animals are excellent mothers and make good breeders. They tend to be clean and less destructive of home furnishings than other animals.

Gemini: The Companion

A bright, quick-witted sign like yours requires an equally interesting and communicative pet. Choose a social animal that adapts well to different environments, since you may travel or have homes in different locations.

Gemini animals can put up with noise, telephones, music, and different people coming and going. They'll want to be part of the action, so place a pillow or roost in a public place. They do not like being left alone, however, so, if you will be away for long periods, find them an animal companion to play with. You might consider adopting two Gemini pets from the same litter.

Animals born under this sign are easy to teach and some enjoy doing tricks or retrieving. They may be more vocal than other animals, especially if they are confined without companionship.

Cancer: The Nurturer

Cancer enjoys a devoted, obedient animal who demonstrates loyalty to its master. An affectionate, home-loving dog or cat who welcomes you and sits on your lap would be ideal. The emotional connection with your pet is most important; therefore, you may depend on your powerful psychic powers when choosing an animal. Wait until you feel that strong bond of psychic communication between you both. The moon sign of the day you adopt is very important for moon-ruled Cancer, so choose a water sign, if possible.

Cancer animals need a feeling of security; they don't like changes of environment or too much chaos at home. If you intend to breed your animal, the Cancer pet makes a wonderful and fertile mother.

Leo: The Prideful Owner

The Leo owner may choose a pet that reminds you of your own physical characteristics, such as similar coloring or build. You'll be proud of your pet, keep the animal groomed to perfection, and choose the most spectacular example of the breed. Noble animals with a regal attitude, beautiful fur, or striking markings are often preferred, such as the Himalayan or red tabby Persian cat, the standard poodle, the chow chow dog. An attention getter is a must.

Under the sign of the King of Beasts, Leo-born animals have proud noble natures. They usually have a cheerful, magnanimous disposition and rule their domains regardless of their breed, holding their heads with pride and walking with great authority. They enjoy grooming, like to show off and be the center of attention. Leo animals are naturals for the show ring, thriving in the spotlight and applause. They'll thrive with plenty of petting, pampering, and admiration.

Virgo: The Caregiver

Virgo owners will be very particular about their pets, paying special attention to requirements for care and maintenance. You need a pet who is clean, obedient, intelligent, yet rather quiet. A highly active, barking or meowing pet that might get on your nerves is a no-no.

Cats are usually very good pets for Virgo. Choose one of the calm breeds, such as a Persian. Though this is a high-maintenance cat, its beauty and personality will be rewarding.

You are compassionate with animals in need, and you might find it rewarding to volunteer at a local shelter or veterinary clinic or to train service dogs.

Virgo animals can be fussy eaters, very particular about their environment. They are gentle and intelligent, and respond to kind words and quiet commands, never harsh treatment.

Virgo is an excellent sign for dogs that are trained to do service work, since they seem to enjoy being useful and are intelligent enough to be easily trained.

Libra: The Beautifier

The Libra owner responds to beauty and elegance in your pet. You require a well-mannered, but social companion, who can be displayed in all of nature's finery. An exotic variety such as a graceful curly-haired Devon Rex cat would be a show-stopper. Libra often prefers the smaller varieties, such as a miniature schnauzer, a mini-greyhound or a teacup poodle.

Pets born under Libra are usually charming, well-mannered gentlemen who love the comforts of home life. They tend to be more careful than other signs, not rushing willfully into potentially dangerous situations. They'll avoid confrontations and harsh sounds, responding to words of love and gentle corrections.

Scorpio: The Powerful

Scorpios enjoy a powerful animal with a strong character. They enjoy training animals in obedience, would do well with service dogs, guard dogs, or police animals. Some Scorpios enjoy the more exotic, edgy pets, such as hairless Sphynx cats or Chinese chin dogs. Scorpios could find rescuing animals in dire circumstances and finding them new homes especially rewarding, as Matthew McConaughey did during Hurricane Katrina.

Animals born under this sign tend to be one-person pets, very strongly attached to their owners and extremely loyal and possessive. They are natural guard animals who will take extreme risks to protect their owners. They are best ruled by love and with consistent behavior training. They need to respect their owners and will return their love with great devotion.

Sagittarius: The Jovial Freedom Lover

Sagittarius is a traveler and one of the great animal lovers of the zodiac. The horse is especially associated with your sign, and you could well be a "horse whisperer." You generally respond most to large, active animals. If a small animal, like a Chihuahua, steals your heart, be sure it's one that travels well or tolerates your absence. Outdoor dogs like hunting dogs, retrievers, and border collies would be good companions on your outdoor adventures.

Sagittarius animals are freedom-loving, jovial, happy-go-lucky types. They may be wanderers, however, so be sure they have the proper identification tags and consider embedded microchip identification. These animals tend to be openly affectionate, companionable, untemperamental. They enjoy socializing and playing with humans and other animals and are especially good with active children.

Capricorn: The Thoroughbred

Capricorn is a discriminating owner, with a great sense of responsibility toward your animal. You will be concerned with maintenance and care, will rarely neglect or overlook any health issues with your pet. You will also discipline your pet wisely, not tolerating any destructive or outrageous antics. You will be attracted to good breeding, good manners, and deep loyalty from your pet.

The Capricorn pet tends to be more quiet and serious than other pets, perhaps a lone wolf who prefers the company of its owner, rather than a sociable or mischievous type. This is another good sign for a working dog, such as a herder, as Capricorn animals enjoy this outlet for their energy.

Aquarius: The Independent Original

Aquarius owners tend to lead active, busy lives and need an animal who can either accompany them cheerfully or who won't make waves. Demanding or high-maintenance dogs are not for you. You might prefer unusual or oddball types of pets, such as dressed-up Chihuahuas who travel in your tote bag or scene-stealing, rather shocking hairless cats. Or you will acquire a group of animals who can play with one another when you are pursuing outside activities, as Oprah Winfrey does. You can relate to the independence of cats, who require relatively little care and maintenance.

Aquarius animals are not loners—they enjoy the companionship of humans or groups of other animals. They tend to be more independent and may require more training to follow the house rules. However, they can have unique personalities and endearing oddball behavior.

Pisces: The Soul Mate

This is the sign that can "talk to the animals." Pisces owners enjoy a deep communication with their pets, love having their animals accompany them, sleep with them, and show affection. Tenderhearted Pisces will often rescue an animal in distress or adopt an animal from a shelter.

Tropical fish are often recommended as a Pisces pet, and seem to have a natural tranquilizing effect on this sign. However, Pisces may require an animal that shows more affection than their fish friends.

Pisces animals are creative types, can be sensually seductive and mysterious, mischievous and theatrical. They make fine house pets, do not usually like to roam far from their owners, and have a winning personality, especially with the adults in the home. Naturally sensitive and seldom vicious, they should be treated gently and given much praise and encouragement.

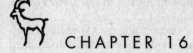

CHAPTER 16

Your Capricorn Personality and Potential: The Roles You Play in Life

The more you understand your Capricorn personality and potential, the more you'll benefit from using your special solar power to help create the life you want. There's a life coach, personal trainer, career adviser, fashion expert, and matchmaker all built into your Capricorn sun sign. Whether you want to make a radical change in your life or simply choose a new wardrobe or paint a room, your sun sign can help you discover new possibilities and make good decisions. You could tap into your Capricorn power to deal with relationship issues, such as getting along with your boss or spicing up your love life. Maybe you'll be inspired by a celebrity sign mate who shares your special traits.

Let the following chapters help you move in harmony with your natural Capricorn gifts. As the ancient oracle of Delphi advised, "Know thyself." To know yourself, as astrology helps you to do, is to gain confidence and strength.

You may wonder how astrologers determine what a Capricorn personality is like. To begin with, we use a type of recipe, blending several ingredients. First there's your Capricorn element: earth. Earth signs are practical, down-to-earth, realistic. Then there's the way Capricorn operates: cardinal—an active doer. Add your sign's polarity: negative, feminine, yin, reactive. Let's not forget your planetary ruler: Saturn, the planet of discipline, structure, order. Add your sign's location in the zodiac: in the tenth house, the place of career, prestige, public life. Finally, stir in your symbol, the Sea Goat, half climbing goat, half fish, with his tail in the waters of the emotions.

This cosmic mix influences everything we say about Capricorn. For example, you could easily deduce that a disciplined earth sign with career emphasis would likely be ambitious, to try to rise to the top of your profession. And that you probably have a deep respect for traditional values.

But all Capricorns are not alike! Your individual astrological personality contains a blend of many other planets, colored by the signs they occupy, plus factors such as the sign coming over the horizon at the exact moment of your birth. However, the more Capricorn planets in your horoscope, the more likely you'll recognize yourself in the descriptions that follow. On the other hand, if many planets are grouped together in a different sign, they will color your horoscope accordingly, sometimes making a low-key, mellow sun sign come on much stronger. So if the Capricorn traits mentioned here don't describe you, there could be other factors flavoring your cosmic stew. (Look up your other planets in the tables in this book to find out what they might be!)

The Capricorn Man: Mr. Achiever

The Capricorn man is an ambitious achiever, a hard methodical worker who is most comfortable in a male-run world. Sometimes the young Capricorn man may appear to be a drifter, but this is usually just a phase where you are learning how the world works and setting serious goals. Later in life, the dignified Capricorn manner takes over. Like Cary Grant, or Humphrey Bogart, you'll embody the elegant tough guy, wise in the ways of the world.

While focused on the top job, you may discount anything or anyone who is not related to your goals. Your personal life is sure to be second to your pursuit of success, at least in the early part of your career. Many Capricorns hold down two jobs at once in a desire to get ahead, or work overtime to move up the ladder of a corporation. Once established, you may decide to make up for lost time and to enjoy the fruits of your labors, allowing your hidden romantic, dreamy side to be revealed.

The Capricorn man generally has an earthy, chauvinistic view of women. You are usually more interested in the physical side of a relationship, and may dismiss women as serious companions or competitors. A woman who can help you in your career or create the right public image is most likely to appeal to you. Though you may experiment sexually with women of a lower class, your wife is usually chosen for her ability to support your cause or elevate your position in some way.

The Capricorn man usually ages very well and is more appealing after forty than before. Then your natural dignity and dry sense of humor shine through. Gray hair or baldness looks distinguished on you. By then you have established yourself financially and feel free to enjoy life. Cary Grant and Humphrey Bogart portrayed the sexy middle-aged Capricorn, the tough guy with a heart and a dry sense of humor.

As a family man, you also improve as you get older, especially when you become the family Rock of Gibraltar, a source of paternal help and wisdom. Family security means a great deal to you. When you are ready to settle down, you'll look for a traditional family relationship.

In a Relationship

The Capricorn man's way of showing love is to share your goals with your mate, and you'll expect her to do everything in her power to help you achieve them. Career comes first, and your wife is expected to adjust to your plans, not vice versa. You won't commit to anyone who doesn't support your goals. Often you'll marry someone who can help you up the mountain with good contacts. You usually don't go for a liberated woman because you need to be the strong figure. It is no surprise that there is often a considerable May–September (or even May–December) generation gap between the Capricorn man and his wife.

The bonus of being with a Capricorn is that this sign gets better as you get older. Many of these older man–younger woman relationships last because the Capricorn mate mellows with age, becoming more fun-loving and easier to live with.

The Capricorn Woman:
A Classy Classic

Capricorn women seem to be born competent, well-organized, and ambitious—on the fast track to success. Elegantly dressed, beautifully groomed, in classic, feminine clothes, the typical Capricorn, like Diane Sawyer, presents a cool, calm image, with everything under control. You give the impression of someone who takes life very seriously. Even those who run counter to type, such as Dolly Parton, are, beneath the glittery facade, shrewd businesswomen who understand the commercial value of their image.

Many Capricorns have followed a rocky road through life, starting out with disadvantages. Yet, with enormous self-discipline, you can muster all your resources for the road ahead and overcome many obstacles to reach a high position. You often have entrepreneurial talent, as you are able to recognize workable projects, follow through on your ideas, and make them happen. Your focus on the path upward puts great value on quality, power, and prestige—and those who have it. But though you'll carefully cultivate contacts with VIPs, you'll remain loyal to anyone who helps you, and you always repay favors in full.

You are most fulfilled when you are using your energy to manage someone or something. You understand how to use and profit from the talents of others, which makes you an excellent manager or supervisor who enjoys directing other lives. On the negative side, Capricorn can also be the stage mother who, when you feel you cannot accomplish goals on your own, will do it vicariously through others in your life. This attitude can cause problems dealing with independent people who have different values or less ambition. However, you are usually a very astute mentor and teacher who can offer valuable practical advice to those who would like to get ahead.

Family relationships mean a great deal to Capricorn women. You are very caring and solicitous of elders, often taking personal care of older relatives. You are proud of your family background, and will make special efforts to keep up appearances and promote traditional family gatherings. You can always be counted on to attend important family-related events and ceremonies.

You are also dedicated to your work. You're the first to arrive in the office and the last to leave, always delivering what you promise. Though you may have conflicts juggling work and family, you'll work hard to ensure that your family is well provided for.

In a Relationship

Capricorn often works out a very complex past relationship with her father and lives out her desire for personal power through a man. You rarely marry impulsively for grand passion. If your husband produces the expected lifestyle, you'll fulfill your responsibilities. And once you learn to stand alone and feel totally secure inside, you make a wise, realistic, and helpful mate. As you mature, you may indulge more in affairs of the heart, allowing yourself more spontaneous pleasure as your earthy, sensual side finally emerges.

But you will not commit yourself until you feel totally secure inside (or until you have established yourself at the top of your profession). Many Capricorn women, once they have a successful career, will marry a much younger husband and be able to keep up with him easily.

Capricorn in the Family

The Capricorn Parent

Your sign of Capricorn is regarded as the father figure of the zodiac just as Cancer, your opposite sign, is regarded as the mother figure. Even female Capricorns have the paternal, responsible, dutiful outlook of the family provider. An ambitious, hard worker yourself, you'll want your children to rise to the top in life, and you'll try to give them the best tools to get there. That includes education, good manners, and knowledge of how to handle finances. You are especially good at teaching your children the perseverance and organizational skills they'll need to achieve their goals. Your children will probably be given an allowance at an early age and taught how to budget their money wisely. As they grow up, you'll provide your children with steady support, though never spoiling or indulging them. For the artistic child who may seem unfocused, you'll provide a sense of direction and a strong dose of reality. Even the more flamboyant Capricorns are solidly rooted in family ties. As a parent, you will impart this sense of lineage and tradition to your children.

The Capricorn Stepparent

Stepchildren can be a big challenge. Your goal as stepparent will be to reestablish a stable family structure, with rules to be followed and lines of authority clarified. (Remember that rules are made to be bent, if not broken, from time to time.) Though you may seem cool and calculating to your stepchildren at first, they will come to respect your strictness and gradual approach to intimacy. Later, they will come to trust you as a mentor and adviser—you're the one who knows what works. Let your stepchildren see your creative side and your delightful dry sense of humor. You're *not* all work, no play! When they get to know you, they will appreciate your sense of values, your realistic outlook, and your sincere support.

The Capricorn Grandparent

Your grandchildren catch you at the mellowest time of your life—you've aged well and lightened up after putting the workaholic days far behind. You're more relaxed and free now that you have reached the top of the mountain, where the air is clear and rarefied. As a grandparent, you'll kick up your heels; you'll enjoy your grandchildren, play with them, and probably be much more openly affectionate than you were with your own children. You welcome your grandchildren's youthful energy; it's like an injection of vitamins. You are the grandparent who goes out dancing (often with a much younger mate). You'll stay in great shape and look terrific—silver hair is sensational on you.

CHAPTER 17

Capricorn Fashion and Decor Tips: Elevate Your Mood with Capricorn Style!

In this year of serious concerns, why not put joy and imagination into your life by creating a harmonious environment and expressing your sun sign's natural flair in everything you do and wear? There are colors, sounds, fashion, and decor tips that fit Capricorn like the proverbial glove and that could brighten every day. Even small changes in decor could make you feel "home at last." A simple change of color in your walls or curtains, your special music in the air, and a wardrobe makeover inspired by a Capricorn designer or celebrity are natural mood elevators that boost your confidence and energy level. Even your vacations might be more fun if you tailor them to your natural Capricorn inclinations. Try these tips to enhance your lifestyle and express the Capricorn stylist in you.

Capricorn Fashion Secrets

Capricorn is concerned with maintaining a specific and appropriate image—and you usually find the one that works for you early in life. It can be as extreme as Dolly Parton's or Diane Keaton's or as elegant as former supermodel Carla Bruni Sarkozy's. Capricorns stay true to this image, rarely varying their basic style throughout life. Consider the eternal glamour of the late Capricorn legends: Marlene Dietrich, Loretta Young, and Ava Gardner. Each had a specific and unforgettable fashion look.

You take a no-nonsense approach to fashion. Your clothes have to project the image that is appropriate for your job or social requirements and be of the highest quality possible. You're a disciplined shopper who'll shop sales and buy wholesale whenever possible. And with your discriminating eye, you'll rarely make a fashion mistake. Your wardrobe contains styles you can wear forever.

Clever Capricorns buy separates that stretch your wardrobe and span the seasons. (Years ago, Marlene Dietrich once counseled women on a budget to stick to black, white, and gray, advice which is still right on target today.) You'll accessorize with real, often antique, jewelry; an elegant bag or briefcase; and beautiful expensive shoes. Your hair and makeup also work for your strong bone structure and busy lifestyle. Capricorn is always in perfect order and projects the best image for the career she chooses.

Capricorn Colors

The colors of deep winter belong to Capricorn. The red of holly berries, black-and-white contrasts, the green of spruce trees. Rich browns, medieval tapestry tones, and earthy hunter greens also complement Capricorn.

Your Capricorn Fashion Role Models

Designer Carolina Herrera is the summit of Capricorn high-fashion style, with her elegant suits and ladylike dresses. Diane Von Furstenberg creates sensual but practical clothing that is ideally suited to the working woman. It is interesting that neither of these designers had formal fashion training. Like the mother of interior decorating, Elsie de Wolfe Mendl, they rose to the top through becoming known for their own personal taste and style, as well as their contacts in the right places. The design team of Badgley and Mishka, both Capricorns, interprets the newest trends for you.

Supermodel Kate Moss, who became a fashion icon, has designed a line of fashionable budget-conscious clothing. Designer Kate Spade is known for stylish accessories. Actress Sienna Miller is a newer fashion trendsetter.

Capricorn men have been equally influential in setting fashion trends. (Nobody wears business suits like Capricorn!) Think of how many men would love to look like Cary Grant or Humphrey Bogart and who still imitate their impeccable style. Singers Elvis Presley, Rod Stewart, David Bowie, and Ricky Martin have defined the way a rock star should look. The moral is to trust your own taste, Capricorn. It's probably just right.

Capricorn Home Makeover Tips

The "House in Good Taste" is the Capricorn ideal. Good taste to a Capricorn generally means a traditional look inspired by classic designs from many ports of call, from the Far East to American folk art.

Capricorn takes home decor seriously and usually has a strong sense of the "right" and proper way to do things. Your trademarks are high ceilings, beautiful dark woods, and the look of old money. Monograms, crests, heraldic motifs, fine antiques, Oriental rugs, and rich colors suit you. Capricorns from the South like columns in front of their houses and a "country club" look (Elvis Presley's Graceland and Dolly Parton's home, for example). In the North, Capricorns love the traditional look of Ivy League Gothic. If the decor is modern, it should still feature fine woods, cabinetry, cathedral ceilings, and a solid, structured look.

Since many of you take work home, space should be set aside for a home office with computer equipment housed in beautiful wood cabinets. Later in life, you may be able to afford a vacation home and may indulge in more escapist fantasy in your decor, like rock star David Bowie, who once built an elaborate Indonesian-style hideaway in the Caribbean.

The woman who created the profession of interior decorating, the legendary Elsie de Wolfe Mendl, was an archetypal Capricorn, with striking silver hair. Lady Mendl's key word was "suitability," which is the perfect description of the typical Capricorn home. Lady Mendl also swept out the overpowering Victorian look and swept in fine French furniture, uncluttered rooms, and a lively use of color. Lady Mendl conveyed such an atmosphere of prestige and "class" that Cole Porter mentioned her in the lyrics of his song "You're the Top."

In decor, Capricorn favors classic colors and fabrics. Lady Mendl was noted for her use of dark green and white, in stripes and lattice patterns. Warm earth tones paired with winter white are another Capricorn decorating look. Capricorns resonate to the jewel tones of Spanish tapestry tones and deep garnet reds. Designer Carolina Herrera's rooms done in an elegant toile fabric are a perfect example of Capricorn elegance.

Capricorn Sounds

Capricorn has eclectic musical tastes. You like classical music, string quartets, and medieval sounds. But earthy country and western also appeals, particularly Capricorn singers Dolly Parton, Barbara Mandrell, and Crystal Gayle. The cool tones of Sade set a romantic mood. As the sign of rock, you kick up your heels to rockers Kid Rock, Rod Stewart, and David Bowie, and the nostalgic records of Elvis Presley. But it is Latin music that really lights your fire.

Capricorn Getaways

Work-oriented Capricorns need to make time for regular vacations. If you are typical of your sign, you like traditional, clubby places with an organized social life and superb service. Capricorn-friendly resorts are where the rich and famous congregate: Newport, Rhode Island; Southampton, Long Island;

Washington, D.C.; Bar Harbor, Maine; Palm Beach, Florida; Monte Carlo; the Caribbean. Both South America and Spain speak to your wild side and could lure you away from business. India, Iowa, Georgia, and Utah are other Capricorn places.

Head for the mountains when you need to be uplifted. High-altitude sports such as mountain hikes, climbing, and skiing can help you leave the workday world far behind and gain perspective.

Or try a yoga retreat where you can stretch your mind and body in a beautiful natural setting. Yoga is a very effective way to relax and take your mind off work.

Spa vacations are another Capricorn specialty, appealing to those who enjoy the structure of a well-planned fitness schedule. Early-morning hikes along mountain and canyon trails, sessions with a personal trainer, and a spa's antiaging therapies could help you get back on the fast track.

Organized Capricorns travel with ease, packing exactly what you need. You tend to take work along with you, so a portable computer with a modem might be a good travel investment. Nothing's wasted with Capricorn, and that includes time—you always have something to do during flight delays. You're the one who has a cell phone or laptop handy, knows where the executive services are in each airport, and is busily doing paperwork while others impatiently pace the waiting room.

Since you're budget-minded (you spend where it counts the most), you may skimp on luxuries while you travel. Remember to pamper yourself once in a while with an in-room movie, a massage, room service, beauty treatments at a local salon, or perhaps a car service waiting to speed you to your destination stress-free and with energy to spare.

CHAPTER 18

The Capricorn Way to Stay Healthy and Age Well

This year we'll be focused on staying healthy to avoid the high costs of health care and to cope with stressful events. Some signs have an easier time than others committing to a health and diet regimen. But Capricorn is naturally disciplined and should be able to incorporate health-building activities into your life. Astrology can clue you in to the specific Capricorn tendencies that contribute to good or ill health. So follow these sun-sign tips to help yourself become the healthiest Capricorn possible.

Disciplined Dieting

It was a Capricorn hostess and decorator, Lady Elsie de Wolfe Mendl, who introduced dieting to America, via the 1920s health guru Gayelord Hauser. Lady Mendl served very small portions of exquisitely prepared health food at her elegant dinner parties, a good tip for you who may need to downsize your portions. One of the skinny signs, Capricorn has amazing self-discipline, a big help in maintaining weight loss. Exercise or active sports should help you keep the pounds off without strenuous dieting. Food and mood are linked with Capricorn, so avoid eating to console or comfort yourself; instead, choose upbeat relaxed companions. Since you are likely to mix business with pleasure, plan your work-related lunches and dinners in advance, so you won't be led astray by the dessert tray.

Your flair for organization should help you make a workable diet plan. Otherwise, you might opt for one of the commercial plans that delivers meals right to your door so you won't be tempted by what is already in the refrigerator.

Aging Well Is a Capricorn Trait

As a Capricorn you naturally take good care of yourself, getting regular medical checkups and tending toward moderation in your lifestyle. You're one of the signs that ages well and remains physically active in your senior years. But Capricorn's fast-paced, action-packed life can be stressful, so here are some ways to unwind and put the spring back into your step.

Since Capricorn is associated with the bone structure, you need to watch for signs of osteoporosis and take preventive measures. Good posture and stretching exercises such as yoga are essential to remain flexible. Another way to counteract osteoporosis is by adding weight-bearing exercise to your routine. If your knees or joints are showing signs of arthritis, calcium supplements may be helpful. For those who enjoy strenuous sports, remember to protect your knees by doing special exercises to strengthen this area, and always warm up beforehand.

Pace Yourself

Capricorn's natural self-discipline is a big help in maintaining good health. Keep a steady, even pace for lasting results. Remember to balance workouts with pleasurable activities in your self-care program. Grim determination can be counterproductive, especially if one of your exercise goals is to relieve tension. Take up a sport for pure enjoyment, not necessarily to become a champion.

Since you probably spend much of your life in an office, check your working environment for hidden health saboteurs like poor air quality, bad lighting, and uncomfortable seating.

Get an ergonomically designed chair to protect your back, or buy a specially designed back-support cushion if your chair is uncomfortable. If you work at a computer, adjust your keyboard and the height of the computer screen for ergonomic comfort.

Stay Young Forever

Capricorn, the sign of Father Time, brings up the subject of aging. If sags and wrinkles are keeping you from looking as young as you feel, investigate plastic surgery to give you a younger look and psychological lift. Teeth are also associated with your sign—a reminder to have regular dental cleanings and checkups.

The Capricorn senior likes to stay actively involved in community life. Yours is a disciplined, organized sign that may not retire from business or may continue your career on a part-time basis. Some may pursue an entirely different career with great success. You could well represent the seniors in your community on boards and committees. It is important for Capricorn to continue doing productive work, even if it is on a volunteer basis. Physically Capricorn is one of the longer-lived signs; it is associated with bones and knees, so protect these areas and watch a tendency toward arthritis and osteoporosis.

CHAPTER 19

Add Capricorn Star Power to Your Career: What It Takes to Succeed in 2010

In today's tight job market, you'll need to pull out all the stops to land a great job. With Pluto giving Capricorn extra power, you're headed for the spotlight, so get used to being the center of attention in 2010. Capricorn has a combination of talents and abilities that can make you a natural winner. At the top of the list are your executive ability and organization skills. You're the one who can make order out of chaos. If you develop and nurture your Capricorn talents, you'll be more likely to find a career you truly enjoy, as well as one that rewards you financially. Here's to your success!

Where to Look for Your Perfect Job

The Capricorn archetype is the original Horatio Alger story, someone who starts out in the mailroom and winds up in the boardroom. You are highly motivated and usually have a clear strategy for reaching the top. You move deliberately, according to plan, with focus and discipline. By using your instinct for spotting potential business opportunities, you often get in on the ground floor of a very profitable venture.

Any job with a power structure, a status product, an organization (a mountain to climb) is a foil for Capricorn talents. Banks, publishing houses, large corporations, politics, and big business of every kind have the terrain you need to climb. Your conservative, high-status tastes could lead you to a career in haute couture, status retailing, interior design. Orthopedic medicine, chiropractic work, and dentistry are possible health-care careers that treat Capricorn-ruled parts of the body, the bones and teeth. Because Capricorn is the sign of age and maturity, you may find a career working with the elderly in some way. You have a special rapport and understanding for this age group, which could point you toward a fulfilling career.

Live Up to Your Leadership Potential

You are a rather formal boss who gives subordinates a strong, definite direction. Your style is all business; many of you literally live for your job. You drive a hard bargain with employees and clients alike, demanding full value for every dollar. You'll stick to the budget, often skipping many of your job's perks, and never stretching your expense account. Since you are very bottom-line oriented, you may undervalue creativity and have trouble understanding freedom-loving creative types. But you are an expert at delegating jobs and can make even the most disorganized worker produce. And you will retain your valued employees, rewarding them for first-class work.

The Capricorn success story is the one who started at the bottom and worked his way to the top. You keep your eye on the top of the mountain all the way. And you have a great talent for spotting potential business opportunities. The Capricorn designer Diane Von Furstenberg saw a little wrap dress as perfect for the modern career woman and then made her fortune with it. Capricorn moves carefully, according to a plan, and often sees opportunity where others see none.

For more inspiration, there's the career of Capricorn Jeff Bezos, who took a loan from his parents to start Amazon.com, which became the paradigm of e-commerce. Bezos believed in the Internet and saw retailing possibilities far ahead of everyone else. He has weathered the ups and downs of the Internet to become an established success.

How to Work with Others

You will be the hardest worker, as long as your job is a stepping-stone to advancement. Otherwise, you may just bide your time, doing the minimum necessary, until a prime opportunity arises. Few Capricorns are content to stay at a low-level job. Capricorn is practical, determined, and superorganized in pursuit of success. No one gets the job done as quickly and economically as you. You function best in a structured situation where you'll strive to be promoted from within. Though you'll take full advantage of any opportunities to develop your talents within the company, you'll never abuse your expense account. You pride yourself in coming in under budget.

The Capricorn Way to Get Ahead

In doing your personal plan of action, think of how you can increase your returns for the effort you put out. Use your special talents and abilities to bring you the highest return on your investment of time and energy. Look for a company that promotes from within and stick with it. Play up these Capricorn attributes:

- Good judgment
- Managerial ability
- Organizational skills
- Reliability
- Concentration
- Persistence
- Ability to produce

CHAPTER 20

Learn from Capricorn Celebrities

You know how much fun it is when you find a famous person who shares your sun sign—and even your birthday! Why not turn your brush with fame into an education in astrology? Celebrities who capture the media's attention reflect the current planetary influences, as well as the unique star quality of their sun sign. Who's in this year may be out next year. You can learn from the hottest stellar spotlight stealers what the public is responding to and what this says about our current values.

If one of your famous sign mates intrigues you, explore his personality further by looking up his other planets using the tables in this book. You may even find his horoscope posted on astrology-related Internet sites like www.astrodatabank. com or www.stariq.com, which have charts of world events and headline makers. Then apply the effects of Venus, Mars, Saturn, and Jupiter to his sun-sign traits. It's a way to get up close and personal with your famous friend, and maybe learn some secrets not revealed to the public.

You're sure to have lots in common with your famous sign mates. The Capricorn take-charge character has produced many TV anchors such as Katie Couric, Diane Sawyer, Matt Lauer, Meredith Vieira, and Charlie Rose. Michelle Obama and Carla Bruni-Sarkozy are prime examples of Capricorn poise in the political arena. Mel Gibson and Kate Moss have survived scandal in recent years.

Get to know these famous Capricorns better and learn what makes their stars shine brightly.

Capricorn Celebrities

Lady Bird Johnson (12/22/12)
Hector Elizondo (12/22/36)
Diane Sawyer (12/22/45)
Maurice and Robin Gibb (12/22/49)
Ralph Fiennes (12/22/62)
Susan Lucci (12/23/49)
Carla Bruni-Sarkozy (12/23/68)
Carey Holm (12/23/71)
Howard Hughes (12/24/1905)
Ava Gardner (12/24/22)
Ricky Martin (12/24/71)
Ryan Seacrest (12/24/76)
Humphrey Bogart (12/25/1899)
Tony Martin (12/25/13)
Hanna Schygylla (12/25/43)
Jimmy Buffett (12/25/46)
Barbara Mandrell (12/25/48)
Sissy Spacek (12/25/49)
Annie Lennox (12/25/54)
Tracy Nelson (12/25/63)
Steve Allen (12/26/21)
Jared Leto (12/26/71)
Marlene Dietrich (12/27/1901)
Mick Jones (12/27/44)
Gerard Dépardieu (12/27/48)
Maggie Smith (12/28/34)
Denzel Washington (12/28/54)
Joe Diffie (12/28/58)
Sienna Miller (12/28/81)
Mary Tyler Moore (12/29/36)
Jon Voight (12/29/38)
Ted Danson (12/29/47)
Jude Law (12/29/72)
Patti Smith (12/30/46)
Meredith Vieira (12/30/53)
Suzy Boggus (12/30/56)
Matt Lauer (12/30/57)
Tracey Ullman (12/30/59)

Tiger Woods (12/30/59)
Heidi Fleiss (12/30/65)
Laila Ali (12/30/77)
Anthony Hopkins (12/31/37)
John Denver (12/31/43)
Ben Kingsley (12/31/43)
Diane von Furstenberg (12/31/46)
Val Kilmer (12/31/59)
Bebe Neuwirth (12/31/59)
Betsy Ross (1/1/1752)
J. Edgar Hoover (1/1/1895)
Frank Langella (1/1/40)
Roger Miller (1/2/36)
Jim Bakker (1/2/40)
Joanna Pacula (1/2/57)
Cuba Gooding Jr. (1/2/68)
Christy Turlington (1/2/69)
Taye Diggs (1/2/70)
Kate Bosworth (1/2/83)
Robert Loggia (1/3/30)
Dabney Coleman (1/3/32)
Victoria Principal (1/3/50)
Mel Gibson (1/3/56)
Trinny Woodall (1/3/65)
Gabriel Aubry (1/4/76)
Jane Wyman (1/4/14)
Floyd Patterson (1/4/35)
Dyan Cannon (1/4/37)
Patty Loveless (1/4/57)
Paramahansa Yogananda (1/5/1893)
Robert Duvall (1/5/30)
Raisa Gorbachev (1/5/34)
Charlie Rose (1/5/42)
Diane Keaton (1/5/45)
Carrie Ann Inaba (1/5/68)
Carl Sandburg (1/6/1878)
Loretta Young (1/6/13)
Katie Couric (1/7/57)
Nicolas Cage (1/7/64)
Nolan Miller (1/8/35)

Elvis Presley (1/8/35)
Stephen Hawking (1/8/42)
Yvette Mimieux (1/8/42)
David Bowie (1/8/47)
Susannah Coustantine (1/8/61)
Simone de Beauvoir (1/9/1908)
Bob Denver (1/9/35)
Joan Baez (1/9/41)
David Johansen (1/9/50)
Crystal Gayle (1/9/51)
Joely Richardson (1/9/65)
Dave Matthews (1/9/67)
Maurice Sendak (1/10/28)
Sal Mineo (1/10/39)
Jim Croce (1/10/43)
Rod Stewart (1/10/45)
Pat Benatar (1/10/53)
Grant Tinker (1/11/26)
Naomi Judd (1/11/46)
Stanley Tucci (1/11/60)
Mary J. Blige (1/11/71)
Kirstie Alley (1/12/51)
Rush Limbaugh (1/12/51)
Howard Stern (1/12/54)
Jeff Bezos (1/12/64)
Olivier Martinez (1/12/66)
Vendela (1/12/67)
Heather Mills (1/12/68)
Horatio Alger (1/13/1834)
Robert Stack (1/13/19)
Julia Louis Dreyfus (1/13/61)
Penelope Ann Miller (1/13/64)
Patrick Dempsey (1/13/66)
Curtis Conway (1/13/71)
Orlando Bloom (1/13/77)
Cecil Beaton (1/14/1904)
Faye Dunaway (1/14/41)
Sydney Biddle Barrows (1/14/52)
Steven Soderbergh (1/14/63)
Emily Watson (1/14/67)

Jason Bateman (1/14/69)
Aristotle Onassis (1/15/1906)
Martin Luther King Jr. (1/15/29)
Chad Lowe (1/15/68)
Sade (1/16/60)
Kate Moss (1/16/74)
Vidal Sassoon (1/17/28)
Maury Povich (1/17/39)
Muhammad Ali (1/17/42)
Mick Taylor (1/17/48)
David Caruso (1/17/56)
Jim Carrey (1/17/62)
Michelle Obama (1/17/64)
Naveen Andrews (1/17/69)
Kid Rock (1/17/71)
Cary Grant (1/18/1904)
Kevin Costner (1/18/55)
Edgar Allan Poe (1/19/1809)
Janis Joplin (1/19/43)
Dolly Parton (1/19/46)
Drea di Matteo (1/19/73)

CHAPTER 21

Your Capricorn Relationships with Every Other Sign: The Green Lights and Red Flags

Are you looking for insight into a relationship? Perhaps it's someone you've met online, a new business partner, a roommate or the proverbial stranger across a crowded room. After an initial attraction, you may be wondering if you'll still get along down the line. Or why supposedly incompatible signs sometimes have a magical attraction to each other. If things aren't working out, astrology could give you some clues as to why he or she is "not that into you."

Astrology has no magic formula for success in love, but it does offer a better understanding of the qualities each person brings to the relationship and how your partner is likely to react to your sun-sign characteristics. Knowing your potential partner's sign and how it relates to yours could give you some clues about what to expect down the line.

There is also the issue of the timing of a new relationship. From an astrological perspective, the people you meet at any given time provide the dynamic that you require at that moment. If you're a practical Virgo, you might benefit from a fun-loving Gemini or a globe-trotting Sagittarius at a certain time in your life.

The celebrity couples in this chapter can help you visualize each sun-sign combination. You'll note that some legendary lovers have stood the test of time, while others blazed, then broke up, and still others existed only in the fantasy world of film or television (but still captured our imagination). Traditional astrological wisdom holds that signs of the same element are naturally compatible. For Capricorn, that would be fellow earth signs Taurus and Virgo. Also favored are signs of complementary elements, such as earth signs with water signs (Cancer, Scorpio, Pisces). In these relationships communication supposedly flows easily, and you'll feel comfortable together.

As you read the following matches, remember that there are no hard-and-fast rules; each combination has perks as well as peeves. So, when sparks fly and an irresistible magnetic pull draws you together, when disagreements and challenges fuel intrigue, mystery, passion, and sexy sparring matches, don't rule the relationship out. That person may provide the diversity, excitement, and challenge you need for an unforgettable romance, a stimulating friendship, or a successful business partnership!

Capricorn/Aries

THE GREEN LIGHTS:

You're both high achievers and hard workers who respect each other's stamina. Capricorn provides the solid organizational skills. Aries provides the enthusiasm and pioneering ideas. The mature Capricorn outlook could offer the stable backup that Aries needs to get there first. In return, innovative Aries methods could pull Capricorn out of the ordinary.

THE RED FLAGS:

Capricorn values the traditional; Aries, the trendy. Aries can seem like a self-centered baby; Capricorn, an old fuddy-duddy. Capricorn rules and structure might seem confining to Aries, whose headstrong methods seem foolhardy to Capricorn.

SIGN MATES:

Capricorn Michelle Williams and Aries Heath Ledger
Capricorn René Angelil and Aries Celine Dion

Capricorn/Taurus

THE GREEN LIGHTS:

Your similar traditional values can make communication easy. This is a combination that works well on all levels. You find it easy to set goals, to organize, and to support each other. There are earthy passions and instinctive understanding.

THE RED FLAGS:

There may be too much earth here, which could make your relationship too dutiful, practical, and unromantic. You both need to expand your horizons occasionally, and may look for stimulation elsewhere. Taurus may resent Capricorn devotion to career.

SIGN MATES:

Capricorn Martin Luther King Jr. and Taurus Coretta Scott King

Capricorn/Gemini

THE GREEN LIGHTS:

Capricorn benefits from the Gemini abstract point of view and lighthearted sense of fun. Gemini shows Capricorn how to enjoy the rewards of hard work. Support and structure are Capricorn gifts to Gemini. (Taking that literally, Capricorn Howard Hughes designed the famous bra that supported Gemini Jane Russell's physical assets!)

THE RED FLAGS:

Capricorn can be ultraconservative and tightfisted with money, which Gemini will not appreciate. Gemini will have to learn to take responsibility and to produce solid results, or Capricorn will tighten the bottom line.

Capricorn Elvis Presley and Gemini Priscilla Presley

Capricorn/Cancer

THE GREEN LIGHTS:

A serious sense of duty, family pride, and a basically traditional outlook bring you together. The zodiac mother (Cancer) and father (Capricorn) establish a strong home base. Cancer's tender devotion could bring out Capricorn's earthy and sensual side. This couple gets closer over the years.

THE RED FLAGS:

Melancholy moods could muddy this picture. Develop a strategy for coping if depression hits. Capricorn is a lone wolf who may isolate emotionally, or withdraw into work, or take on an overload of duties. Cancer could look elsewhere for comfort and consolation.

SIGN MATES:

Capricorn Kid Rock and Cancer Pamela Anderson

Capricorn/Leo

THE GREEN LIGHTS:

Here's the perfect mix of business and pleasure. Dignified, refined Capricorn has energy and discipline to match Leo passion. Leo comes to the rescue of your ambitious workaholic sign, adding confidence, poise, and joie de vivre. Capricorn reciprocates with the royal treatment.

THE RED FLAGS:

Since Capricorn prefers underplayed elegance to glitter and glamour, Leo may have to tone down the flamboyant style. Capricorn cuts off the cash flow when Leo become extravagant, and may not pour out the megadoses of affection that Leo requires. Leo can't bear a partner who is stingy with love or money!

SIGN MATES:

Capricorn David Bowie and Leo supermodel Iman
Capricorn Michelle Obama and Leo Barack Obama

Capricorn/Virgo

THE GREEN LIGHTS:

This looks like a sure thing between two signs who have so much in common. You're both good providers. You both have a strong sense of duty and respect for order, and similar conservative tastes and a basically traditional approach to relationships. You could accomplish much together.

THE RED FLAGS:

You may be too similar! Cary Grant (Capricorn) and Sophia Loren (Virgo) had strong chemistry, but finally opted for other commitments. Romance needs challenges to keep the sparks flying.

SIGN MATES:

Capricorn Humphrey Bogart and Virgo Lauren Bacall

Capricorn/Libra

THE GREEN LIGHTS:

Capricorn is quick to spot Libra potential as a social asset as well as a romantic lead. Libra loves your dignified Capricorn demeanor and elegant taste. You can climb the heights together, helping each other get the lifestyle you want.

THE RED FLAGS:

Capricorn is a loner and a home lover, while Libra is a party person who likes to do things in tandem. Expensive Libra tastes could create tension with your frugal Capricorn ways, unless Libra learns to consider the budget as well as the beauty.

SIGN MATES:

Capricorn Faye Dunaway and Libra Marcello Mastroianni

Capricorn/Scorpio

THE GREEN LIGHTS:

Sexy Scorpio takes your Capricorn mind off business. Though you could get wrapped up in each other, you are also turned on by power and position, and you'll join forces to scale the heights.

THE RED FLAGS:

Capricorn has no patience for intrigue or hidden agendas. Scorpio will find you too focused on your own goals. As a Capricorn you won't be easily diverted, even if this means leaving Scorpio emotional needs and ego in the backseat.

SIGN MATES:

Capricorn Diane Sawyer and Scorpio Mike Nichols
Capricorn Jim Carrey and Scorpio Jenny McCarthy

Capricorn/Sagittarius

THE GREEN LIGHTS:

Capricorn has a built-in job organizing Sagittarius. But the challenge of doing something for the greater good could bring Capricorn status and recognition. Sagittarius encourages Capricorn to elevate goals beyond the material, and also brings out both the spiritual side and the humor of your sign.

THE RED FLAGS:

Optimistic Sagittarius meets pessimistic Capricorn and you cancel each other out! Ultimately, you can't play it for laughs. Capricorn pushes Sagittarius to produce and commit. And Sagittarius runs off to do his or her own thing.

SIGN MATES:

Capricorn Carolyn Bessette Kennedy and Sagittarius JFK Jr.

Capricorn/Capricorn

THE GREEN LIGHTS:

You two mountain goats can climb to the top together. You'll share the same traditional values. You'll appreciate each other's thrifty, practical ways and excellent organization. You'll bring out each other's dry sense of humor and earthy sensuality.

THE RED FLAGS:

Too much earth (sameness) could bury the romance. You both need the inspiration and stimulation of different kinds of energies to keep climbing. Otherwise, you two will be all work and no fun.

SIGN MATES:

Capricorns Laila Ali and Curtis Conway

Capricorn/Aquarius

THE GREEN LIGHTS:

When the Capricorn lone wolf and the Aquarius oddball team up, the romantic route takes an unpredictable detour. Aquarius discovers that your Capricorn know-how and organizational skills can make wild dreams come true. Capricorn finds that an Aquarius shake-up can have productive results.

THE RED FLAGS:

After the initial fascination, these two signs may go off in opposite directions unless there are shared goals or a project to get done. Capricorn may push for a traditional relationship, while Aquarius follows a different drummer.

SIGN MATES:

Capricorn Carla Bruni and Aquarius Nicholas Sarkozy

Capricorn/Pisces

THE GREEN LIGHTS:

Your Capricorn organizational abilities and worldly knowhow impress Pisces. You can help this foggy, creative sign find a clear direction. The Pisces romance, tenderness, and knowledge of the art of love bring out the gypsy in you—a fair exchange.

THE RED FLAGS:

You've got your work cut out for you with free-floating Pisces, who avoids nets of any kind. What spells security for Capricorn could look like a gilded cage to Pisces, who doesn't play by the same rules. If you can make allowances for radical differences, you'll go far together. Don't try to make each other over!

SIGN MATES:

Capricorn Rod Stewart and Pisces Penny Lancaster

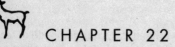

CHAPTER 22

The Big Picture for Capricorn in 2010

Welcome to 2010! This is your year for building foundations, for solidifying your ambitions and dreams, and for manifestation!

There are significant transits this year that will impact your life in challenging ways, but first let's take a look at what your ruler, Saturn, will be doing this year and how it will affect you. Saturn entered Libra and the career sector of your chart late last year, so you've gotten a taste already of how this is influencing your professional life. It's necessary to meet your obligations and responsibilities and to learn how to be a team player (the Libra part of the equation!). Saturn will then help you to solidify your career ambitions, and to manifest your dreams and wishes. There could be some delays or restrictions while Saturn is in your tenth house, particularly in terms of recognition.

On January 13, Saturn turns retrograde and remains that way until May 30. During this period, you may be revisiting professional issues you thought were resolved. It's also likely that you will be scrutinizing elements of your professional life in an attempt to improve things.

Jupiter enters Pisces on January 17, zooms through it, enters Aries on June 6, retrogrades on July 23, and remains in Pisces for the rest of the year. By January 2011, it has entered Aries again. What all this means for you is that while Jupiter is in Pisces, in your third house, your conscious mind is absorbing information at the speed of light and that your daily life is expanding in some way. Perhaps you go back to school or enter college or graduate school. You might move into a large community or neighborhood.

Once Jupiter enters Aries, the expansiveness is transferred to your home and family. There could be a birth in the family or someone moves in. You may sell your home and move into a larger home. You may buy real estate as an investment. You don't hesitate to take chances, and the risks you take pay off.

Pluto begins the year in your sign, where it has been since late 2008 and where it will be until 2024. Pluto is the great transformer, and during its transit in your sign, every facet of your life will change in some way. The changes will be subtle, because Jupiter moves so slowly. For instance, in 2010, Pluto travels from three to five degrees of Capricorn, so those of you born between December 24 and December 28 will feel the transit most strongly.

Pluto turns retrograde on April 6 and doesn't turn direct again until September 13. During this retrograde period, pay close attention to everything that happens. Note repeating patterns. Follow synchronicities; listen to your intuition.

Uranus—the planet that symbolizes our individualism and sudden and unexpected change—enters Aries on May 27, for a period of about seven years. This transit will create sudden, unexpected changes in your home life—moves, marriage or divorce, or issues with a parent. You may decide to set up a home office, for example, and your home-based business becomes outrageously successful! You may also start putting certain principles to work in your life—the law of attraction, for example, and reading books that explain these principles and how to use them.

Even though Uranus will retrograde back into Pisces from August 13 to the end of the year, you'll get a taste of what kind of excitement this planet will usher into your life between May 27 and mid-August.

Neptune—the planet that symbolizes our illusions, idealism, all forms of escapism, and our higher selves—continues its journey through Aquarius, your second house. Neptune has been in this position since 1998, so by now you're well aware of how it impacts your finances and your attitudes toward money. There can be psychic experiences with Neptune, so be prepared to explore your gut feelings, impulses, and dreams, particularly where money is concerned. When Neptune turns retrograde between May 31 and November 6, it enters a period of dormancy. Your finances may not function as smoothly during this period.

If you have a copy of your natal chart, by all means check to see where both Pisces and Aries fall in your chart. This will tell you a great deal about the specific area of your life where expansion is happening.

Mercury begins the year retrograde in your sign, a holdover from 2009 that may mess up your plans the first two weeks of the year. But on January 15, it turns direct, where Venus is at that time, and suddenly everything looks much rosier, particularly your love life!

Romance and Creativity

There are two notable time periods this year that favor romance and creative endeavors. Between January 1 and January 18, Venus is in your sign, marking one of the most romantic and creative periods for you all year. Yes, Mercury is retrograde in your sign during this period, but Venus's presence helps to mitigate some of the annoyance associated with the retrograde. Creatively, your best bet is to revise and review what you're doing.

While Venus is in your sign, your sex appeal, charisma, and general self-confidence are bolstered significantly. You get another boost toward the end of the year, from December 7 into January 2011, when Mars transits your sign. This transit should ramp up your sex life and also help you professionally and personally to be more aggressive in obtaining what you want. Mars in your sign accentuates all your normal traits and characteristics. If you get involved under this transit, your passions will be running the show! But your intuition and emotions will be your guidance system.

The second great time period for romance and sex falls between March 31 and April 25, when Venus is transiting your fifth house of romance and creativity. This transit should bring smoothness and ease to your life in general. But it certainly adds all kinds of spice to your love life, and your muse is up close and very personal.

Career

The best career dates this year occur when Venus transits your tenth house and Libra, from August 6 to September 8. This period should bring about a lot of communication with bosses and peers, increased networking, and perhaps some business travel. Other people will be receptive to your ideas. This is the time to make sales pitches. Venus brings ease and artistic sensibilities to your career. With Jupiter spending part of this year in Pisces, in the communication section of your chart, you'll have the communication skills to push professional matters forward.

Another great time falls around the new moon in your sign on January 15. This also happens to be a solar eclipse in your sign, which portends a double whammy of new opportunities. But you may have to give up something first. This moon happens just once a year and sets the tone for the next year. It should usher in new opportunities for your personal life and for many other areas of your life as well. You'll feel more appreciated, more recognized, more applauded!

Best Times For

Buying or selling a home: December 7 to the end of the year while Mars transits your sign. This transit energizes everything that's important to you personally and gives you practically unlimited energy.

Family reunions: March 7 to March 31, while Venus transits Aries, in the home section of your chart.

Financial matters: January 18 to February 11, when Venus transits the financial sector of your chart.

Signing contracts: When Mercury is moving direct! Especially good between November 30 and December 9, while Mercury is moving direct through your sign.

Overseas travel, publishing, and higher-education endeavors: July 10 to August 6.

Mercury Retrogrades

Every year, Mercury—the planet of communication and travel—turns retrograde three times. During this period, it's wise not to sign contracts (unless you don't mind renegotiating when Mercury is moving direct), to check and recheck travel plans, and to communicate as succinctly as possible. Refrain from buying any big-ticket items or electronics during this time too. Often, computers and appliances go on the fritz, cars act up, data is lost—you get the idea. Be sure to back up all files before the dates below:

April 17–May 11: Mercury retrograde in Taurus, your fifth house of love and romance, creativity and kids.

August 20–September 12: Mercury retrograde in Virgo, your ninth house, your worldview. Impacts education and overseas travel.

December 10–December 30: Mercury retrograde in Capricorn. Ouch. Whenever Mercury turns retrograde in your sign, the impact tends to exacerbate all the usual delays and sudden upsets and miscommunications that ride with Mercury's retrograde.

Eclipses

Solar eclipses tend to trigger external events that bring about change according to the sign and the house in which they fall. Lunar eclipses trigger inner, emotional events according to the sign and house in which they fall. Any eclipse marks both beginnings and endings. The solar and lunar eclipse in a pair fall in opposite signs.

If you were born under or around the time of an eclipse, it's to your advantage to take a look at your birth chart to find out exactly where the eclipses will impact you.

Most years feature four eclipses—two solar, two lunar, with the set separate by about two weeks. In 2009, there was a lunar eclipse in Cancer on December 31, so the first eclipse in 2010 is a solar eclipse in the opposite sign, Capricorn. That's you! This year, three of the eclipses occur either in Cancer or in Capricorn. Below are the dates for this year's eclipses:

January 15: solar, Capricorn. Events concerning you personally are highlighted. New opportunities surface. Since Venus is close to the eclipse degree, this eclipse should be quite pleasing to you.

June 26: lunar, Capricorn. Emotions stirred concerning your personal life.

July 11: solar, Cancer, your seventh house of partnerships. New opportunities surface in this area—perhaps through a business or romantic partner.

December 21: lunar, Gemini, your sixth house of daily work and health.

Luckiest Day of the Year

There's at least one day a year when the sun and Jupiter link up in some way. This year, March 2 looks to be that day, with a nice backup on July 26.

Now let's find out what's in store for you, day by day.

CHAPTER 23

Eighteen Months of Day-by-Day Predictions: July 2009 to December 2010

Moon sign times are calculated for Eastern Standard Time and Eastern Daylight Time. Please adjust for your local time zone.

JULY 2009

Wednesday, July 1 (Moon in Libra to Scorpio 1:20 p.m.) Uranus goes retrograde in your third house, which suggests you'll be thinking from time to time about your behavior in the past related to your brothers and sisters. Your communication was probably erratic, and you realize that affects your relationships. Cooperation is highlighted.

Thursday, July 2 (Moon in Scorpio) Friends play an important role in your day. Group activities work in your favor, especially if you join a group of like-minded people. Focus on your wishes and dreams. Make sure that your goals are an expression of who you really are.

Friday, July 3 (Moon in Scorpio to Sagittarius 11:12 a.m.) Mercury moves into your seventh house. You relate well to the public and get your ideas across. You're also good at working with people and arbitrating any disputes. It's a good day for sales and public relations.

Saturday, July 4 (Moon in Sagittarius)   You could be dealing with institutions, such as hospitals, courts, government offices, or large corporations. Stay out of the public eye. Work behind the scenes. Keep your feelings to yourself.

Sunday, July 5 (Moon in Sagittarius to Capricorn 11:08 p.m.)   Venus moves into your sixth house, which suggests romantic involvement in the workplace. Alternately, you could be in love with your job and working long hours, especially if it involves helping others.

Monday, July 6 (Moon in Capricorn)   The moon is on your ascendant. The way you see yourself is the way others see you. Your face is before the public. You're recharged for the month ahead, which makes you more appealing to the public.

Tuesday, July 7 (Moon in Capricorn)   There's a lunar eclipse in your first house. You react strongly to an emotional event related to your personal life. You may feel moody. It's all about your health and your emotional self: how you feel and how you feel about yourself.

Wednesday, July 8 (Moon in Capricorn to Aquarius 12:04 p.m.)   Clear up odds and ends. Make room for something new, but don't start anything until tomorrow. Take time to look beyond the immediate. Visualize the future, set your goals, and get to work.

Thursday, July 9 (Moon in Aquarius)   You identify emotionally with your possessions, which provide a sense of security. It's not the objects themselves that are important, but the feelings that you associate with them. It's a good time to invest. Collect what's owed you and make payments.

Friday, July 10 (Moon in Aquarius)   The emphasis is on cooperation and understanding. Let things develop with a partner. Marriage is particularly important. Don't make waves, rush about, or show resentment. Just go with the flow. Money issues could be a factor.

Saturday, July 11 (Moon in Aquarius to Pisces 12:44 a.m.)   Mars joins Venus in your sixth house, suggesting high energy and aggressive actions at work. This fits well with your native tendencies. However, it could cause problems with fellow workers. You love what you do, but you have no patience for laziness from others. Control your temper, or you could find your position untenable.

Sunday, July 12 (Moon in Pisces)   Enjoy a social gathering. Take what you know and share it with others. You communicate well, but be careful not to get overemotional when making your point, especially on matters related to the past. You have contact with neighbors and maybe relatives.

Monday, July 13 (Moon in Pisces to Aries 11:40 a.m.)   Approach the day with an unconventional mind-set. Experiment; promote new ideas. You're feeling versatile and changeable, but be careful not to diversify too much. You'll be in a hurry all day, so watch your step.

Tuesday, July 14 (Moon in Aries)   You're dealing with your home life and the foundations of who you are. Do something special with your family. You feel emotionally secure in your home. Retreat and meditate.

Wednesday, July 15 (Moon in Aries to Taurus 6:30 p.m.)   A mystery could be unfolding before your eyes. If you look closely, you might uncover secrets and confidential information. Follow your intuition. Knowledge is essential for success. Be aware of possible deception; don't act until you have the facts.

Thursday, July 16 (Moon in Taurus)   It's a great day for romance or pursuing a creative endeavor. Just try to be yourself in your dealings with others. You have the ability to tap deeply into your emotions to bring out the best. Children and animals play a role.

Friday, July 17 (Moon in Taurus to Gemini 11:42 p.m.)   A mystery that caught your attention on Wednesday comes up again. You investigate and dig deeper this time. You get to the truth of the matter. Finances, insurance, taxes, or an inheritance could play a role. You also could be digging into the deeper meaning of life.

Saturday, July 18 (Moon in Gemini)   Attend to daily details, and be of service today. Help others where you can, but don't overlook your own needs. Pay attention to your health and diet.

Sunday, July 19 (Moon in Gemini)   It's a number 2 day. The spotlight is on cooperative efforts and partnerships. Be kind, understanding, patient, and supportive. Let things develop. Don't make waves. Don't rush or show resentment.

Monday, July 20 (Moon in Gemini to Cancer 12:52 a.m.) Yesterday's energy related to partnerships flows on and takes center stage. There could be discussions about contracts and legal matters, possibly a marriage. Try to avoid any conflicts.

Tuesday, July 21 (Moon in Cancer)   There's a solar eclipse in your seventh house. That means there's more partnership activity. If one business relationship ends, another begins. You could find a new romantic partner, if you're looking for one. You also have stronger feelings about your home, your roots, and your parents.

Wednesday, July 22 (Moon in Cancer to Leo 12:28 a.m.) The moon is in your eighth house. You may attract power people. An interest in metaphysics could play a role. Your energy is more intense than usual. Your emotions could affect your feelings about belongings that you share with others.

Thursday, July 23 (Moon in Leo)   Be of service to others. You offer advice and support. Your hard work is appreciated. Visit someone who is ill or in need of your help. But avoid scattering your energies. Dance to your own tune.

Friday, July 24 (Moon in Leo to Virgo 12:24 a.m.) Your mind is active; you yearn for new experiences. Plan a long trip.

Sign up for a workshop or seminar. An interest in ideas, religion, mythology, or philosophy plays a role.

Saturday, July 25 (Moon in Virgo)   Take care of details, especially related to your health. Start exercising; watch your diet. Stop fretting. Take time to write in a journal. You write from a deep place now with lots of details and colorful descriptions. Dig deep for info.

Sunday, July 26 (Moon in Virgo to Libra 2:26 a.m.)   Don't start anything new. Use the day for reflection, expansion, and concluding projects. Make room for something new. Spiritual values surface. Strive for universal appeal.

Monday, July 27 (Moon in Libra)   The moon is in your tenth house. Your tenacity is recognized. You gain an elevation in prestige related to your profession and career. Material success and financial security play a role. You make a strong emotional commitment to your profession or to a role in public life.

Tuesday, July 28 (Moon in Libra to Scorpio 8:57 a.m.) Help comes through a partner or loved one. Cooperation wins the way. Be kind and understanding. Marriage is particularly important. Don't make waves, rush about, or show resentment. Just go with the flow.

Wednesday, July 29 (Moon in Scorpio)   With the moon in your eleventh house, friends play an important role, especially a Taurus and another Capricorn. Take a look at your goals and make sure that they're still an expression of who you are. You do well in a group setting. You could be dealing with an issue involving social consciousness.

Thursday, July 30 (Moon in Scorpio to Sagittarius 5:10 p.m.) Put your organizational skills to use. Revise and rewrite. Tear down in order to rebuild. Be methodical and thorough. Stay focused and emphasize quality. You're in the right place at the right time.

Friday, July 31 (Moon in Sagittarius)   Venus moves into your seventh house. You end the month on a high note. You find harmony in a professional or personal relationship. You get along well with others. You could gain financially through a marriage or partnership.

AUGUST 2009

Saturday, August 1 (Moon in Sagittarius)   Retreat and work on a creative project. Stay close to home and out of the public view. You could be dealing with secret sorrows, hidden fears, or worries. You could be thinking about a secret romance.

Sunday, August 2 (Moon in Sagittarius to Capricorn 5:09 a.m.)   Mercury moves into your ninth house, the home of higher learning. You're full of ideas now on matters such as philosophy, religion, the law, or publishing. You also have a strong interest in foreign travel or a foreign nation.

Monday, August 3 (Moon in Capricorn)   With the moon on your ascendant, you're recharged for the month ahead. You're more appealing to the public. You're feeling physically vital; relations with the opposite sex go well. Your thoughts and feelings are aligned.

Tuesday, August 4 (Moon in Capricorn to Aquarius 6:08 p.m.)   It's a number 6 day. Domestic purchases are highlighted. Focus on making people happy. It's a service day, so direct your energy toward helping others. Be generous and tolerant, even if it goes against your nature.

Wednesday, August 5 (Moon in Aquarius)   There's a lunar eclipse in your second house, your money house. You react emotionally to a matter related to your personal finances. Your values play an important role. Whatever you value takes on greater importance. You feel best surrounded by your things.

Thursday, August 6 (Moon in Aquarius)   Yesterday's energy flows on. You could gain a financial boost through an investment or some other money matter. It provides you with a sense of security. However, it's best to put off making any big purchases for a few days.

Friday, August 7 (Moon in Aquarius to Pisces 6:35 a.m.) Look beyond the immediate. Let go of preconceived notions. Strive for universal appeal. Spiritual values surface. Finish a project in order to make room for something new.

Saturday, August 8 (Moon in Pisces)   You could attend a social event related to relatives and neighbors. You tend to be more assertive than usual, but make sure you control your emotions. Avoid road rage on short trips.

Sunday, August 9 (Moon in Pisces to Aries 5:24 p.m.)   Use your intuition to get a sense of your day. You're feeling very emotional about a partnership. Your relations with a mate are highlighted. Be kind and understanding, even if others nag. Don't rush or show resentment.

Monday, August 10 (Moon in Aries)   You're somewhat moody. Spend time with your family; work on a home project. But also find a quiet space for meditation. Go with the flow.

Tuesday, August 11 (Moon in Aries)   You're extremely persuasive, especially if you're passionate about what you're doing or selling or trying to convey. Brainstorm or launch a new idea. You do your best work at home.

Wednesday, August 12 (Moon in Aries to Taurus 1:51 a.m.) Freedom of thought and action is highlighted. Experiment and take a risk. Approach the day with an unconventional mind-set. A change of scenery would do you good.

Thursday, August 13 (Moon in Taurus)   Pursue a romance or dive into a creative project. There's greater emotional depth in whatever you pursue. Lend a hand to help others, especially children. Pets play a role.

Friday, August 14 (Moon in Taurus to Gemini 7:27 a.m.) Look behind the scenes regarding confidential information.

Secret meetings and intrigue could play a role. See things as they are, not as you wish them to be. Maintain your emotional balance. Think before you act.

Saturday, August 15 (Moon in Gemini)   Be of service to others, but don't let your fears hold you back. Confront them and move on. Do a good deed; visit someone who is ill or in need of assistance. Tend to your personal health needs as well.

Sunday, August 16 (Moon in Gemini to Cancer 10:14 a.m.) It's a number 9 day. Clear your desk and make room for the new, but don't start anything until tomorrow. Spend some time in deep thought. Consider how you can expand your base.

Monday, August 17 (Moon in Cancer)   It's all about partnerships and working together. Loved ones and partners play a significant role. You could be dealing with a contract. Any conflicts can be more emotional than usual, especially when dealing with women. It'll be difficult to stay objective and detached.

Tuesday, August 18 (Moon in Cancer to Leo 10:57 a.m.) Yesterday's energy related to partnerships flows on. Process everything that happened yesterday. Help comes through a partner or loved one. Cooperation wins the way. Show your appreciation to others. Maintain your emotional balance.

Wednesday, August 19 (Moon in Leo)   The moon is in your eighth house. You could be attracting powerful people. Your experiences could be intense, especially related to shared belongings. An interest in metaphysics plays a role.

Thursday, August 20 (Moon in Leo to Virgo 11:01 a.m.) Yesterday's intense energy rolls on, and there's a new moon. That suggests an opportunity related to shared belongings or metaphysics opens. You might explore mysteries of life, including what happens at the end of life. Inheritance, taxes, and insurance issues might take up some of your day.

Friday, August 21 (Moon in Virgo)   The moon moves into your ninth house. You're feeling as if you need to break out of your usual routine. Travel or higher education plays a role. Plan a trip or sign up for a seminar or workshop. A foreign country or person of foreign birth could play a role.

Saturday, August 22 (Moon in Virgo to Libra 12:12 p.m.) Time to lighten up. Focus on making people happy, but avoid scattering your energies. Be diplomatic and helpful, but dance to your own tune. Domestic purchases are highlighted. Some change or adjustment in the home scene works out for the best. Be generous and tolerant.

Sunday, August 23 (Moon in Libra)   You get along now with the public. You're thinking a lot about success and achievement. You have a strong desire for recognition. You're concerned about your reputation. You're particularly responsive to the needs of a group.

Monday, August 24 (Moon in Libra to Scorpio 4:17 p.m.) It's your power day. Expect a financial coup. Unexpected money comes your way.

Tuesday, August 25 (Moon in Scorpio)   You tend to get aggressive and defensive as Mars moves into your seventh house. You communicate well, especially in a work setting. Hold your tongue at home, or you and your partner might get in a major squabble.

Wednesday, August 26 (Moon in Scorpio)   Venus moves into your eighth house, suggesting that you gain financially through a marriage or partnership. You could be in a position to control or manipulate another person's money. Alternately, you could join a social movement to improve the well-being of others in need.

Thursday, August 27 (Moon in Scorpio to Sagittarius 12:16 a.m.)   Your interest in the occult, the mystical, and the mysteries of the unknown plays a role. You communicate your ideas to someone with similar interests. Keep such activities undercover. Pursue your interests behind the scenes.

Friday, August 28 (Moon in Sagittarius)   Make use of your sense of humor. You see the big picture, not just the details. You're restless, impulsive, and inquisitive. Don't limit yourself. Stay optimistic and remain flexible. Attitude determines everything. Think abundance.

Saturday, August 29 (Moon in Sagittarius to Capricorn 11:45 a.m.)   It's a number 4 day. That means the emphasis is on your organizational skills. In romance, your persistence pays off. You're building a foundation for the future. Control your impulses to wander; fulfill your obligations. You could find missing papers.

Sunday, August 30 (Moon in Capricorn)   It's all about the emotional self. You have strong feelings related to your appearance and self-awareness. You also could be feeling strongly about a personal health issue or about details regarding a matter of importance that you've overlooked.

Monday, August 31 (Moon in Capricorn)   Be diplomatic rather than confrontational. It's a service day. You're resourceful and helpful, but avoid scattering your energies. A domestic change works out for the best. Be generous and tolerant; avoid acting confrontational.

SEPTEMBER 2009

Tuesday, September 1 (Moon in Capricorn to Aquarius 12:43 a.m.)   Money and material possessions take on new importance. They bring you emotional security. Any financial problems can result in disruption of your domestic life. Watch your spending. You feel best surrounded by your things.

Wednesday, September 2 (Moon in Aquarius)   Friends offer advice and support. Your association with a group or a social event plays a role. You're dealing with new options.

Thursday, September 3 (Moon in Aquarius to Pisces 12:59 p.m.)   It's another service day. You offer advice and support. Focus on making people happy. Be sympathetic, kind, and compassionate. A domestic adjustment works out for the best.

Friday, September 4 (Moon in Pisces)   There's a full moon today in your third house. You reap what you have sown. Your strong intellectual curiosity about the past reaps results. You connect with relatives and accept an invitation to a social event. Control your emotions when talking with neighbors.

Saturday, September 5 (Moon in Pisces to Aries 11:15 p.m.) It's a number 8 day, your power day. Expect a financial windfall. Business dealings go well; a new approach brings in big bucks.

Sunday, September 6 (Moon in Aries)   Mercury goes retrograde in your tenth house. Expect some confusion and disruption at work over the next three weeks. You could be facing delays related to communication with fellow workers and computer glitches. Keep in mind that it's temporary.

Monday, September 7 (Moon in Aries)   Emotional issues arise related to your home life. Try not to get overagitated or overaggressive. You could be feeling emotionally possessive of loved ones. Take time to retreat to a private place for quiet meditation. Find a new way to beautify your home scene.

Tuesday, September 8 (Moon in Aries to Taurus 7:19 a.m.)   It's a number 2 day. Cooperation is highlighted. Use your intuition to get a sense of your day. Be kind and understanding. Show your appreciation to others. There could be some soul-searching related to relationships.

Wednesday, September 9 (Moon in Taurus)   The moon is in your fifth house. Your love life takes off. There's an idealistic turn to whatever you do for pleasure. It's a great time for a creative project, especially fiction writing. You could be somewhat possessive of loved ones and children.

Thursday, September 10 (Moon in Taurus to Gemini 1:18 p.m.) It's a number 4 day. Persevere to get things done. Tear down the old in order to rebuild. You're building a creative base for your future. Be methodical and thorough. Missing papers or objects are found.

Friday, September 11 (Moon in Gemini) Pluto goes direct in your first house. You can integrate your personal power into your life more effectively. Your personality is more intense than usual. You work hard, but you have more difficulty working with others.

Saturday, September 12 (Moon in Gemini to Cancer 5:20 p.m.) It's a number 6 day. Service to others is the theme. Focus on making people happy. You offer advice and support. Be diplomatic rather than confrontational. Do a good deed for someone. Visit someone who is ill or in need of help.

Sunday, September 13 (Moon in Cancer) With the moon in your seventh house, you get along well with others. Your partner allows you to expand your horizons. Material gains are likely, especially through marriage or a partnership. You and a spouse or partner work well together and succeed at whatever you are doing together.

Monday, September 14 (Moon in Cancer to Leo 7:40 p.m.) It's your power day. Open your mind to a new approach, and you can gain financially in a big way. You have a chance to gain recognition, fame, and power. You're playing with power, so be careful not to hurt others.

Tuesday, September 15 (Moon in Leo) You gain an elevation in prestige related to your profession and career. Material success and financial security play a role. You make a strong emotional commitment to your profession or to a role in public life.

Wednesday, September 16 (Moon in Leo to Virgo 8:56 p.m.) It's a number 1 day. Take the initiative to start something new.

Individuality is stressed. Get out and meet people; make contacts. Make room for a romance, if you're ready for it.

Thursday, September 17 (Moon in Virgo)   You yearn for a break from the usual routine. Your mind is active. You can create positive change through your ideas. An interest in philosophy, religion, or mythology captivates you.

Friday, September 18 (Moon in Virgo to Libra 10:26 p.m.)   There's a new moon in your ninth house. That could mean you get an opportunity for long-distance travel or continuing your education. A foreign-born person or a foreign country plays a role. Worldviews are emphasized.

Saturday, September 19 (Moon in Libra)   You're more responsive to the needs and moods of a group and the public in general. You get an elevation in prestige for your hard work. Your thoughts and especially your feelings are more exposed.

Sunday, September 20 (Moon in Libra)   With Venus moving into your ninth house, your love of travel and study abroad is highlighted. Plan a long trip. You're a dreamer and a thinker. Your mind is active. You yearn for a change from the status quo.

Monday, September 21 (Moon in Libra to Scorpio 1:52 a.m.)   Start off the week by doing a good deed for someone. Diplomacy wins your way. It's all about service to others. Be understanding and avoid confrontations.

Tuesday, September 22 (Moon in Scorpio)   You make deeper contact with friends. Join a group of like-minded individuals. You find strength in numbers. You find meaning by pursuing a joint project for the common good.

Wednesday, September 23 (Moon in Scorpio to Sagittarius 8:44 a.m.)   It's your lucky day. Expect something wonderful out of the blue: a financial windfall, an unexpected check, a generous bonus, or a gift.

Thursday, September 24 (Moon in Sagittarius)   Keep your feelings secret. Work behind the scenes, and finish a project. Unconscious attitudes could be difficult. Think positive, even if you're feeling down. It's a great day for a mystical or spiritual discipline.

Friday, September 25 (Moon in Sagittarius to Capricorn 7:19 p.m.)   It's a number 1 day. You get a fresh start. Don't be afraid to take the lead or turn in a new direction. You connect with creative people. Get out and meet people; have new experiences. A flirtation could turn serious.

Saturday, September 26 (Moon in Capricorn)   The moon is on your ascendant. Your face could be in front of the public. You focus on your self-awareness and appearance. Your feelings and thoughts are aligned. You're physically vital; relations with the opposite sex go well.

Sunday, September 27 (Moon in Capricorn)   It's all about your health and your emotional self: how you feel and how you feel about yourself. You're more sensitive to other people's feelings than usual. You could be feeling stressed and overworked. Other earth signs, a Taurus and a Virgo, play a prominent role.

Monday, September 28 (Moon in Capricorn to Aquarius 8:07 a.m.)   Your organizational skills are highlighted. You're building foundations for the future. Persevere to get things done. Self-discipline is stressed; quality work is emphasized. You're developing outlets for your creativity.

Tuesday, September 29 (Moon in Aquarius)   Mercury goes direct. Confusion, miscommunication, and delays recede into the past. Things move more smoothly. You get along with others better, and you get your message across. Everything works better, including computers and other electronic equipment.

Wednesday, September 30 (Moon in Aquarius to Pisces 8:27 p.m.)   The month ends on a service day. Help others, but avoid scattering your energies. Dance to your own tune. Diplomacy wins the way. Focus on making people happy.

OCTOBER 2009

Thursday, October 1 (Moon in Pisces)   Your mental abilities are strong. You have an emotional need to reinvigorate your studies, especially regarding the past. You're attracted to historical or archaeological studies. Contact with relatives is likely. You accept an invitation to a social event. Neighbors may be involved in your day.

Friday, October 2 (Moon in Pisces)   The moon is in your third house. You're busy interacting with neighbors or relatives. You get your ideas across, but try not to get too emotional. A female relative plays an important role.

Saturday, October 3 (Moon in Pisces to Aries 6:21 a.m.) It's a number 7 day. You journey into the unknown and investigate something hidden going on behind the scenes. You dig deep. You're launching a journey into the unknown and exploring a mystery. Knowledge is essential to your success.

Sunday, October 4 (Moon in Aries)   The full moon in your fourth house sheds light on your home life. Tension between your personal and professional obligations could be highlighted. Take time to retreat to a private place for meditation. It's a good day for dream recall.

Monday, October 5 (Moon in Aries to Taurus 1:34 p.m.) Use the day for reflection, expansion, and concluding projects. But don't start anything new. Like yesterday, spiritual values are emphasized. Strive for universal appeal; look beyond the immediate.

Tuesday, October 6 (Moon in Taurus)   Just try to be yourself. There's greater quality in a relationship. If you're working on a creative project, you have the ability to tap deeply into your emotions to bring out the best. Children and animals play a role.

Wednesday, October 7 (Moon in Taurus to Gemini 6:47 p.m.) It's a number 2 day. The spotlight shines on cooperative efforts. If you're married, your marriage takes on more significance. If you're not married, there could be some soul-searching related to a relationship, or a new relationship develops. Help comes through friends.

Thursday, October 8 (Moon in Gemini) With the moon in your sixth house, the emphasis turns to your daily work and service to others. Attend to all the details. Be careful not to overlook any seemingly minor matters that could take on importance. Keep up with your exercise plan; watch your diet.

Friday, October 9 (Moon in Gemini to Cancer 10:48 p.m.) Take care of your obligations. Focus on getting organized. Persevere to get things done. Don't get sloppy in your work. You may need to tear down in order to rebuild. Revise and rewrite.

Saturday, October 10 (Moon in Cancer) Partnership and cooperation are highlighted. Go with the flow. Let things develop in their own time. Think of yourself as part of the process. Through a partnership, you become whole. You realize your full potential.

Sunday, October 11 (Moon in Cancer) You're moody and sensitive to other people. You feel best near water. You're intuitive and nurturing. Your home life is important to you.

Monday, October 12 (Moon in Cancer to Leo 2:03 a.m.) Jupiter goes direct in your second house. The emphasis is on money as you expand your financial base. Material gains are likely. Whatever you value or your values take on greater importance. Think abundance.

Tuesday, October 13 (Moon in Leo) Your experiences are more intense than usual. You could be channeling your energy through a powerful sex drive. Be aware that emotions can be intense, especially related to shared possessions. Matters related to death and rebirth are highlighted.

Wednesday, October 14 (Moon in Leo to Virgo 4:46 a.m.)
As Venus moves into your tenth house, you're attracted to a creative project in your career, especially something involving the arts or entertainment. You gain public attention or recognition. You're seen as appealing to the public.

Thursday, October 15 (Moon in Virgo) Matters related to college or any type of higher education take on greater importance. Philosophy, mythology, and worldviews play a role. In romance, you could be attracted to a foreign-born person or a particular foreign land.

Friday, October 16 (Moon in Virgo to Libra 7:30 a.m.)
With Mars moving into your eighth house, you're an investigator and a problem solver. You dig deep for information in whatever area that interests you or is of greatest importance. Your sex drive is strong. However, tension arises in any dealings related to joint resources or an inheritance.

Saturday, October 17 (Moon in Libra) The moon is in your tenth house. Your focus turns to professional matters. You could be dealing with a matter related to your reputation. You get a boost in prestige. You're received well by others, but avoid making an emotional display in public.

Sunday, October 18 (Moon in Libra to Scorpio 11:23 a.m.)
Yesterday's energy flows on. With a new moon in your tenth house, an opportunity comes your way. You get along well with others, but be careful not to cross the line between your personal and professional lives.

Monday, October 19 (Moon in Scorpio) Friends can help you reach your goals. Group activities work in your favor. Focus on your wishes and dreams. Make sure that your goals are an expression of who you really are.

Tuesday, October 20 (Moon in Scorpio to Sagittarius 5:50 p.m.)   It's all about service. Help others where you can, but dance to your own tune. A domestic change works out for the best. Be diplomatic, resourceful, and helpful, but avoid scattering your energies.

Wednesday, October 21 (Moon in Sagittarius)   Stay out of the public eye. Work behind the scenes. Keep your feelings to yourself. Be aware that relations with women can be difficult. Pursue a mystical or spiritual discipline.

Thursday, October 22 (Moon in Sagittarius)   The moon is in your twelfth house. Work behind the scenes; avoid any conflict. You could be dealing with a matter from the past that has returned to haunt you. Keep your feelings secret. Follow your intuition.

Friday, October 23 (Moon in Sagittarius to Capricorn 3:40 a.m.)   Take time for reflection. Conclude projects and consider ways to expand your base. Clear out the old in preparation for a fresh start. But don't start anything new just yet. Strive for universal appeal; look beyond the immediate. You're up to the challenge.

Saturday, October 24 (Moon in Capricorn)   The sun is on your ascendant, and you're at the top of your cycle. You're feeling physically vital. Relations with the opposite sex go well. The way you see yourself is the way others see you. Your face is in front of the public; you get a fresh start.

Sunday, October 25 (Moon in Capricorn to Aquarius 3:08 p.m.)   It's a number 2 day. Partnerships and cooperation rule the day. Use your intuition to get a sense of your day. Be kind and understanding. Don't make waves. Let things develop. Focus on your direction and motivation.

Monday, October 26 (Moon in Aquarius)   The moon is in your second house. Expect emotional experiences related to money. You identify emotionally with your possessions or whatever you value. Look at your priorities in handling your income. Put off making any major purchases.

Tuesday, October 27 (Moon in Aquarius)   Groups and social events are highlighted. Your individuality is stressed. Your visionary abilities are heightened. You're dealing with new ideas.

Wednesday, October 28 (Moon in Aquarius to Pisces 3:46 a.m.)   Mercury moves into your eleventh house. Your mind is quick; you pursue a variety of ideas. You communicate well with members of a group. Friends provide you with a variety of opinions and a wide range of perspectives.

Thursday, October 29 (Moon in Pisces)   Saturn moves into your tenth house. Your professional responsibilities increase, but there might be delays in getting the recognition you seek and deserve. But if you work hard you'll reap the benefits later.

Friday, October 30 (Moon in Pisces to Aries 1:57 p.m.) You're launching a journey into the unknown and exploring a mystery. You dig deep for information, looking into a secret or hidden matter. Knowledge is essential to your success.

Saturday, October 31 (Moon in Aries)   Stick close to home and spend time with your family. Work on a project to beautify your home. Take time to retreat to a private place for meditation.

NOVEMBER 2009

Sunday, November 1—Daylight Saving Time Ends (Moon in Aries to Taurus 7:45 p.m.)   You start the month on a service day. Diplomacy wins the way. A domestic adjustment works out for the best. Be understanding and avoid confrontations. Dance to your own tune. An adjustment in your domestic life may be necessary.

Monday, November 2 (Moon in Taurus)   There's a full moon in your fifth house. You get a break on a creative project. A burst of creative energy motors you ahead. It's a good day to take a risk, especially one that can pay off in a big way. Sex for pleasure is highlighted. You're more possessive of loved ones.

Tuesday, November 3 (Moon in Taurus to Gemini 11:53 p.m.) It's a number 8 day. It's your power day; business dealings go well. You can go far with your plans and achieve financial success. You have a chance to gain recognition, fame, and power. You're playing with power, so be careful not to hurt others.

Wednesday, November 4 (Moon in Gemini)   Neptune moves into your second house. Be emotionally honest, especially when dealing with money issues that cropped up yesterday. If you bend the truth, it can cost you financially. Be aware of self-deception, especially related to money issues. Watch out for get-rich-quick schemes.

Thursday, November 5 (Moon in Gemini)   Service is the order of the day. Help others, but don't deny your own needs. Your health occupies your attention. Visit someone who is sick or in need of your help.

Friday, November 6 (Moon in Gemini to Cancer 2:43 a.m.) It's a number 2 day. Use your intuition to get a sense of the day. The spotlight is on cooperation. There could be some soul-searching related to a relationship. Show your appreciation to others.

Saturday, November 7 (Moon in Cancer)   Venus moves into your eleventh house. Social activities are highlighted, possibly in your own home. You get along well with others and put new acquaintances at ease. You work smoothly with a group and show your affection to friends.

Sunday, November 8 (Moon in Cancer to Leo 5:23 a.m.) It's a number 4 day. Get things organized for the week ahead.

Revise; rewrite. Clean a closet, the garage, or the attic. Be methodical and thorough. Be practical with your money.

Monday, November 9 (Moon in Leo) You're dealing with shared assets or belongings in any joint venture, such as a marriage or a business partnership. Taxes, insurance, or an inheritance could play a role. You expand your horizons with the help of a loved one or partner. You're intrigued by mysteries of life, including what happens at the end of life.

Tuesday, November 10 (Moon in Leo to Virgo 8:31 a.m.) It's a number 6 day. Service to others is the theme. You offer advice and support. Do a good deed for someone. Focus on making people happy. Domestic purchases are highlighted.

Wednesday, November 11 (Moon in Virgo) With the moon in your ninth house, look to the big picture. Break away from your routine. You could be feeling restless and looking for a broader approach. A foreign-born person or a foreign country could play a role.

Thursday, November 12 (Moon in Virgo to Libra 12:23 p.m.) It's your power day. Be courageous. Business dealings work in your favor. A windfall comes your way. You have a good chance to expand your base. Financial success is at hand.

Friday, November 13 (Moon in Libra) You gain a boost in prestige at work: a promotion, a raise, or more responsibilities. It could relate to your work with a colleague. It's a good day for sales and public relations. You're in the public eye. Be careful about getting too emotionally involved with someone in the office.

Saturday, November 14 (Moon in Libra to Scorpio 5:25 p.m.) You're at the top of your cycle. You get a new perspective. Explore and discover; creativity is highlighted. Get out and meet new people; have new experiences.

Sunday, November 15 (Moon in Scorpio) Mercury moves into your twelfth house. Your past and your unconscious mind strongly influence your thoughts and actions. Emotions, rather than logic, dictate your decisions.

Monday, November 16 (Moon in Scorpio)   There's a new moon in your eleventh house. Thanks to your friends, you get a nice break. Your sense of security is tied to your relationships. You work well with a group, especially if you're working for the common good.

Tuesday, November 17 (Moon in Scorpio to Sagittarius 12:23 a.m.)   Time to get organized so you can move ahead. It takes hard work to succeed. Stay focused and avoid any tendencies to wander. Be methodical and thorough. Fulfill your obligations.

Wednesday, November 18 (Moon in Sagittarius)   Work behind the scenes and avoid any confrontations. It can be a difficult time with secrets from the past revisited. You could be dealing with the mysteries of life and death as well as matters related to higher awareness.

Thursday, November 19 (Moon in Sagittarius to Capricorn 10:01 a.m.)   You could face emotional outbursts or someone making unfair demands on your time. Be sympathetic, kind, and understanding, but dance to your own tune. An adjustment in your domestic life may be necessary.

Friday, November 20 (Moon in Capricorn)   The moon is in your first house. You are sensitive and responsive regarding the needs of others. But you're restless and somewhat uncertain what to do. Your self-awareness and appearance are important. It's all about your health and your emotional self.

Saturday, November 21 (Moon in Capricorn to Aquarius 10:11 p.m.)   You can go far with your plans and achieve financial success. You have a chance to gain recognition, fame, and power. Open your mind to a new approach that could bring in big bucks.

Sunday, November 22 (Moon in Aquarius)   The moon is in your second house. You identify emotionally with your values or whatever you value. You tend to equate your assets with emotional security. You feel best when surrounded by familiar objects, especially in your home. It's not the objects themselves that are important, but the feelings and memories you associate with them.

Monday, November 23 (Moon in Aquarius)   Groups and social events are highlighted. You have a greater sense of freedom. You're dealing with new ideas. You get a new perspective.

Tuesday, November 24 (Moon in Aquarius to Pisces 11:08 a.m.)   You work well with others. Cooperation is the key word. Go with the flow. Don't make waves. Use your intuition, especially concerning a partnership. Show others that you appreciate them, but don't forget your own needs.

Wednesday, November 25 (Moon in Pisces)   No doubt you're running around taking care of your everyday needs. Be especially careful when driving. Stay grounded. Control your emotions when talking with relatives or neighbors.

Thursday, November 26 (Moon in Pisces to Aries 10:11 p.m.) Focus on your organizational skills. Fulfill your obligations. Persevere to get things done. Emphasize quality. You're building a creative base for your future, but it takes hard work.

Friday, November 27 (Moon in Aries)   It's a great time for initiating projects, launching new ideas, and brainstorming. Emotions could be volatile. You're passionate, but impatient. Be careful about accidents. Avoid reckless behavior.

Saturday, November 28 (Moon in Aries)   The moon is in your fourth house. Emotional issues that arise relate to the domestic scene. You could be feeling possessive of loved ones. Retreat to a private place for quiet meditation. Find a new way to beautify your home scene.

Sunday, November 29 (Moon in Aries to Taurus 5:35 a.m.) It's a number 7 day. You investigate, analyze, or simply observe what's going on. You quickly come to a conclusion and wonder why others don't see what you see. You detect deception and recognize insincerity with ease.

Monday, November 30 (Moon in Taurus)   The moon is in your fifth house as the month comes to an end. You can reach greater depths in a relationship. A creative project blossoms. Spend time with children.

DECEMBER 2009

Tuesday, December 1 (Moon in Taurus to Gemini 9:24 a.m.) You love your solitude and need time to yourself to reflect. Any secrets you possess are well hidden. Meanwhile, Uranus goes direct in your seventh house. That means you might encounter sudden and unexpected changes in a relationship, either personal or business. An unexpected legal matter could come to your attention.

Wednesday, December 2 (Moon in Gemini)   There's a full moon in your sixth house. It's harvesttime. All your hard work pays off. Others respect you and turn to you for help. You improve, refine, and edit their work. But don't ignore your own needs. A health checkup will give you the answers you're hoping for.

Thursday, December 3 (Moon in Gemini to Cancer 11:01 a.m.)   It's a good day to clear your desk, complete projects, and get ready for something new. Take time to consider how to expand and achieve universal appeal, but don't start anything new.

Friday, December 4 (Moon in Cancer)   The focus is on partnerships. You get a fresh start. A legal matter or contract is at hand. Women play a prominent role. Be careful not to let others manipulate your feelings. It's difficult to remain detached and objective. You need to be determined and courageous.

Saturday, December 5 (Moon in Cancer to Leo 12:08 p.m.)
Your mind is active as you reflect on your personal life. You're inventive; you make connections that others overlook. You adapt quickly to changing circumstances. You're mentally restless as you focus on your self-awareness and appearance.

Sunday, December 6 (Moon in Leo)   You attract the attention of powerful people. Be aware that your experiences could be more intense than usual. Matters related to shared belongings, investments, taxes, or insurance could play a role. An interest in a metaphysical subject attracts your attention.

Monday, December 7 (Moon in Leo to Virgo 2:07 p.m.)   It's a number 4 day. Get organized. Focus on advertising and publicity. Be adventurous. But also be methodical and thorough. You're building a creative base for the future.

Tuesday, December 8 (Moon in Virgo)   Break away from your usual routines, and escape for a day or two. Sign up for a workshop or seminar that interests you. Something related to publishing works to your favor. Pursue a new idea. Are you ready to plan a long trip?

Wednesday, December 9 (Moon in Virgo to Libra 5:48 p.m.)
It's another service day. Do a good deed for someone. Visit someone who is ill or in need of help. Be sympathetic, kind, and compassionate. Avoid confrontations; avoid scattering your energy.

Thursday, December 10 (Moon in Libra)   Professional concerns weigh heavily. Your life is more public. You're more responsive to the needs and moods of a group and the public in general. Keep your profession and personal lives separate.

Friday, December 11 (Moon in Libra to Scorpio 11:32 p.m.)
It's a number 8 day, your power day. You pull off a financial coup. You're being watched by people in power. Be aware that fear of failure or fear that you won't measure up will attract tangible experiences that reinforce the feeling.

Saturday, December 12 (Moon in Scorpio)   Friends play an important role, and they may help you in surprising ways. Focus on your wishes and dreams; make sure that they are an expression of who you really are.

Sunday, December 13 (Moon in Scorpio)   You're passionate today; your sexuality is heightened. Intense emotional experiences are in store for you. Control issues arise. Be aware of things happening in secret. Forgive and forget; try to avoid going to extremes.

Monday, December 14 (Moon in Scorpio to Sagittarius 7:25 a.m.)   The emphasis is on working together. You can get more accomplished that way. Use your intuition to get a sense of your day. Be kind and understanding. Partnerships play an important role.

Tuesday, December 15 (Moon in Sagittarius)   Work behind the scenes. Avoid any confrontations, especially with women. Use your intuition to get a sense of your day. Go deep within to look for answers. Keep your opinions to yourself, but confide in a close friend.

Wednesday, December 16 (Moon in Sagittarius to Capricorn 5:32 p.m.)   There's a new moon in your first house. An opportunity comes your way; it could involve working at home, on your own, or behind the scenes. It could involve a connection from the past. Your reaction to the offer could bring success and also help you deal with rejection or failure.

Thursday, December 17 (Moon in Capricorn)   The moon is in your first house. The focus turns to the self, particularly your emotional self. You're sensitive to other people's feelings, and you may feel moody.

Friday, December 18 (Moon in Capricorn)   With the moon on your ascendant, the way you see yourself is the way others see you. It's all about what you show of yourself. You're recharged for the month ahead, which makes you more appealing to the public. You're physically vital, and relations with the opposite sex go well.

Saturday, December 19 (Moon in Capricorn to Aquarius 5:39 a.m.)   Dig deep into a mystery. You could be dealing with confidential information, secrets, and intrigue. Maintain your balance. Gather information, but don't make any immediate decisions based on what you learn.

Sunday, December 20 (Moon in Aquarius)   Mars goes retrograde in your eighth house. Be careful about applying for mortgages or loans. You could be revisiting tax or insurance issues. Avoid any confrontations related to shared belongings.

Monday, December 21 (Moon in Aquarius to Pisces 6:42 p.m.)   Finish whatever you've been working on. Clear up odds and ends; make room for something new. Get ready for a new cycle. Accept what comes your way, but don't start anything new.

Tuesday, December 22 (Moon in Pisces)   You write from a deep place. Your mental abilities are strong, you have an emotional need to reinvigorate your studies, especially regarding the past. A female relative plays a role. Expect a visit from a relative or neighbor or an invitation to a social event.

Wednesday, December 23 (Moon in Pisces)   Your imagination is highlighted. Watch for psychic events. Don't fall into a trap of self-deception. Keep track of your dreams. Ideas are ripe. You're feeling inspired.

Thursday, December 24 (Moon in Pisces to Aries 6:40 a.m.)   It's a number 3 day. Ease up on your routines; spread your good news. You communicate well. You're warm and receptive to what others say. Your imagination is keen. You're curious and inventive. Enjoy the harmony, beauty, and pleasures of life. Beautify your home.

Friday, December 25 (Moon in Aries)   Venus moves into your first house. You're friendly and outgoing, moving from one gathering to another. Your charm and wit are appreciated. Your attitude determines everything. Your vitality is strong; you have a natural ability to express yourself. Merry Christmas!

Saturday, December 26 (Moon in Aries into Taurus 3:27 a.m.)   Mercury goes retrograde in your first house. You're reflecting on everything that's happened recently. You retreat and relax, but your mind is active. You mentally connect different ideas and different people. But you're forced to wait before you can act on your thoughts.

Sunday, December 27 (Moon in Taurus)   You're emotionally in touch with your creative side. You're easily impressed, so make sure that you don't allow anyone to influence you on a speculative matter. Tend to children and loved ones. There's a lot of emotion in a romantic relationship.

Monday, December 28 (Moon in Taurus to Gemini 8:15 p.m.)   It's a number 7 day. You become aware of confidential information and secret meetings. You investigate. Gather information, but don't act on what you learn until tomorrow.

Tuesday, December 29 (Moon in Gemini)   Others rely on you for help. You're the go-to person to improve or refine what others are working on. Just make sure that the ones you're helping don't take advantage of your willingness. Know when to say enough is enough.

Wednesday, December 30 (Moon in Gemini to Cancer 9:46 p.m.)   It's a number 9 day. Finish the year by wrapping up a project and preparing for something new. Take time to reflect on everything that's been going on. Look for a way to expand your horizons, but don't start anything new until the New Year.

Thursday, December 31 (Moon in Cancer)   There's a lunar eclipse in the seventh house. You can expect to experience an emotional reaction to an event related to a partnership.

241

You comprehend the nuances of a situation, but it's difficult to go with the flow. Be careful that others don't manipulate your feelings.

HAPPY NEW YEAR!

JANUARY 2010

Friday, January 1 (Moon in Cancer to Leo 10:42 p.m.) With the moon in Cancer most of the day, you're in the mood to spend time with the one you love. You actually could be somewhat moody today, your sensitivity triggered by the smallest things; a misplaced word or look, a feeling that you're not good enough. You know the drill. Let these moods work their way through you. By tomorrow, you're on fire.

Saturday, January 2 (Moon in Leo) You're more than willing to share your time and expertise with others today. You'll find other people are receptive to your ideas, to your energy, to *you*. Mercury is retrograde in your sign until January 15, so there may be some miscommunication.

Sunday, January 3 (Moon in Leo to Virgo 10:53 p.m.) The focus is on your worldview, your spiritual beliefs, and your educational goals. If you're on your way to college or graduate school in the fall, then now is the time to wind up all the bureaucratic stuff that's required. If you're a writer in search of a publisher, get busy preparing your manuscript for submission.

Monday, January 4 (Moon in Virgo) Mercury started the year retrograde in your sign and doesn't turn direct until January 15. So keep new projects under wraps till then, and save your traveling until after that date as well. But virtual travel all you want. It'll bring an element of peace to your soul.

Tuesday, January 5 (Moon in Virgo) The moon forms a harmonious angle to your sun, bolstering your emotions and intuition. Others see you as a leader, as someone who has answers and a plan. You nearly always have a backup plan and you may have to fall back on it today.

Wednesday, January 6 (Moon in Virgo to Libra 12:59 a.m.) Your career and professional relationships take center stage today. You may have to make a decision that is difficult, but you have a strong sense of what's right and wrong with this issue and know exactly what to do. Bottom line? You win the day.

Thursday, January 7 (Moon in Libra)　Cooperation and balance are called for with a boss or peer. It may be that you're called upon to get involved in a team project. If it interests you, of course, you dive in and probably end up running the show. If it doesn't interest you, you'll still have to put in an appearance.

Friday, January 8 (Moon in Libra to Scorpio 6:01 a.m.) The moon enters your eleventh house and forms a nice angle to your sun. Your social calendar should heat up today, with activities being planned for the weekend. You'll have your pick of invitations. You and a friend may decide to get out of town for the weekend, perhaps in a search for something unusual—a piece of art, a rare book, or even some food delight not available in your area.

Saturday, January 9 (Moon in Scorpio)　With Venus in your sign until February 11 and the moon in compatible water sign Scorpio, your love life is cranked up several notches today. You and a partner may be discussing bottom-line issues in your relationship. Or perhaps you're deciding whether to move in together. Whatever your decisions, it has to feel right to you.

Sunday, January 10 (Moon in Scorpio to Sagittarius 2:10 p.m.)　The moon enters your twelfth house this afternoon. This is probably a day when you stick close to home, kick back to relax, and end up doing stuff around your home. You always need a goal, and even when you relax, you've got one.

Monday, January 11 (Moon in Sagittarius)   You're looking for the big picture today concerning motives—your own
or someone else's. You actually have the big picture, but just
don't know it. So take a few minutes today to sit quietly, your
mind empty of thought, and ask that the universe show you
what you need to know.

Tuesday, January 12 (Moon in Sagittarius)   The Sagittarius moon forms a nice angle to Mars in Leo. This combination of energies should allow you to grasp the larger spectrum
of a spiritual issue or of some motive that you have and may
not quite understand. With Venus still in your sign, you're on
a creative roll.

*Wednesday, January 13 (Moon in Sagittarius to Capricorn
12:54 a.m.)*   Saturn turns retrograde in Libra, in the career
sector of your chart, and will be that way until May 30. During
the retrograde, you may be reviewing professional issues and
matters that you thought were resolved. Or a project may go
on a back burner. Your responsibilities at work are increasing
steadily this year, and you rise to the challenge.

Thursday, January 14 (Moon in Capricorn)   A power
day. Get moving on whatever stirs your blood. Your head and
heart are in complete unison today, so it's an excellent opportunity to tackle difficult stuff—at work, at home, and within
yourself.

*Friday, January 15 (Moon in Capricorn to Aquarius 1:17
p.m.)*   The solar eclipse in your sign is like a double new
moon and ushers in all kinds of opportunities for you. These
opportunities can occur in virtually any area of your life. It
depends on where your focus is. So don't waste your energy
today. Dive into the areas that matter to you most of all. Mercury turns direct in your sign, a major plus overall.

Saturday, January 16 (Moon in Aquarius)   The moon
joins Venus in your second house of finances. You may feel
somewhat vulnerable financially, but there's really nothing to
worry about. Your money is in good shape; your earning ca-

pacity is strong. All you need to do right now is resist spending on big-ticket items.

Sunday, January 17 (Moon in Aquarius)   Jupiter enters Pisces today, forming a beneficial angle with your sun. Read more about this under the big-picture section. But for today, celebrate this transit by doing something special for another person. Do it without any thought of compensation or reward. Pisces loves and appreciates that kind of gesture.

Monday, January 18 (Moon in Aquarius to Pisces 2:18 a.m.) Venus enters Aquarius and your second house today. Lucky you. Between now and February 11, your financial picture should improve. You might land a nice bonus, a raise, or even a promotion that puts extra money in your pocket.

Tuesday, January 19 (Moon in Pisces)   The moon joins Jupiter in Pisces, in your third house. Jupiter expands whatever it touches. If you find yourself getting emotional today, understand that your feelings are exaggerated. Wait until the moon enters Taurus to figure it all out.

Wednesday, January 20 (Moon in Pisces to Aries 2:37 p.m.) Just when you're starting to feel the afternoon doldrums setting in, the moon enters Aries, and suddenly you're fired up and ready to go. You're so ready, in fact, that you may take the rest of the day off and head home to launch improvement projects that have been on the back burner.

Thursday, January 21 (Moon in Aries)   This moon forms a beautiful angle to Venus in Aquarius and helps you to take care of financial business that demands your attention. Whether it's balancing your checkbook or taking a deeper look into your savings situation, you're on the case. You may be brainstorming with someone about how to increase your earnings.

Friday, January 22 (Moon in Aries)   It's not about burning bridges or even crossing the same bridges that others cross.

Today, you're forging new paths. There's an entrepreneurial spirit in the air.

Saturday, January 23 (Moon in Aries to Taurus 12:41 a.m.) You're very comfortable with the Taurus moon. Remember the story of the little engine that said, "I think I can. I think I can." But with this moon, your litany is: I *know* I can.

Sunday, January 24 (Moon in Taurus) The moon forms a beautiful angle with Jupiter in Pisces and highlights your love life, your conscious mind, and your creativity. It's as if you have the Midas touch in all these areas today. Notice, for instance, the patterns that your thoughts follow. If they seem to veer too easily into negativity, nudge them back into a more positive vein.

Monday, January 25 (Moon in Taurus to Gemini 7:12 a.m.) Your focus shifts to your daily work routine and to the maintenance of your health. You may be on an information-gathering kick, looking for some nutritional or exercise program that provides the magic bullet. Maybe it's time to join a gym, if you don't have an exercise routine already.

Tuesday, January 26 (Moon in Gemini) Gathering information isn't the same thing as research. Your search is quite specific, but the information you're collecting covers a wide swath of areas. That's a good thing. Collect and then toss out what isn't relevant. Then make your decisions.

Wednesday, January 27 (Moon in Gemini to Cancer 10:02 a.m.) The moon enters your opposite sign, bringing your attention to nurturing of others. The focus of your nurturing may be a partner in business or in romance who could be at loose ends or simply caught in a difficult situation. You offer your perspective and advice.

Thursday, January 28 (Moon in Cancer) Intuitively, you understand exactly what's going on in a partnership. You listen to your feelings and hunches about it and then act on them.

But do so in a gentle, nonthreatening way. The result will be more to your liking.

Friday, January 29 (Moon in Cancer to Leo 10:10 a.m.)
The resources, time, and money of a partner or spouse are the issues today. This person may be facing challenges with taxes or insurance, and you pitch in to help out in some way. It's the kind of thing you do because you care about this individual and not because you want something in return.

Saturday, January 30 (Moon in Leo)   Today's full moon in Leo may feel a bit nuts. There's a lot of activity, running around, and talk. Mars is within a degree of this moon, suggesting that you're really pushing forward with something. The insights you gain concerning shared resources are helpful in making a decision.

Sunday, January 31 (Moon in Leo to Virgo 9:23 a.m.)
Feeling picky and critical? If so, turn that focus to details. Connect the dots, figure out the pattern, and look for the deeper motive. Then take a deep breath.

FEBRUARY 2010

Monday, February 1 (Moon in Virgo)   Details, details. That's where your work lies today. Whether you're dealing with work, family, your personal life, or money, the devil really is in the details. If it's winter where you are, you may be feeling the need to get somewhere sunny and warm. Be sure to travel on either side of the next Mercury retrograde—April 17 to May 11.

Tuesday, February 2 (Moon in Virgo to Libra 9:42 a.m.)
The moon joins Saturn retrograde in your tenth house of career. There could be a kind of oppressive texture to the day. Blame Saturn. It asks that you take responsibility for your thoughts and actions, that you fulfill your obligations, and that you be disciplined. If you're doing what Saturn asks already, then the day will just be busy, and you'll get a whole lot done.

Wednesday, February 3 (Moon in Libra)   Teamwork may not be what you want to do today, but in some way, shape or form, it's what you'll be doing. It could be teamwork through a webcast or podcast, through e-mail, or even conference calls. People are receptive to your ideas and agenda.

Thursday, February 4 (Moon in Libra to Scorpio 12:56 p.m.) The Scorpio moon is a friendlier moon for you, although perhaps a tad too intense! You may end up meeting a romantic interest through friends or through a group to which you belong. If so, be aware that the relationship will be sexually charged.

Friday, February 5 (Moon in Scorpio)   It's a bottom-line sort of day. You're after something: information, research, or the real scoop on an event, situation, or relationship. Your need will take you where you need to go and with a minimum of effort if you follow your intuition. If you feel an urge to search in a particular place, even if that place is unfamiliar to you, do so.

Saturday, February 6 (Moon in Scorpio to Sagittarius 8:04 p.m.)   Whenever the moon enters your twelfth house, there's a sense of pulling back—a need, perhaps, for solitude or down time. Indulge it. Honor it. You're preparing for the moon entering your sign on Tuesday.

Sunday, February 7 (Moon in Sagittarius)   Since the Sagittarius moon can be restless, you may want to consider taking a car trip today. Alone. Just drive. Let your mind wander. Try not to name objects and things that you see. Just observe in the moment. Be fully present.

Monday, February 8 (Moon in Sagittarius)   Time to tie up loose ends and prepare yourself for tomorrow's power day. Make a list of what you would like to accomplish tomorrow through Friday. It can be related to anything. But because you tend to be so directed and focused, it probably will be connected to a goal that you have.

Tuesday, February 9 (Moon in Sagittarius to Capricorn 6:45 a.m.)   Okay, here it is! You awaken with a sense of purpose and embrace everything that comes your way. Try to get through the day without attaching labels to situations and people. Just *be*.

Wednesday, February 10 (Moon in Capricorn)   Mercury enters Aquarius and the financial sector of your chart, where it'll be until March 1. During this period, you'll be thinking and talking a lot about money: how you earn it, spend it, your attitudes toward it. It's possible that you can earn money through communication now—like with writing or public speaking.

Thursday, February 11 (Moon in Capricorn to Aquarius 7:25 p.m.)   Venus enters Pisces, where it will remain until March 7. During this period, a romance is possible with someone who lives as close as your backyard! You may also get involved in some sort of creative project with a sibling or neighbor.

Friday, February 12 (Moon in Aquarius)   Today's new moon in Aquarius should usher in financial opportunities for you. This could be anything from a better-paying job, a raise, an investment that pays off, to royalties you receive. Neptune is within a degree of this new moon, indicating a spiritual or creative component to this new opportunity.

Saturday, February 13 (Moon in Aquarius)   Follow your hunches today, and you'll be thinking outside the box in no time. This can lead you to doing unusual things to boost your earnings. You find a niche that your talents or expertise can fill, or you find a venue that is in line with your values and beliefs. Or both.

Sunday, February 14 (Moon in Aquarius to Pisces 8:24 a.m.) Happy Valentine's Day! Be sure to make time for that special person in your life. If you're not involved, then get together with friends or family members, and express your appreciation for their being in your life.

Monday, February 15 (Moon in Pisces)   You may get together with relatives or neighbors at some point today. You feel a need for connecting with people on an intuitive level. Your imagination comes into play in ways you don't expect. Suddenly, your world looks brighter.

Tuesday, February 16 (Moon in Pisces to Aries 8:31 p.m.) With Venus now in Pisces and your third house, and the moon in Aries and your fourth house, your love life should be humming along quite nicely. Your muse is up close and personal, whispering suggestions and guiding you to do this or that. Keep a notebook handy tonight. Your dreams will be vivid and provide information.

Wednesday, February 17 (Moon in Aries)   Emotionally, you're on fire. Whether this fire is triggered by an idea, project, relationship, or something else, you're on the case. And there's no holding you back. You rush forward with all the pioneering spirit of an astronaut on a space walk.

Thursday, February 18 (Moon in Aries)   You may be redoing your home environment—fresh paint, new furniture, new appliances, whatever you feel needs to be spiffed up. You may want to choose the paint colors when the moon is in a fellow earth sign. Otherwise, you could end up with fire-color rooms.

Friday, February 19 (Moon in Aries to Taurus 6:56 a.m.) Your comfort level increases with this moon. You feel more grounded. Your focus shifts to your love life, specifically to a certain someone who interests you. If you're involved already, then you and your partner should get out and do something that you both enjoy.

Saturday, February 20 (Moon in Taurus)   You may want to spend today just being creative. The stars are lined up in favor of it, and it doesn't matter what kind of creativity is involved. In fact, with Mercury still transiting the financial sector of your chart, you may want to consider a creative project or thrust that will put more money in your pocket.

Sunday, February 21 (Moon in Taurus to Gemini 2:47 p.m.)   Today's answers lie in information. Not just in gathering information, but in connecting the dots. For you, it's like putting together a jigsaw puzzle. And the information comes to you in both conventional and unconventional ways.

Monday, February 22 (Moon in Gemini)   Are you feeling the impact of the new moon on February 13 yet? Any financial opportunities surfacing? If not, then it's time for you to take action. One simple action you can take is almost ritualistic: spend a little money on yourself. Treat yourself. Make this a gesture of your newfound abundance.

Tuesday, February 23 (Moon in Gemini to Cancer 7:29 p.m.) You and a business partner may not be seeing eye to eye on things. It's a good idea to sit down and discuss things now, while Mercury is direct in visionary Aquarius. Make lists. Get it all down on paper or in a computer file so you both know exactly what the terms are.

Wednesday, February 24 (Moon in Cancer)   You may be nurturing your mother or some other woman in your life who has nurtured you in the past. This person is insightful and seems to have a solid understanding of who you are and what makes you tick. Listen closely to what she has to say.

Thursday, February 25 (Moon in Cancer to Leo 9:09 p.m.) The dramatic Leo moon stirs up theatrics today. If you have natal planets in Leo, then the ante is raised even higher. The best course of action—unless you love drama—is to take a deep breath, listen to both sides of the story, and make your decisions when the moon is in fellow earth sign Virgo.

Friday, February 26 (Moon in Leo)   Your emotions are all over the place. It would be smart to back off a bit today on just about everything. Hang out with a few close friends, and plan something special for tomorrow, when the moon is in a fellow earth sign.

Saturday, February 27 (Moon in Leo to Virgo 8:53 p.m.)
Get prepared for tomorrow's full moon in Virgo. You can expect news from abroad, news about your education goals, and insight into your spiritual beliefs. Today, stay to the straight and narrow.

Sunday, February 28 (Moon in Virgo)   Today's full moon in Virgo receives a powerful angle from Pluto, so this one is a packed house. Use all this energy wisely and judiciously.

MARCH 2010

Monday, March 1 (Moon in Virgo to Libra 8:32 p.m.)
Mercury enters Pisces and your third house and remains there until March 17. During this transit, your communication with relatives increases significantly. You may be in discussions concerning a contract. Your conscious mind is now like a sponge, absorbing other people's moods and feelings. So it's important to hang out only with upbeat individuals.

Tuesday, March 2 (Moon in Libra)   You're very focused on a professional issue or project. You may have to engage others in whatever this is, so choose your team carefully. You need competent individuals who are as directed as you are. You'll have a clearer sense of where everything stands by March 4.

Wednesday, March 3 (Moon in Libra to Scorpio 10:12 p.m.)
The Scorpio moon is more to your liking because it's energy you understand. A bit intense probably, but it bolsters all the qualities for which you're known. Friends are helpful today, and a certain someone in a group to which you belong may have an eye on you.

Thursday, March 4 (Moon in Scorpio)   There seem to be rumblings among your friends that you hear through the grapevine. Don't bother listening to gossip. Go directly to the source to find out what's going on. Be up front, but not confrontational. Use your people skills!

Friday, March 5 (Moon in Scorpio)   Your intuition is right on today. So if you have an impulse to do something you've never done before, to drive a route you've never gone before, go for it. It's your intuition speaking. Make notes about what you discover so that next time you feel this kind of impulse, you act on it quickly.

Saturday, March 6 (Moon in Scorpio to Sagittarius 3:37 a.m.)   Is it time to chill yet? You bet. Not only is it Saturday, but you've earned some relaxation time. Of course, relaxation for you rarely lasts very long. Even when you're chilling, you find something to do, a small goal to move toward.

Sunday, March 7 (Moon in Sagittarius)   Venus enters Aries, where it will be until March 31. During this period, your love life at home should ramp up and you become what was once called a nester. If you're not involved right now, then the energy can be put to creative use. You may decide, for instance, to set up a home office and do your creative work there.

Monday, March 8 (Moon in Sagittarius to Capricorn 1:15 p.m.)   A power day. The moon enters your sign early this afternoon, and the difference in energy is immediately apparent to you. Gone is whatever angst you may have been feeling. Your mind and your heart are in complete agreement. So use today and the next few days to take on difficult tasks. You'll get them done in record time.

Tuesday, March 9 (Moon in Capricorn)   Your ruler, Saturn, is still moving retrograde in Libra, in the career sector of your chart. This movement may be creating some challenges for you. But with the moon still in your sign today, you have an opportunity to tackle these issues in a positive, productive way.

Wednesday, March 10 (Moon in Capricorn)   Mars finally turns direct in Leo and now forms a nice angle to Venus in Aries. Whenever these two planets are supporting each other, chemistry between you and someone else is strong. Since both planets are in fire signs, there should be plenty of passionate encounters.

Thursday, March 11 (Moon in Capricorn to Aquarius 1:44 a.m.) There's plenty to think about and mull over today. The most basic element to remember is to be present in whatever you do, to be fully rooted in the moment. Make your decisions from a point of stillness rather than from that noise in your head.

Friday, March 12 (Moon in Aquarius) With Neptune also in Aquarius, there may be a confusing element to many days when the moon is in this sign. Or you can experience profound compassion and idealism. Or both. A great deal depends on your state of mind, what you're doing, and how you approach what you're involved in.

Saturday, March 13 (Moon in Aquarius to Pisces 2:44 p.m.) Whatever you imagine can manifest itself in your life. But, like the old saying goes, be careful what you wish for because you may just get it. So be mindful of your wishes and desires. Be prepared to dive deeply into your own psyche today.

Sunday, March 14—Daylight Saving Time Begins (Moon in Pisces) Your emotions run deep today and may concern a relative. Or if you're thinking about moving to a different area, there could be emotional reactions surrounding that. Whatever you're feeling should be positive since the Pisces moon is compatible with your sun sign.

Monday, March 15 (Moon in Pisces) Today's new moon in Pisces ushers in experiences related to your daily conscious life (as opposed to what's unconscious or hidden from you). Mercury forms a tight and positive angle with this moon, suggesting considerable debate and discussion. A contract may be in the offing.

Tuesday, March 16 (Moon in Pisces to Aries 3:32 a.m.) The moon joins Venus in Aries, in your fourth house. The combination of planets should bring depth and energy to any creative project in which you're involved right now. It could also nudge you into brainstorming about how to beautify your home or personal surroundings in some way without spending a ton of money to do it.

Wednesday, March 17 (Moon in Aries)   Mercury enters Aries, joining Venus and the moon in your fourth house. This trio really snaps your attention toward doing your own thing, forging your own path, and doing it alone and with passion and determination. You are being asked to acknowledge your own expertise, talents, and skills.

Thursday, March 18 (Moon in Aries to Taurus 1:30 p.m.)
You may be feeling like a mush head today when it comes to pets and animals. You have a soft spot for strays and may be feeding all the strays in your neighborhood. Perhaps there's creative fodder here—something about how our animal companions help to illuminate the fundamental truths in our lives.

Friday, March 19 (Moon in Taurus)   Resolute. Look up that word. Think about it. It describes how you feel today about a relationship, a creative project, or a child. It defines the actions you take, the decisions you make. You're stubborn, and the situation probably calls for it. Don't back down.

Saturday, March 20 (Moon in Taurus to Gemini 9:29 p.m.)
The Gemini moon forms a nice angle with Mars in Leo and with the planets presently in Aries. It brings fuel to the fire signs, so your energy is undoubtedly more impassioned than usual, more directed and focused. Today wouldn't be favorable for group work, unless it's conducted by e-mail or by phone.

Sunday, March 21 (Moon in Gemini)   Network, network. Social networking, that is. Make new contacts with people who share your interests and passions. And since your time is often at a premium, the best way to do this is through the Internet.

Monday, March 22 (Moon in Gemini)   You may be spending more time than usual with employees or coworkers, all of you trying to figure something out. Overall, a productive way to use your time.

Tuesday, March 23 (Moon in Gemini to Cancer 3:16 a.m.)
The moon enters your opposite sign, which can be a weird
time of the month for you. The focus suddenly shifts from
yourself to *others*. The primary other is a partner in business
or romance, but if you're a teenager, then others can mean
friends.

Wednesday, March 24 (Moon in Cancer)   Nurturing is the
name of the game. And your nurturing today will be directed
toward others. Or your mother or some other nurturing female
in your life needs additional emotional support today. You give
the support gladly and without thought of recompense.

Thursday, March 25 (Moon in Cancer to Leo 6:40 a.m.)
The Leo moon is conjunct to Mars and forms terrific angles
to Venus and Mercury. The combination brings passion and
enthusiasm to whatever you take on today. Your interactions
with coworkers, with the people in your personal environment, and even with yourself are infused with this energy.

Friday, March 26 (Moon in Leo)   Strut your stuff. People
are eager to hear what you have to say. So dress for success,
believe in your own abilities and talents, and don't hesitate
to share. Just resist the urge to actively seek the limelight. It
won't do much in the long run.

Saturday, March 27 (Moon in Leo to Virgo 7:58 a.m.)   If
you're a writer in search of a publisher, today should bring
news or insights into the publishing industry or news from an
editor. If you haven't submitted yet, dust off that manuscript
and whip it into shape.

Sunday, March 28 (Moon in Virgo)   You're good at piecing things together today; others realize it and may come to
you to piece together *their* stuff. In fact, if that's how events
unfold, think of it as a service you're doing for someone else.
And when you're done, get on with your own agenda.

Monday, March 29 (Moon in Virgo to Libra 8:22 a.m.)   Today's full moon in Libra brings news and insights related to

your career. Teamwork of some kind becomes evident today, a situation where you may have to draw on the expertise of others. Saturn forms a wide conjunction to this moon, indicating that events that unfold are serious, grounded, and deserve your judicious consideration.

Tuesday, March 30 (Moon in Libra) Can you feel spring in the air yet? If not, then buy something artistic for yourself today—fresh flowers, for instance, or something else that reminds you that spring is on the way. Your artistic sensibilities are integrated into your career.

Wednesday, March 31 (Moon in Libra to Scorpio 9:42 a.m.) Venus enters Taurus and your fifth house, marking the beginning of one of the most romantic and creative periods for you all year. This transit ends on April 25. Read more about it under the big-picture section.

APRIL 2010

Thursday, April 1 (Moon in Scorpio) Your passion may frighten that special person in your life. You'll feel that you should tamp it down a notch, but really, if the other person can't deal with your emotions, maybe he or she isn't the right one for you. Perhaps it's time to revisit your needs about the relationship.

Friday, April 2 (Moon in Scorpio to Sagittarius 1:54 p.m.) Mercury joins Venus in your fifth house. This combination is practically guaranteed to create a fertile atmosphere for discussion with a romantic partner—or with someone with whom you're working on a creative project.

Saturday, April 3 (Moon in Sagittarius) It's that twelfth-house moon again. Not your favorite moon, unless you have planets in fire or in Sagittarius in your natal chart. The interesting thing about this moon is that it forms a beautiful angle to Mars in Leo, infusing you with enthusiasm and passion. Use this energy to clear your desk, tie up loose ends, and clear the decks. The moon enters your sign tomorrow.

Sunday, April 4 (Moon in Sagittarius to Capricorn 10:08 p.m.)   A power day begins tonight. You're ready for it. Whether you're taking a few days off, diving into a new project, or starting an exercise routine, you're on top of things. Your only challenge is what to get to first! Since the moon will be in your sign until Wednesday morning, take it one item at a time.

Monday, April 5 (Moon in Capricorn)   The moon is traveling now with Pluto and will do so every month until early 2024. So observe the pattern that unfolds today. If you don't like what you see, figure out how to change it. If you like it, then figure out how to enhance it.

Tuesday, April 6 (Moon in Capricorn)   Pluto turns retrograde in Capricorn and will remain that way until September 13. During this period, you'll have a chance to scrutinize what you really want in your personal life and how you would like to spend the rest of your years on the planet.

Wednesday, April 7 (Moon in Capricorn to Aquarius 9:51 a.m.)   Money is on your mind today. There could be a bit of obsession about it, actually. So take a deep breath and ask yourself why you're obsessed.

Thursday, April 8 (Moon in Aquarius)   You may be taking a deeper look at what you value. What are your priorities? Values are often intimately connected to belief systems, so this inner scrutiny could veer into the beliefs that you hold. Are they really *your* beliefs or have you adopted what you believe from family and friends?

Friday, April 9 (Moon in Aquarius to Pisces 10:48 p.m.)   Part of this weekend may include relatives or neighbors. If the contact is personal rather than through calls or e-mail, you may have to bolster yourself, because there could be some sob stories coming your way. You'll be playing counselor.

Saturday, April 10 (Moon in Pisces)   Today you're the counselor. But you also may be counseled by someone else who is quite intuitive and provides penetrating insights into some facet of your life. It would be to your benefit to learn a divination system if you haven't done so already.

Sunday, April 11 (Moon in Pisces)   Your imagination soars to new heights. It could happen as the result of a dream you have or something that occurs to you while daydreaming, driving, or doing some other activity that frees your creative mind from your rational mind. Be sure to record whatever occurs to you. You'll be able to use it later.

Monday, April 12 (Moon in Pisces to Aries 10:31 a.m.) Things at home demand your attention. In your usual, careful way, you get to the root of the problem and find the appropriate solution. And then you lay down some rules to make life a bit easier.

Tuesday, April 13 (Moon in Aries)   Feeling restless? Then figure out why and indulge yourself. Burn off that energy. Find an outlet for it. But don't take it out on the people around you. You're in that groove called independence and probably should steer clear of sycophants.

Wednesday, April 14 (Moon in Aries to Taurus 7:55 p.m.) Today's new moon in Aries ushers in opportunities related to home, family, and your roots. Neptune forms a beneficial angle to this moon, suggesting that your compassion and ideals are involved in the events that unfold.

Thursday, April 15 (Moon in Taurus)   Oh, how you love the Taurus moon. Not only does it put you in a creative frame of mind; it also brings your thoughts to romance and children and everything you do for fun and pleasure. Even more to the point, you feel much more grounded under the influence of this moon.

Friday, April 16 (Moon in Taurus)   Tomorrow, Mercury turns retrograde in Taurus, in your fifth house. So take precautions. Back up all computer files today, explain to your romantic partner that you'll be silent for the next three weeks, and if you'll be traveling between then and May 11, keep your sense of humor. Other than that, be flexible. You may need it!

Saturday, April 17 (Moon in Taurus to Gemini 3:09 a.m.)
Mercury turns retrograde in Taurus. Between now and May 11, your job is to revise, review, and rewrite. Old friends you haven't seen for a while may resurface. Ditto for former lovers. You may revamp the things you do for fun and pleasure.

Sunday, April 18 (Moon in Gemini)   Connections are what you're about today: how to connect this person to that person, how to connect this dot with that dot. It's not the detailed work at which you often excel, but a kind of holistic approach to living and finding solutions.

Monday, April 19 (Moon in Gemini to Cancer 8:40 a.m.)
The moon enters your opposite sign. You may be piecing together information or insights about a partner or what you're looking for in a partnership. Don't make any decisions until after Mercury turns direct on May 11.

Tuesday, April 20 (Moon in Cancer)   At the end of next month, Saturn will turn direct again. Until then, if possible keep new projects under wraps at work and lay the ground work in a subtle way for anything new you want to launch. Expansive Jupiter is pouring ideas into your head; be sure to record them all. They'll come in handy this summer when Saturn is moving direct again.

Wednesday, April 21 (Moon in Cancer to Leo 12:43 p.m.)
Fretting about the taxes you had to pay on April 15? Waiting for your tax refund and anticipating what you're going to do with it? Don't look backward or forward today. Stay rooted in the moment. Be still. Be present. Become nothing more than a vehicle for sensations.

Thursday, April 22 (Moon in Leo)   Enjoy the rest of Venus's transit through Taurus while it lasts. In three days, will enter Gemini. So even though Mercury is retrograde, plan something with that special person in your life. Venus won't be in Taurus again for another year.

Friday, April 23 (Moon in Leo to Virgo 3:25 p.m.)   Just when you think you have the universe all figured out, you have to do it over again! Whether your worldview has been sculpted by a traditional religion or a nontraditional spirituality, you may be wrestling with big questions. The ultimate riddle, of course, is your place in the universe.

Saturday, April 24 (Moon in Virgo)   Off you trot to your local bookstore or Internet café today. Whether you're looking for a particular book or information from whomever you meet at the café, it's the outing that you're after—that sensation of being out in the world, searching, living.

Sunday, April 25 (Moon in Virgo to Libra 5:18 p.m.)   Venus enters Gemini and your sixth house, where it will be until May 19. During this period, your daily work life should move along with relative smoothness and will be focused on communication. This transit favors the pitching of ideas, sales, socializing, networking, and the gathering and disseminating of information.

Monday, April 26 (Moon in Libra)   The moon entered your tenth house yesterday. By now you should have a good idea what this means and how it impacts your decisions and attitudes toward professional matters. If you feel vulnerable—insecure, for instance, with your job—don't worry about it. The feelings really will pass by tomorrow night.

Tuesday, April 27 (Moon in Libra to Scorpio 7:30 p.m.) Your friends and any groups to which you belong are helpful in attaining your goals and dreams. You may not realize it at the time, but even strangers that you befriend can turn out to be beneficial to what you want to do with your life. Don't approach friendship with an end result in mind, however. Just go with the flow.

Wednesday, April 28 (Moon in Scorpio)   Today's full moon in Scorpio sheds light on a friendship or one of your dreams. Pluto forms a beneficial angle to this moon, indicating that you're in the power seat. Show yourself what you're made of.

Thursday, April 29 (Moon in Scorpio to Sagittarius 11:36 p.m.)   Here's that twelfth-house moon again—the one that urges you to do one of several things. You can retreat, seek solitude, or hit the road. That's the Sagittarius part of the equation—an urge to travel. If you go that route, it probably will be a trip you take alone.

Friday, April 30 (Moon in Sagittarius)   Animals and pets may take center stage today. Whether you have pets of your own or you're feeding all the strays in the neighborhood, animals are one of your soft spots. You care for them as you would your own kids.

MAY 2010

Saturday, May 1 (Moon in Sagittarius)   Time to clean house—not your literal house, but the internal stuff. Get out that metaphorical broom and start clearing away cobwebs, beliefs that no longer serve their purpose. You're clearing space for your power days, when the moon enters your sign. Engage your family and friends, if you're so inclined. Have a garage sale.

Sunday, May 2 (Moon in Sagittarius to Capricorn 7:00 a.m.) The moon joins Pluto in your first house. On a personal level, there's just no stopping you today. You're a powerhouse of energy and resolve. And since it's a weekend, put the energy to good use doing whatever you have neglected the past few weeks.

Monday, May 3 (Moon in Capricorn)   You're the leader today. Everyone comes to you for answers and insights, and you may spend a good part of the day counseling others. You excel at working with others at this level.

Tuesday, May 4 (Moon in Capricorn to Aquarius 5:52 p.m.) If you've been annoyed by Mercury's retrograde, just hold on for a while longer. It turns direct on May 11. After that, you can move forward with your new projects, ideas, and travel. For today, be sure to check your bank statements carefully. There could be errors or charges that need to be corrected.

Wednesday, May 5 (Moon in Aquarius) This moon forms a harmonious angle with Venus in Gemini, and provides you with the emotional detachment you may need right now. Don't hesitate to delegate tasks at work and at home. You often tend to shoulder all the responsibility yourself. But really, it's okay to ask for help.

Thursday, May 6 (Moon in Aquarius) Your visionary stuff surfaces through conscious thinking today, by being present in each moment. It's important to appreciate everything around you. Only in this way will you attract more to appreciate!

Friday, May 7 (Moon in Aquarius to Pisces 6:34 a.m.) You may be celebrating spring with a barbecue or a party at your place this weekend. Invite the neighbors. Your siblings. People in your community. Make it a real social event. With Jupiter also in Pisces, you're doing things in a big way.

Saturday, May 8 (Moon in Pisces) In three days, Mercury turns direct again. So start doing your virtual traveling now, get your contracts lined up and ready to sign, and keep backing up your computer files. Then wait until May 12, when Mercury will be stabilized, to move forward.

Sunday, May 9 (Moon in Pisces to Aries 6:30 p.m.) Various options are open to you today. You may choose the one that allows you to work independently, free to pursue your own ideas and course. But a word of caution: You may have to seek advice from someone you trust about this course you choose.

Monday, May 10 (Moon in Aries)   There's plenty of passion and enthusiasm on the home front today. A parent, a partner, a child, or someone else within your personal environment may need additional support. Or perhaps the family group—your tribe—gets together to accomplish a specific thing. However events unfold, think before you speak.

Tuesday, May 11 (Moon in Aries)   Mercury turns direct today. It's safe to pack your bags, sign those contracts, and start pushing ahead with everything you've held on the back burner for the last three weeks. For travel plans, remember that the next Mercury retrograde falls between August 20 and September 12.

Wednesday, May 12 (Moon in Aries to Taurus 3:49 a.m.)
By early next month, both Jupiter and Uranus will be in Aries, in your fourth house. So take advantage of these two planets still being in Pisces, a water sign compatible with your earth-sign sun. Allow your thinking to expand, to spill out of the box. Take a course or workshop in something that interests you. Allow yourself to follow impulses.

Thursday, May 13 (Moon in Taurus)   Today's new moon in Taurus is a beauty for your love life and creativity. It brings opportunities in both areas. Saturn, Uranus, and Jupiter form beneficial angles to this moon, indicating that the opportunities that surface are serious, occur suddenly, and somehow expand your current venues.

Friday, May 14 (Moon in Taurus to Gemini 10:19 a.m.)   If you're sending out résumés and actively searching for a new job, the new moon in Gemini on June 12 is the date to watch. If you can't wait that long to land a new position, then take something temporary to cover yourself.

Saturday, May 15 (Moon in Gemini)   Communication with coworkers, employees, or anyone in your work environment is essential today. Even if you're not at work, you should touch base with everyone by e-mail or phone. You're gearing up for something next week that will require the support of others.

Sunday, May 16 (Moon in Gemini to Cancer 2:47 p.m.) Today's moon is opposite your sign sun, which is usually a low time of the month. But if you learn to use the Cancer-moon energy to nurture self and others, it's less low. Also, because Cancer is a water sign, it's smart to honor that element in some way. Buy a small fountain and place it somewhere you can hear the sound of the flowing water.

Monday, May 17 (Moon in Cancer) In a few days, Venus will enter Cancer and your seventh house, marking the start of a romantic and creative period for you and your partner. It will be in that position until June 16, so sometime during that period, have something special planned for just the two of you.

Tuesday, May 18 (Moon in Cancer to Leo 6:07 p.m.) Someone in your life may need your expertise or emotional support. You provide it without thought of compensation, because it's the right thing to do. Or someone else provides this service for you.

Wednesday, May 19 (Moon in Leo) Venus enters Cancer and your seventh house. Read the entry for May 17. To this, add that you now get a tremendous creative boost if you're working on a project with a partner. If you're trying to launch your own business, this transit, which lasts until June 14, should be a tremendous help.

Thursday, May 20 (Moon in Leo to Virgo 8:59 p.m.) Listen closely. Can you hear it? Can you hear the little gremlins in your closet informing you there are dust bunnies accumulating in their throats? Time to clean your personal space. If you feel you don't have the time, then hire someone to do it.

Friday, May 21 (Moon in Virgo) Time to schedule dentist and doctor appointments or, if you go the way of alternative medicine, to get an acupuncture treatment or see your homeopath. You could be trying out a new nutritional program or an exercise routine, or signing up for yoga classes. In other words, today's energy favors the maintenance of your health.

Saturday, May 22 (Moon in Virgo to Libra 11:50 p.m.) You bring your work home this weekend. You could be preparing for something you have to deliver or present on Monday, or perhaps you're just catching up on paperwork. Whatever it is, be sure to schedule fun time too. You're one of the hardest workers in the zodiac, and you can sometimes forget that life is also about pleasure.

Sunday, May 23 (Moon in Libra)   Balance may elude you today, but it's what you most covet. The Libra moon always strives to see things from other people's perspectives, to feel what they do, so they bend over backward to please someone else. Avoid this. Treat yourself to something artistic and beautiful.

Monday, May 24 (Moon in Libra)   As you head into the last week of May, change is undoubtedly in the air. If you have kids, then they probably are preparing for end-of-the-year exams and may need your help and attention. This could create an emotional conflict for you because you have professional matters to attend to as well.

Tuesday, May 25 (Moon in Libra to Scorpio 3:18 a.m.)   The intensity of the Scorpio moon fits your serious mind-set today. You're determined to achieve certain things by the day's end, and this moon provides the resolve to do exactly that.

Wednesday, May 26 (Moon in Scorpio)   Psychic experiences are often part and parcel of the Scorpio moon. Whether you experience them depends on how attuned you are to the environment in which you live and how open you are to these sorts of experiences. A hunch, an impulse to do something different, a déjà vu—all of these manifestations are part of intuition and psychic ability.

Thursday, May 27 (Moon in Scorpio to Sagittarius 8:16 a.m.)   Today's full moon in your twelfth house coincides with Uranus's transit into Aries and your fourth house. Read about the Uranus transit in the big-picture section. What's especially nice is that Uranus forms a wide but beneficial angle to this moon, suggesting a lot of physical energy, movement, excitement, and surprises.

Friday, May 28 (Moon in Sagittarius)　　Sink into yourself or hit the road. Read a book, or write your own. You're preparing for tomorrow's power day, when the moon enters your sign, and whatever you need to do to charge your batteries, do it.

Saturday, May 29 (Moon in Sagittarius to Capricorn 3:44 p.m.)　　Early this afternoon, the moon enters your sign, joining Pluto in your first house. By now you should know something about the patterns that unfold when these two planets are together. Power issues may crop up, but rituals, deep emotions, and a gradual evolution toward something better are also possible.

Sunday, May 30 (Moon in Capricorn)　　Saturn turns direct in Virgo, your eleventh house. As the ruler of your sign, this planet's movements are important for you. You should have a clearer picture now of the kinds of things you would like to achieve and how to do so. Saturn provides the structure.

Monday, May 31 (Moon in Capricorn)　　Neptune turns retrograde in Aquarius. The impact will be subtle, but between now and November 6, you may be trying to find a way to integrate your idealism more firmly into the way you earn your living. Not always an easy thing to do, but you've never been about *easy*.

JUNE 2010

Tuesday, June 1 (Moon in Capricorn to Aquarius 2:08 a.m.)
Summer is almost here. The rhythm of life now changes, slows down, and you have some space to breathe, to tackle whatever got squeezed out during the busier part of the year. If you

have kids of working age, you may be helping them to scope out summer jobs.

Wednesday, June 2 (Moon in Aquarius)   With Neptune now retrograde in Aquarius, you may be casting about for ways to bring more compassion and spirituality into how you earn your living. But the bottom line may be that it's enough to bring those qualities into your daily life.

Thursday, June 3 (Moon in Aquarius to Pisces 2:34 p.m.) In another three days, Jupiter joins Uranus in Aries, so today and the next two days should be reserved for anything you want to expand in your life. They're excellent days for reading, for absorbing knowledge, and for communication. If you're a writer, hurry up and finish that book!

Friday, June 4 (Moon in Pisces)   Your imagination takes off today. Maybe it's due to Jupiter's final fling through Pisces. Maybe you're just in the mood for creative soaring. Whatever the cause, go with it. See where it leads. Be sure to have a recorder or pen and paper handy.

Saturday, June 5 (Moon in Pisces)   You're after creative freedom. Whatever it takes to be able to do a project your way, through the lens of your vision, is your goal. Funny thing is, creative freedom starts in your mind, in your heart and soul, and no one can take it away from you.

Sunday, June 6 (Moon in Pisces to Aries 2:51 a.m.)   Jupiter enters Aries and your fourth house. First, read about this transit in the big-picture section. Then pay close attention to events that begin to unfold over the next several weeks. Sometimes when Jupiter enters a new sign, its most obvious manifestation is excess.

Monday, June 7 (Moon in Aries)   Mars enters Virgo and your ninth house and will be there until July 29. During this period, you'll actively pursue participation in groups and organizations that support your interests and beliefs. You'll be spending more time with friends and engaged in social activities. Of course, you always have one eye on how all of this may benefit you professionally.

Tuesday, June 8 (Moon in Aries to Taurus 12:42 p.m.) You dig in your heels today and refuse to budge. Whether it's an opinion you're holding on to, a process, a relationship, or a situation, try not to be stubborn just to be contrary. Be stubborn only if you know it's the right thing to do, and you really object to whatever is being put forward.

Wednesday, June 9 (Moon in Taurus) There's a sensuous quality to the Taurus moon. It may have to do with sex, but could just as likely be connected to other pleasures—the taste of certain types of foods, for instance, or certain kinds of drinks. The point is the senses. Delight yours today. Just don't overindulge!

Thursday, June 10 (Moon in Taurus to Gemini 7:12 p.m.) Mercury enters Gemini and your sixth house, where it will be until June 25. This transit places a lot of emphasis on communication in its myriad forms. Whether you're writing or communicating verbally, it's important to include employees and coworkers. You may discover information about them that surprises you.

Friday, June 11 (Moon in Gemini) The Gemini moon often makes you feel more sociable. If that's how you feel today, then look for a party to attend. Or throw a party. That way you control the guest list!

Saturday, June 12 (Moon in Gemini to Cancer 10:51 p.m.) Today's new moon in Gemini ushers in opportunities in your daily work. You land a job for which you've applied, you get a promotion, or you're recognized by coworkers for something you've done. Neptune forms a wide but beneficial angle to this moon, suggesting there's an element of spirituality and idealism in the opportunities that surface.

Sunday, June 13 (Moon in Cancer) Today it's best to go with your hunches rather than trying to figure it all out rationally. You've got the answers inside. You just have to access them intuitively. Your dreams may be particularly vivid and insightful now. Keep track of them.

Monday, June 14 (Moon in Cancer)   Venus enters Leo, where it will be until July 10. During this period, it will be easier to obtain mortgages, loans, and even tax refunds. Your spouse or partner or someone else with whom you share finances or other resources could get a raise.

Tuesday, June 15 (Moon in Cancer to Leo 12:55 a.m.) You're out in front of the public more than usual today. If your daily job is behind a desk, then today you're away from the desk, perhaps engaged in public relations or some other activity that deals with the public. If your usual job takes you out in front of the public, then today and tomorrow it's even more so. So look your best. People are watching you.

Wednesday, June 16 (Moon in Leo)   This moon forms a beneficial angle to both Jupiter and Uranus in Aries, so you've got plenty of energy and whatever you do is larger than life, with abrupt changes in direction. Your love life could be heating up in a major way too.

Thursday, June 17 (Moon in Leo to Virgo 2:41 a.m.)   The moon joins Mars in Virgo. Emotionally, you're a stickler for details today. The danger here is that you'll turn that quality onto others and may be somewhat too sharp-tongued, blurting what shouldn't be said. Best to turn the energy to a project.

Friday, June 18 (Moon in Virgo)   You're shuffling pieces of a puzzle around and around in your head, carrying on inner dialogues, and not finding the answers you want or the information you need. So step back, quiet the noise in your mind, and sit silently for a few minutes with yourself. Then request that the information come to you.

Saturday, June 19 (Moon in Virgo to Libra 5:13 a.m.)   Today the game is yours. Be judicious in your actions toward others, mediate situations fairly, and you'll do fine. Saturn won't return to your tenth house and Libra until next month, so between now and then, give some thought to what you would like to achieve professionally before the end of the year.

Sunday, June 20 (Moon in Libra)   A coworker or boss takes center stage today. And since it's a Sunday, you may feel a bit peeved about it, particularly if you have to go into work. On the other hand, if you love your work, it's no big deal. So the question you really have to ask yourself, if the first possibility fits you, is, what would you rather be doing in your career?

Monday, June 21 (Moon in Libra to Scorpio 9:14 a.m.) The day seems charged, almost electrical, as if there's so much energy in the air that the planet can't accommodate all of it. That's an illusion, of course, and the energy is actually within you. Use it to charm everyone in your circle of friends and coworkers today.

Tuesday, June 22 (Moon in Scorpio)   Your emotional intensity needs an outlet. Dive into a creative project, go for a long walk or take a yoga class. If all else fails, walk into your closet, close the door, and scream. Then you're fit to deal with whatever you feel.

Wednesday, June 23 (Moon in Scorpio to Sagittarius 3:11 p.m.)   In three days, there will be a lunar eclipse in your sign. Depending on how sensitive you are to eclipses, you could be feeling the effects already. If so, understand it's the eclipse and that your emotions, if negative, will pass. If what you're feeling is positive, and it should be, then you are in for a treat.

Thursday, June 24 (Moon in Sagittarius)   Clearing the decks and making space for the new are what this moon is often about for you. Today, keep your nose to the grindstone and your opinions to yourself.

Friday, June 25 (Moon in Sagittarius to Capricorn 11:22 p.m.)   Mercury enters Cancer, your opposite sign, where it

271

will be until July 9. This will be a nice transit for that long July Fourth weekend, when family and friends often get together. It should also bring about conversations with your partner or spouse that are stripped of artifice.

Saturday, June 26 (Moon in Capricorn)   Today's lunar eclipse in Capricorn looks very nice for you—and quite powerful. Pluto is exactly conjunct to the degree of the moon, adding an intensity to whatever you do and feel. Lunar eclipses are about emotions, our inner worlds, and your insights and discoveries today will be positive.

Sunday, June 27 (Moon in Capricorn)   If you landed a job around the time of the eclipse or got married, engaged, or experienced some other event that made you happy, then it's to your advantage to keep track of how these eclipses impact your life. Actually, even if you experience something negative around an eclipse, keep track of the patterns that unfold.

Monday, June 28 (Moon in Capricorn to Aquarius 9:53 a.m.)   There's emotional detachment with the Aquarius moon, and it's exactly what you need right now. You can focus more clearly on the task at hand and silence that nagging voice in your mind that whispers whatever it is you don't want to hear.

Tuesday, June 29 (Moon in Aquarius)   Pursue your dream, whatever it may be. You're here to learn how to manifest your desires, to enjoy the pleasures of physical existence. But you were born with Saturn as your ruler, and it's difficult at times for you to relax. Maybe it's time to take a few days off.

Wednesday, June 30 (Moon in Aquarius to Pisces 10:11 p.m.) The moon is alone in Pisces today, now that Jupiter and Uranus have moved on into Aries. And it's actually quite happy in its solitude, so you can count on a dreamy, peaceful day.

Thursday, July 1 (Moon in Pisces)   The moon is now opposite Mars in Virgo, so there could be something of a struggle while you balance various obligations. A brother or sister or someone who visits from a foreign country could be involved. Just try to go with the flow.

Friday, July 2 (Moon in Pisces)   Intuitively, you're on your game today. You may have to rely on your intuition, in fact, to resolve an issue in your neighborhood or community or perhaps with a sibling. If you try to solve things with your left brain, through reason, the results may not be as positive.

Saturday, July 3 (Moon in Pisces to Aries 10:45 a.m.)   The moon joins both Jupiter and Uranus in Aries, in your fourth house. This appropriate combination for the July Fourth weekend places your focus squarely on family and home. There should be a lot of excitement—and excitable people around you—but it's all about expansion now: expanding your communication venues, expanding your existing relationships, and forging your own path forward.

Sunday, July 4 (Moon in Aries)   Whether you're out of town or sticking close to home, you're intent on doing your thing today, and you hope that everyone else follows along. If you're the host this weekend, you may have to relent a bit and do what the group wants to do. Yes, it probably will run contrary to your own desires. Then again, you can be diplomatic and very much of a team player when you need to be.

Monday, July 5 (Moon in Aries to Taurus 9:30 p.m.)   Uranus turns retrograde in Aries and begins its movement back into Pisces, which occurs on August 13. Once Uranus turns direct on December 5, it moves toward its appointment with Aries again early in 2011. What all this means is that between August 13 and the end of the year you'll have Uranus in a beneficial angle to your sun again, and that will attract unusual people and experiences. Just think back over the last seven years, and you'll have a clearer understanding what to expect during Uranus's last hurrah in Pisces.

Tuesday, July 6 (Moon in Taurus)   You may find yourself eyeing some expensive item today that you would like to buy for someone special in your life. Just be sure the money is in the bank! If it's not, then treat yourself to something less expensive that still satisfies your need for beauty.

Wednesday, July 7 (Moon in Taurus)   With the moon, Mars, and Saturn all in fellow earth signs, you're feeling quite grounded, your ideas feel solid, tangible, and real, and your goals seem to be within your reach. In a few days, Venus will also be in a fellow earth sign, and your heart will be singing. Just take things a moment at a time. If you feel overwhelmed in any area of your life, don't hesitate to delegate. You can relinquish some control. It's really okay.

Thursday, July 8 (Moon in Taurus to Gemini 4:51 a.m.) You and a partner in romance or business may embark on some new chapter in your relationship. You may be trying to expand your relationship, services, or product to different markets, and each of you has unique ideas. Open and honest communication about your respective needs and goals will take you farther than working in solitude.

Friday, July 9 (Moon in Gemini)   Mercury enters Leo, where it will be until July 27. This transit brings your attention toward how you appear to others, and urges you to examine mundane areas like taxes and insurance. It's a good time to have a will drawn up too.

Saturday, July 10 (Moon in Gemini to Cancer 8:38 a.m.) Venus enters Virgo, a very nice transit that lasts until August 6. During this period, your social calendar should be packed. You may be doing more publicity and promotion, and the public is receptive to you and your ideas. If you're not involved, you may meet a potential romantic interest through friends or through a group to which you belong.

Sunday, July 11 (Moon in Cancer)   Today's solar eclipse in Cancer should trigger external events that usher in opportunities in partnerships, either romantic or professional. Mars forms an exact and beneficial angle to the eclipse degree, suggesting a lot of frenetic activity around this date. Some possibilities: You land a new job, you and a partner launch your own business, you sell a book or screenplay, you move, or you sell your home.

Monday, July 12 (Moon in Cancer to Leo 9:54 a.m.)   You feel the change in lunar energy today. You feel confident, but may be a bit more flamboyant than usual, with brighter colors in your clothes, for instance, or more posturing. If you're seeking support for a project, wait until the moon is in a fellow earth sign.

Tuesday, July 13 (Moon in Leo)   You're pushing forward along a particular track in life, and then something happens that alters your perception of that path. What do you do? It's likely that you don't panic. Instead, you find a detour around whatever the obstacle might be and move on with the relentlessness for which you're famous.

Wednesday, July 14 (Moon in Leo to Virgo 10:15 a.m.) Now that the moon is entering a fellow earth sign, you'll be in a stronger position to make decisions you avoided or put off. The Virgo moon asks that you be meticulous about emotional details—connect the dots about why you feel as you do. Or connect the dots about why you were avoiding a particular issue.

Thursday, July 15 (Moon in Virgo)   If you're feeling restless and nomadic today, it may be time to get out of town. It can be as close to or as far from home as you like. Right now farther will be more satisfying. Another way this energy could manifest itself is in dealing with foreign countries or foreign-born individuals. If you're a writer, it's a good day to contact your editor.

Friday, July 16 (Moon in Virgo to Libra 11:25 a.m.)   The moon enters the career sector of your chart and could neces-

sitate having to work with several other individuals in a clos
situation. If anyone in this group bothers you, ask yoursel
about the traits you find distasteful in this individual. Is it pos
sible these traits may be part of who you are as well?

Saturday, July 17 (Moon in Libra) Among your peer
you're perceived as the person who gets things done. It isn'
just that your physical energy is excellent, but that you're a
exceptionally organized and efficient person who gets th
most done in the least amount of time. So today capitalize o
that, and don't allow others to distract you from the task a
hand.

Sunday, July 18 (Moon in Libra to Scorpio 2:43 p.m.) Wit
Venus, Mars, Pluto, and the moon in earth signs or signs tha
are compatible with yours, you have a distinct advantage ove
the competition. Your pragmatic approach to projects, situ
ations, relationships, and events is impossible to dispute. O
a personal level, there could be some inner tension betwee
your professional and family obligations. But you'll deal wit
it just as you do with everything else.

Monday, July 19 (Moon in Scorpio) Bottom lines—that'
what you're all about today. You may be digging into the em
ployment or work history of an employee or someone you'r
thinking about hiring. You eventually find what you're lookin
for and could discover that your hunch was right.

Tuesday, July 20 (Moon in Scorpio to Sagittarius 8:49 p.m.
Here it is again, that Sagittarius moon. By now you have som
idea of the possibilities it presents. Forget connecting the dot
Forget looking at the trees. Today, you're in search of the fo
est. Once you've got that big picture in your mind, you can im
plement whatever you need to in order to achieve the goal.

Wednesday, July 21 (Moon in Sagittarius) Things ar
in flux. And that's fine with you. With the Sagittarius moo
you're able to remain emotionally flexible and to blend wit
your surroundings. You become the mirror through whic
others recognize their own truths.

Thursday, July 22 (Moon in Sagittarius)   You're dealing with loose ends, leftovers, and trying to figure out what to do with the overflow of e-mail. Your drawers may be stuffed with papers that need your attention. Can you get it all done today? Try. Tomorrow, the moon enters your sign, and you need to start fresh.

Friday, July 23 (Moon in Sagittarius to Capricorn 5:40 a.m.) Whether you're planning a trip, taking care of kids, diving into work and creative projects, or just hanging out with friends, it's your day. You feel anchored in your own skin. Can it get any better than this?

Saturday, July 24 (Moon in Capricorn)   The moon and Pluto team up again and have both Venus and Mars in the earth-sign court as well. This could be another one of those days when things all click into place, seemingly of their own volition, with hardly any effort from you. So enjoy it. You've earned a day like this!

Sunday, July 25 (Moon in Capricorn to Aquarius 4:39 p.m.) Today's full moon in Aquarius brings news and insights about finances. Both Uranus and Jupiter form beneficial angles to the degree of this moon, indicating that the news is positive and could result in a check in your mailbox!

Monday, July 26 (Moon in Aquarius)   This moon is opposed to Mercury in Leo, so your mind is moving in one direction and your emotions in another. But the contrast may be good for you, if you can look at it in that light. Contrast helps define what you want. What you desire. And once you know that, you can make attitude and thought adjustments to create more of what you want.

Tuesday, July 27 (Moon in Aquarius)   Mercury enters Virgo, and yesterday's angst is history. You're in the groove again, doing, plotting, planning, and examining details. You may not even be after a particular result. You're just digging around and gathering information and opinions.

Wednesday, July 28 (Moon in Aquarius to Pisces 5:00 a.m.)   All the digging you did yesterday and whatever you unearthed can be put to good use today. Take your cues from your immediate environment. Look for metaphors in whatever happens. Do these metaphors reflect your inner thoughts and beliefs in some way?

Thursday, July 29 (Moon in Pisces)   Mars enters Libra and will be transiting the career sector of your chart until September 14. During this period, all professional concerns are energized. Your career is the central focus. You may be working longer hours, perhaps to meet a deadline. Or, if you've been dissatisfied with your job and have sent out résumés, you could land a job that would be more satisfying.

Friday, July 30 (Moon in Pisces to Aries 5:42 p.m.)   The moon links up with Uranus and Jupiter in your fourth house. Nice that it happens on a Friday, when all this energy can be put to excellent use—to enjoy yourself or to get back in touch with your family. In fact, a party may be in order.

Saturday, July 31 (Moon in Aries)   A parent or someone else within your most intimate circle has suggestions and insights that you should listen to. Or this person needs your help and support for some reason. Whichever it is, take this person along with you today—get out of town!

AUGUST 2010

Sunday, August 1 (Moon in Aries)   Change may be in the air. If you have children, they may be preparing to return to school. You may be planning a final vacation fling for summer. If so, travel on either side of the next Mercury retrograde dates: August 20 to September 12. It will be retrograde in Virgo, in your ninth house of overseas travel.

Monday, August 2 (Moon in Aries to Taurus 5:13 a.m.)   In a few days, Venus will join Mars in Libra, a certain recipe for romance. Since the two planets will be transiting your career sector, this could indicate the advent of a relationship with a coworker or boss. It can be risky to mix business and pleasure.

Tuesday, August 3 (Moon in Taurus)   Sensuality is often a part of the Taurus moon. Today's dose of sensuality could be something as simple as the feel of silk against your skin or the warmth of the sun against your face. Or it could be as complex as the foods you prepare to seduce someone!

Wednesday, August 4 (Moon in Taurus to Gemini 1:54 p.m.) As the poem says, you've got miles to go before you sleep. It's part of that relentless work ethic that you have, always moving and doing. You always have some sort of goal, even when you're vague about what it is.

Thursday, August 5 (Moon in Gemini)   If you've got a child headed off to college this fall, you may be running around, buying supplies for the dorm, gathering the final paperwork, and basically consolidating things to get the job done more quickly. The point is information—culling it and disseminating it. Again, look for cues within your environment about the path you're on.

Friday, August 6 (Moon in Gemini to Cancer 6:50 p.m.) Venus joins Mars in Libra, in your tenth house. In addition to the romantic implications, this is a nice creative match that could result in some sort of joint project with a peer or boss. The creative component should be quite powerful and could appeal to a number of people across the board.

Saturday, August 7 (Moon in Cancer)   With the moon in cardinal sign Cancer, Venus, Mars, and Saturn all in cardinal sign Libra, and your natal sign in cardinal sign Capricorn, you are in very rare form indeed. There's a lot of pressure on you to succeed. It may not even be external pressure, but some sort of inner pressure cooker. Once you pop off the lid, watch out!

Sunday, August 8 (Moon in Cancer to Leo 8:23 p.m.)   It's that time of month again when the day can go one of several ways. You can tend to mundane stuff like taxes, insurance, and paying bills. Or you can delve into the truly mysterious realms of reincarnation, life after death, communication with the dead, and the like.

Monday, August 9 (Moon in Leo)   Today's new moon in Leo ushers in new opportunities to research the really big cosmic questions. Seek the kind of wisdom and knowledge you need for this new journey. Or if that doesn't interest you, head out and enjoy the summer weather.

Tuesday, August 10 (Moon in Leo to Virgo 8:02 p.m.)   If you're a writer in search of a publisher, today's lineup of planets favors submissions or news about a submission you've made. If you're traveling overseas, the day should be very good, indeed, with lot of stimulation for heart and head and soul.

Wednesday, August 11 (Moon in Virgo)   As your summer winds down, you could be feeling that nostalgia or whatever it is that people sometimes feel about the passage of time and of summer. But instead of looking back, be rooted in the moment and look forward. What would you like to see for yourself?

Thursday, August 12 (Moon in Virgo to Libra 7:44 p.m.) The moon joins Mars and Venus in Libra, in your tenth house. This trio certainly ramps up your professional energy and your focus on career matters. With Mars, you have the physical stamina to work long and hard. Venus causes events to unfold more smoothly. And the moon provides the emotional nourishment you need to get to where you want to go.

Friday, August 13 (Moon in Libra)   You're a team player today. You almost have to be with the lineup of planets in Libra. But the team may not stick around at work. It may decide to hit the closest restaurant or pub to celebrate Friday. And there, in a casual setting, the various elements all come together. Everyone on the team has a part to play, and the combination of ideas proves productive.

Saturday, August 14 (Moon in Libra to Scorpio 9:27 p.m.)
Your sexuality is heightened today and plays a major part in what you do. If you're involved, you'll be spending the day with your partner. If you're not involved, then you may be sequestered in your office, writing that steamy romance novel.

Sunday, August 15 (Moon in Scorpio)   If you're planning to purchase a new computer or laptop, do it before August 20, when Mercury turns retrograde in Virgo. And you might consider buying a backup external hard drive on which to store documents, photos, and any other computer files that are of the utmost importance to you.

Monday, August 16 (Moon in Scorpio)   If you have any health issues, look for the inner triggers for illness and unhappiness. Take a deeper, more penetrating look at your own life. That's something the Scorpio moon does very well.

Tuesday, August 17 (Moon in Scorpio to Sagittarius 2:35 a.m.)   It's a good day to communicate with clients, coworkers, and employees through e-mail. If you have to go into work, fine, but keep your mouth shut. The Sagittarius moon can bring out your sharp wit, which may not be appreciated by the people around you. If you can confine communication to the written word, you'll be better able not to offend anyone.

Wednesday, August 18 (Moon in Sagittarius)   Start backing up those computer files. Mercury turns retrograde the day after tomorrow. You might want to buy a flash drive as a second backup. Think it's redundant? You won't think that if your computer crashes.

Thursday, August 19 (Moon in Sagittarius to Capricorn 11:18 a.m.)   The moon enters your sign, and over the course of the next two days, the world is at your feet. Make good use of this energy. You should start planting seeds now for the fall, which will carry you to the end of the year. Back up computer files!

Friday, August 20 (Moon in Capricorn)   Mercury turns retrograde in Virgo, in your ninth house, and stays like that until September 12. You know the drill by now, and hopefully, you've taken steps before today to protect your computer files. On other fronts, it's a great time to dive into anything that needs to be revised, reviewed, or rewritten.

Saturday, August 21 (Moon in Capricorn to Aquarius 10:38 p.m.)   Every month for several days, the moon is conjunct to Neptune, and the two planets urge you to think about money and idealism. In addition, with Pluto in your sign now, you may witness the collapse of established institutions and try to figure out how to create a safe haven for *your* money. The secret lies in what you think and feel about money.

Sunday, August 22 (Moon in Aquarius)   Keep abreast of politics. Even if you're apolitical and prefer to believe it's got zero to do with your daily life, think again. The Internet, political blogs, and TV political commentary have changed the landscape. Legislation, the decisions of the Supreme Court, and the activities of the Congress all impact your life.

Monday, August 23 (Moon in Aquarius)   The deal seems simple. It also may seem too good to be true. And if that's the case, run in the opposite direction. You know the routine—you're supposed to get something for practically nothing. Remember your cardinal rule: Nothing is free.

Tuesday, August 24 (Moon in Aquarius to Pisces 11:11 a.m.)   Today's full moon in Pisces brings news concerning a communication project and insights into how your conscious mind works. Pluto forms a close and beneficial angle to this moon, so the insights should be quite positive and powerful for you.

Wednesday, August 25 (Moon in Pisces)   Whenever the moon is in Pisces, your intuition is exceptional, and it's easier to zip through issues, agendas, situations, and events because you draw on information and insights in nontraditional ways. Sometimes, you can grasp the fuller picture by conceptualizing it in your imagination. Try not to shy away from this kind of knowing. It benefits you.

Thursday, August 26 (Moon in Pisces to Aries 11:49 p.m.) The moon joins Jupiter in your fourth house. Pretty soon, Jupiter will retrograde back into Pisces, but while it's here, make full use of it. Plan to expand your personal space in some way. If you own your home, look for ways to expand the space you have. If you're renting, add mirrors or use colors that create the illusion of more space.

Friday, August 27 (Moon in Aries)   Continuing yesterday's theme, you may want to buy a feng shui book or talk to someone who's an expert in it and practice some of the techniques on different areas of your life. What areas would you like to enhance: creativity, prosperity, family, career, or reputation? Sounds like you have a renovation project on your hands.

Saturday, August 28 (Moon in Aries)   As you're working your way toward the Labor Day weekend, it's smart to take a few moments for reflection. Have you done what you intended to do so far this year? Have certain areas of your life improved? Are you happy? If the answer to any of these questions is no, then you've got your work cut out for you for the last four months of 2010.

Sunday, August 29 (Moon in Aries to Taurus 11:36 a.m.) Time to join a gym, create an exercise routine you'll stick to, sign up for yoga classes, or start running or walking or something. On the other hand, if you already have your exercise routine, you're ahead of the game and now need to ask yourself how you can enhance it. The Taurus moon makes you more aware of your physical appearance, so if your body is in good shape, what about the rest of you? New wardrobe in your future? New skin creams?

Monday, August 30 (Moon in Taurus)   About those skin creams mentioned yesterday: Do some online research. Figure out your skin type; see what products apply to you. This will make the Taurus moon joyful. It's the sort of thing Taurus really enjoys.

Tuesday, August 31 (Moon in Taurus to Gemini 9:20 p.m.) If you have a close Virgo friend or a family member whose birthday is today, do something special for this person. He or she would enjoy the gesture and probably has insights and commentary you need to hear.

SEPTEMBER 2010

Wednesday, September 1 (Moon in Gemini) Chatty Gemini moon always seeks someone to talk to. The urge can be satisfied in any number of ways—face-to-face, through e-mail, by phone, or through writing. In fact, writing might be the best way today. You can vent on paper or in a computer file. You can imagine your audience and address them in your mind.

Thursday, September 2 (Moon in Gemini) Mercury is still retrograde, but even so, it's possible to communicate whatever you need to say to a coworker or employee, as long as you're clear and concise in what you're saying. Maybe e-mail is the best alternative. That way you can think about what you want to say.

Friday, September 3 (Moon in Gemini to Cancer 3:51 a.m.) The moon enters your opposite sign, so once again your focus shifts to others. If you're not married, the others could be your friends. If you're involved or married, the other would be your partner. If you're in business with someone else, the other could be your business partner. This person may need emotional support at this time.

Saturday, September 4 (Moon in Cancer) If you're traveling over this long Labor Day weekend, it's best to maintain flexibility and your sense of humor. Not only is this one of the busiest travel times, but Mercury is retrograde. If you do experience an abrupt change in plans, go with the flow.

Sunday, September 5 (Moon in Cancer to Leo 6:46 a.m.)
As the moon enters Leo today, you may feel the need for recognition from peers, family, and friends. Even if you aren't entirely clear what you should be recognized for, the feeling persists. But the bottom line here is that you don't need the approval of others to validate your work, your being, or your existence.

Monday, September 6 (Moon in Leo) If you've got decisions to make about insurance or taxes, delay until tomorrow, when the moon will be in fellow earth sign Virgo. Or, better yet, wait until the new moon in Virgo on September 8. If you're launching something new or have ideas to pitch, wait until the new moon as well.

Tuesday, September 7 (Moon in Leo to Virgo 6:54 a.m.)
Tomorrow, there's not only a new moon, but Venus enters Scorpio. This transit will last through the end of the year, because Venus will retrograde between October 8 and November 18. But while it's moving direct, romance may be as close as your backyard or your own neighborhood. This transit bolsters your self-confidence and your appeal to others.

Wednesday, September 8 (Moon in Virgo) Today's new moon in Virgo attracts opportunities to travel abroad, to do business with foreign countries, and to broaden your spiritual knowledge, and opportunities for higher education. Whether you're a teen bound for college, already in college, or an adult who wants to return to college, this new moon should be beneficial for you.

Thursday, September 9 (Moon in Virgo to Libra 6:02 a.m.)
With the new moon in Virgo yesterday and today's moon in the career sector of your chart, you should be seeing results of seeds you planted weeks or even months ago. Don't make any moves until after September 12, when Mercury turns direct.

Friday, September 10 (Moon in Libra) The moon, of course, is now traveling with Saturn through the career sector of your chart. While the combination can sometimes feel oppressive and serious, there's an upside to it. Saturn strengthens whatever professional structures you have in place and allows you to work well within the parameters you've established.

Saturday, September 11 (Moon in Libra to Scorpio 6:22 a.m.) Here it is again, that intense Scorpio moon. By now you have a pretty clear idea how you feel on these particular days. This moon should bring insights into your closest friendships or into some wish or dream that you hold. One thing is for sure. If you encounter a naysayer who says that your dreams are unrealistic, you'll have the inner certainty to just laugh it all off.

Sunday, September 12 (Moon in Scorpio) Mercury turns direct today in Virgo. Pack your bags and get out of town. What's especially nice about this movement is that Mercury, the moon, and Uranus are all in signs compatible with your sun sign. This combination brings heightened intensity and excitement to anything you undertake today.

Monday, September 13 (Moon in Scorpio to Sagittarius 9:52 a.m.) Pluto turns direct in your sign. The effects will be subtle, but fairly soon you should begin to notice that whatever has been stalled in your personal life should begin to move forward once again. You'll be able to integrate your own power successfully into whatever you do without being obnoxious or dictatorial about it.

Tuesday, September 14 (Moon in Sagittarius) Mars enters Scorpio, where it will be until October 28, and joins Venus in your eleventh house. This transit is certain to energize your social life and to act as a booster for the achievement of at least some of your wishes and dreams. Even if you don't achieve them now, you'll make significant strides.

Wednesday, September 15 (Moon in Sagittarius to Capricorn 5:30 p.m.) The moon enters your sign this afternoon and joins Pluto, now moving direct, in your first house. You should notice the difference of this combination now, the first time it's happened (with Pluto direct) since April 6. You'll feel more powerful and centered, and you should be able to make swifter, more focused decisions.

Thursday, September 16 (Moon in Capricorn)   You're grounded today. Feels good, doesn't it? Just be sure that you don't overstep your boundaries with bosses, peers, or others who have authority over you. With the planets lined up like this in your favor, there can be a tendency to believe that no matter what you do, nothing will go wrong.

Friday, September 17 (Moon in Capricorn)   In love, as in life, you like to be the captain of the ship. And today that tactic probably will work well for you. But tomorrow, it may not. So don't burn any bridges. And be careful what you wish for.

Saturday, September 18 (Moon in Capricorn to Aquarius 4:35 a.m.)   It's one of those days when you're fairly detached emotionally, which makes it good for dealing with emotional stuff. You'll have the distance you need. Since the issue could involve money, a subject about which you can be emotional, dive into your financial records. Get everything straightened out to your satisfaction. Figure out your financial goals.

Sunday, September 19 (Moon in Aquarius)   You're coming up on a full moon in Aries, and you may notice increased activity and perhaps a bit of chaos at home. Not to worry. If you're warned, you can be forearmed and deal with whatever comes up. But mark September 23 on your calendar.

Monday, September 20 (Moon in Aquarius to Pisces 5:15 p.m.)   With both Mars and Venus in Scorpio, your love life and creativity should be humming along very much to your satisfaction. Romance, in fact, may be as close as the house next door, or a flirtation could be heating up with someone you meet through a relative.

Tuesday, September 21 (Moon in Pisces)   Lucky you. With both Jupiter and Uranus back in Pisces for the rest of the year, any time the moon enters Pisces should be exciting, expansive, and generally a good luck day. So do something special today for yourself and for the people in your immediate environment. Practice appreciation. The more often you do that, the more likely it is that the universe will send more stuff your way to appreciate!

Wednesday, September 22 (Moon in Pisces)   Your head longs to go in one direction, your heart in another. It's the classic dilemma for the Pisces moon. So who wins: the head or the heart? You can't satisfy both. This is where you have to test your desires against your intuition.

Thursday, September 23 (Moon in Pisces to Aries 5:47 a.m.) Today's full moon in Aries is at zero degrees, a rather powerful full moon that stimulates three other areas in your chart. You become the intrepid explorer and may find that by handling a challenge differently from the way you usually do, things are settled much more quickly.

Friday, September 24 (Moon in Aries)   Combine the Aries moon with both Venus and Mars in passionate Scorpio, and you've got high-tension emotions. The Aries moon can be volatile, restless, and sharp-tongued. It can also be jealous. So walk a careful line. If you feel yourself getting jealous, breathe. Try to understand why you feel threatened. Don't lash out.

Saturday, September 25 (Moon in Aries to Taurus 5:17 p.m.) Here's that beautiful Taurus moon again, all prepared to stir your sensuality, your romanticism, and your sexuality. Even if you're not involved right now, you probably will be before the end of the year. In terms of creativity, this moon brings new insights into a current project and the emotional stamina to see it through to the end.

Sunday, September 26 (Moon in Taurus)   Today is all about fun and pleasure. Make sure that any activity today is one in which you engage because you want to and not out of sense of obligation. These Taurus moon days are supposed to open you up to your own desires so that you act on them.

Monday, September 27 (Moon in Taurus)   Mars and Venus are opposed to this moon, meaning they are in Taurus's opposite sign. That can create some tension between your desires and your outward actions, your needs and the needs of a partner. It's often a fine balance. But you manage to find it.

Tuesday, September 28 (Moon in Taurus to Gemini 3:12 a.m.)   If you live in the northern hemisphere, are you still enjoying warm, beautiful weather? Take notice of your environment. Then communicate what you feel to others.

Wednesday, September 29 (Moon in Gemini)   Things at work seem to loosen up a bit today, and you have a chance to socialize with coworkers or employees. You may be surprised to discover the commonalities that you share with the people you work alongside of day after day. It would behoove you to begin keeping a journal. Nothing fancy. A paragraph a day about your inner world.

Thursday, September 30 (Moon in Gemini to Cancer 10:47 a.m.)   The moon enters your opposite sign. This can be a low point in the month for you, so it's important to get enough rest and to eat right. Your digestive system is ruled by the moon and Cancer, so if your stomach is bothering you, perhaps a change in diet is in order.

OCTOBER 2010

Friday, October 1 (Moon in Cancer)   With the moon still in your opposite sign, the month gets off to a hectic start. It seems you've got a lot to do and not much time in which to do it. But instead of taking your work home with you this weekend, try leaving everything at the office and resolve to enjoy yourself for the next two days.

Saturday, October 2 (Moon in Cancer to Leo 4:22 p.m.)
You may be helping out someone else today. This person could be moving or need help with taxes or insurance issues. What-

ever it is, you're delighted to lend a helping hand and may be back tomorrow to finish up the job.

Sunday, October 3 (Moon in Leo)   Mercury enters Libra, and the career area of your chart, where it will be until October 20. During this period, you may be meeting more frequently with bosses and peers and could be traveling for business. This is a great time to pitch ideas, to boost your sales, and to generally consolidate your mental energy toward career and professional matters.

Monday, October 4 (Moon in Leo to Virgo 5:00 p.m.)   In a few days, Venus will turn retrograde in Scorpio, in your eleventh house. There are a couple of ways to prepare for this. If you're in the market for a computer, a car, or any other big-ticket item, buy before October 8. While it's possible to get good deals sometimes under a Venus retrograde, you may have to jump through hoops to do it. Best to buy now or wait until after November 18.

Tuesday, October 5 (Moon in Virgo)   Hungry for adventure or a break in your routine? Feeling a bit of wanderlust? Then today is the day to head out of town by car, train, plane, or even on foot. You're primed for new experiences, and even though you don't actually have to leave town to have them, it's guaranteed to stir up your perceptions.

Wednesday, October 6 (Moon in Virgo to Libra 3:52 p.m.) The moon joins Mercury and Saturn in Libra, in your tenth house. The combination of planets snaps your focus to professional matters, teamwork, and social structures and relationships. With Saturn in your career court, any offers you receive deserve serious consideration.

Thursday, October 7 (Moon in Libra)   Today's new moon in Libra should attract professional opportunities: a new job, a new career path, new contacts, a move, a promotion, a raise, a sale, an audition. You get the idea. Both Saturn and Mercury form wide conjunctions to this new moon, suggesting contracts, discussion, and debate and the new, stronger structures within which to work.

Friday, October 8 (Moon in Libra to Scorpio 3:52 p.m.) Venus turns retrograde in Scorpio, in your eleventh house. One possible repercussion for this retrograde is that former lovers or ex-spouses appear in your life. Or old friends you haven't seen in years suddenly get in touch. It's also possible that someone you consider a friend becomes something much more.

Saturday, October 9 (Moon in Scorpio) The moon joins Venus retrograde in your eleventh house. If you hang out with friends or meet with a group to which you belong, there could be some bumps and bruises in personal relationships—the wrong words said at the wrong time, or a silly misunderstanding gets blown out of proportion. You may decide to beautify your surroundings in some way. Be careful about buying any expensive items to do this!

Sunday, October 10 (Moon in Scorpio to Sagittarius 6:09 p.m.) Tie up loose ends, complete projects, finish up answering your e-mails, and schedule appointments with your health-care practitioners. Today, tomorrow, and Tuesday are the days to do whatever has been placed on a back burner. Clear the decks. You're preparing yourself for the moon entering your sign on Wednesday.

Monday, October 11 (Moon in Sagittarius) You're delving into your own psyche, looking for your true motives. Or you may be digging around in your own unconscious, looking for clues to a past life. Or you're making plans for your Halloween costume. Maybe a crazy astrologer?

Tuesday, October 12 (Moon in Sagittarius) Your quest for deeper answers spills over into other areas of your life. You're at a bookstore and a particular book falls at your feet. You turn on the radio, and the first thing you hear actually answers a question that's been bugging you. Synchronicities abound.

Wednesday, October 13 (Moon in Sagittarius to Capricorn 1:17 a.m.)   The moon enters your sign, and for the next two and a half days, you're in charge. Whenever the moon is in your sign, you may feel that you're the only one who can get the job done or meet the deadline. Or that you have to do everything. Resist that kind of thinking. Delegate.

Thursday, October 14 (Moon in Capricorn)   The moon forms beneficial angles to Mars, Jupiter, Uranus, Pluto, and Venus. With this sort of lineup, things aren't just exciting. Your life may be moving at the speed of light, with events unfolding so quickly that you can barely keep pace. But keep pace you do, of course, because few signs in the zodiac have your gift for getting things done.

Friday, October 15 (Moon in Capricorn to Aquarius 11:24 a.m.)   If you're feeling a financial pinch right now, it's probably only in your mind. What's really going on is that you're aware of what you need to feel emotionally secure. Is it a certain amount of money in the bank, a solid family life, or friends or a partner upon whom you can depend? Answer these questions.

Saturday, October 16 (Moon in Aquarius)   If you don't have to work weekends, then get together with friends and brainstorm for new ways to make money. You're feeling entrepreneurial today, and chances are that the people around you are as well. With that kind of energy humming through the air, indulge in some group brainstorming. Be as outrageously creative as you dare!

Sunday, October 17 (Moon in Aquarius to Pisces 11:52 p.m.)   Enjoy. That's the day's message. The moon joins Uranus and Jupiter in your third house. One of the best uses for this energy is to feed your intellect by attending a seminar or workshop or just settling in with a great book. You're a psychic sponge today, so be sure to associate only with upbeat, positive people.

Monday, October 18 (Moon in Pisces)   There's usually an air of unpredictability with Uranus involved in an astrological lineup, and today is no exception. But because Uranus forms such a beneficial angle to your sun and is conjunct to expansive Jupiter, the unknown works in your favor. You attract unusual people and experiences, and in some way, these people or experiences expand your understanding of your world. You're finally beginning to understand your place in the scheme of things.

Tuesday, October 19 (Moon in Pisces)   Intuitively, you're paying closer attention to what you think. Sounds contradictory, doesn't it? But it really isn't. You're able to catch yourself now when some negative loop keeps playing in your head—something that probably has no basis in reality but for which you feel you should be prepared. Remember that you get what you concentrate on.

Wednesday, October 20 (Moon in Pisces to Aries 12:24 p.m.) Mercury enters Scorpio and your eleventh house, where it will be until November 8. During this transit, you really do become a psychic sponge, absorbing information intuitively, and honing right in on the bottom line concerning issues and in relationships that are important to you. Friends take a more central role during this transit.

Thursday, October 21 (Moon in Aries)   You're on your own track today, wearing blinders that block your peripheral vision. It's likely that whatever you're doing requires a concentrated focus and determination, but you may have to remove those blinders before the end of the day to get some sense of how far you've gone.

Friday, October 22 (Moon in Aries to Taurus 11:31 p.m.) This is the second full moon in Aries this year. The one last month was at zero degrees, this one is at twenty degrees. Expect news or some sort of culmination related to your family, your home, and your roots. Neptune forms a close and beneficial angle to this moon, indicating that you may not have all the information you need to make an informed decision.

Saturday, October 23 (Moon in Taurus)   It's smart to remind yourself that the Taurus moon days are the universe's gifts to you. It's as if some higher power is making it clear that it's okay to take a day off and have fun. So with that in mind, let this be a day with nothing scheduled.

Sunday, October 24 (Moon in Taurus)   You're learning that it's fine to live rooted in the moment. Yes, we all still need plans and goals and dreams toward which we can strive. But the moment is the only certainty, and the more present you are, the greater your sense of fulfillment and joy. And the more joyful you are, the more likely it is that you'll experience more joyful events and relationships.

Monday, October 25 (Moon in Taurus to Gemini 8:48 a.m.) If you absolutely love what you do, it puts you leagues ahead of most people. It also helps you to maintain a positive attitude and belief in your own abilities, which then makes it easier to attract more experiences that feed this joy. But if you *are* looking for a job, today is the day to submit résumés and begin networking. Maintain your confidence. Keep believing in yourself. See yourself in the job you want.

Tuesday, October 26 (Moon in Gemini)   Jupiter is still moving retrograde through Pisces, making it likely that today you'll be communicating with a relative. If you and this person don't get along well, it's time to mend the relationship so that you both can move forward.

Wednesday, October 27 (Moon in Gemini to Cancer 4:15 p.m.)   This moon forms a harmonious angle with both Venus and Mars in Scorpio. It boosts your intuitive abilities and also your nurturing qualities. But are you nurturing someone else out of a sense of obligation or because it's what you want to do?

Thursday, October 28 (Moon in Cancer)   Mars moves into Sagittarius and your twelfth house, where it will be until December 7. During this transit, you're urged to delve into your own unconscious. Therapy and meditation are excellent ways to do this. But so are dream recall, some sort of mind-body discipline like yoga, and even taking workshops in the development of psychic abilities.

Friday, October 29 (Moon in Cancer to Leo 9:39 p.m.) This evening, the moon enters Leo and forms a beneficial angle with Mars in Sagittarius. You may be somewhat short-tempered or, at the very least, more irritable. Try not to take your irritability out on the people around you. Use the energy to do something constructive.

Saturday, October 30 (Moon in Leo)   You may be looking for end-of-the-year tax cuts. But it's best to wait until after Venus turns direct again on November 18 if you're buying expensive items that you can write off on your taxes. For now, just discuss your options with an accountant or someone with expertise in this area.

Sunday, October 31 (Moon in Leo)   Happy Halloween! Today, it all comes down to fun and games. If you have kids, then get into the Halloween celebrations. Even if you don't have kids, celebrate in some way.

NOVEMBER 2010

Monday, November 1 (Moon in Leo to Virgo 12:51 a.m.) As you enter the final two months of the year, the Virgo moon asks you to evaluate where you have been this year, what you have learned, and where you're headed now. In other words, it's time to take stock. If you're feeling really detail-oriented, you may want to open a computer file and take notes.

Tuesday, November 2 (Moon in Virgo)   In-laws or an out-of-town visitor may show up today. Whether the visit is expected or unexpected, you may feel pressured to take some time off work and show them around. Remind yourself that it's okay *not* to work around the clock.

Wednesday, November 3 (Moon in Virgo to Libra 2:19 a.m.) Before Saturn leaves Libra in 2012, you should see progress in your professional life—a raise, a promotion, or recognition by peers or bosses. But Saturn can also cause delays.

Thursday, November 4 (Moon in Libra) You may be juggling a lot of different balls today. Work, home, personal life, and everything in between. The balance you're seeking may elude you. But if you can keep your eye on the goal, then by tomorrow the balls all fall into place.

Friday, November 5 (Moon in Libra to Scorpio 3:16 a.m.) If you celebrate Thanksgiving, then you may be in discussions with friends and family members about who will host the festivities and who will bring which piece of the dinner. If you have to fly to your destination for Thanksgiving, know that Mercury will be in direct motion, always a bonus. But traveling over the Christmas holidays may be another matter. Mercury will be retrograde from December 10 to December 30.

Saturday, November 6 (Moon in Scorpio) Today's new moon in Scorpio should attract new friends and groups into your life. You'll have opportunities to develop your intuitive ability, to conduct research and investigation, and to expand your creative venues. Neptune also turns direct today in Aquarius, in the financial sector of your chart. The impact of this movement will be subtle, but you'll begin to find ways to integrate your spirituality more readily into the way you earn your living.

Sunday, November 7—Daylight Saving Time Ends (Moon in Scorpio to Sagittarius 4:28 a.m.) Communion with your hidden self is part of what unfolds today. It's possible that you finally understand what has motivated you in a relationship or situation. Whether or not you like what you find is really irrelevant. The important thing is that a question is answered.

Monday, November 8 (Moon in Sagittarius) Mercury enters Sagittarius and your twelfth house, where it will be until November 30. This transit certainly favors writers and writing and communication of all kinds. It would be a good time to get involved with publicity and promotion for your company's service or product. There could be some travel related to something you're working on.

Tuesday, November 9 (Moon in Sagittarius to Capricorn 9:37 a.m.) The transition is palpable. Midmorning, you suddenly are in your element again. The moon enters your sign once more. Work like a maniac, because that last Mercury retrograde this year will be in your sign, and that will be a time for lying low and sticking close to home!

Wednesday, November 10 (Moon in Capricorn) Organization is the key. It doesn't matter whom or what you're organizing—you do it with your usual efficiency and drive. People around you marvel at how easy you make it all seem.

Thursday, November 11 (Moon in Capricorn to Aquarius 6:33 p.m.) If possible, take some time today for reflection. You'll have the emotional detachment to do it, which will make it easier to deal with anything you discover that you don't like. But you tend to be tough on yourself and may ask for input from a trusted family member or friend.

Friday, November 12 (Moon in Aquarius) Vision is a quality of the Aquarius moon. Today you can put this quality to good use by trying to figure out where to invest your money. In the end, you may opt for what seems safest.

Saturday, November 13 (Moon in Aquarius) You know your priorities. You live according to your priorities. But today, the priorities may get switched around somewhat. A challenge surfaces at home, at work, or with a partner, and you have to deal with it.

Sunday, November 14 (Moon in Aquarius to Pisces 6:25 a.m.) E-mails are flying back and forth through cyberspace as everyone in your environment gets dates and times for arrival set for the long Thanksgiving weekend. It may be that this year's table is open to neighbors and people in your community who live too far from their own families to go home.

Monday, November 15 (Moon in Pisces)   With Mars now in jubilant Sagittarius, your sex life could be heating up, but behind the scenes, in a relationship that may have an element of secrecy to it. That's fine. Unless you're being secretive because the relationship is illicit. Then you have to ask yourself if all the sneaking around is really worth it.

Tuesday, November 16 (Moon in Pisces to Aries 7:00 p.m.) This evening, the moon enters your fourth house, and things at home suddenly seem to be on an unexpected track. It throws you off your game. But by the end of tomorrow, you find a unique and creative way to deal with whatever it is.

Wednesday, November 17 (Moon in Aries)   You're emotionally charged today, a knight armed for battle. Things could be somewhat volatile with someone close to you, so it might be best to sit out a round or two. In fact, wait until Friday to deal with this. The moon will be in Taurus then.

Thursday, November 18 (Moon in Aries)   Both Venus and Jupiter turn direct today, certainly a cause for celebration. You now have a much clearer idea about what you're looking for romantically and creatively. Both Venus and Jupiter now head toward their appointment with Aries early in 2011, so enjoy these two planets traveling in harmony with your sun sign through the end of the year. Life will unfold more smoothly.

Friday, November 19 (Moon in Aries to Taurus 6:05 a.m.) Any decision you put off should be tackled now, while the moon is in fellow earth sign Taurus. Your resolve will be helpful in dealing with whatever the issue is. Also, other earth-sign individuals may be helpful now—anyone with a Taurus, a Capricorn, or a Virgo sun. On the romantic front, it's the day to plan something special with the person who is most special to you.

Saturday, November 20 (Moon in Taurus)   You could be feeling the effects of tomorrow's full moon already. If so, then your day is sure to be fast-paced, with e-mail filling your in-box, your phone ringing constantly, and your calendar getting crowded. You're in demand.

Sunday, November 21 (Moon in Taurus to Gemini 2:46 p.m.) Today's full moon in Gemini should be splendid for you. It falls in your fifth house of romance and creativity, so in those areas, there should be news and some sort of culmination. Perhaps you and a partner decide to take your relationship to a deeper level of commitment. Maybe you decide it's time to start a family. With friendly angles from both Jupiter and Uranus, excitement and serendipity are sure to be part of the events.

Monday, November 22 (Moon in Gemini)   Network. Even if you're not up to it, do it anyway. It will benefit you in the long run and take your mind off other issues and concerns. Besides, once you start socializing and talking with people, you find that you enjoy it.

Tuesday, November 23 (Moon in Gemini to Cancer 9:14 p.m.)   If you're taking time off this week to head out of town for Thanksgiving—or to prepare for the arrival of guests—then you may be in a frenetic mood today. Rushed. Trying to get stuff done. Relax. You have a partner who is willing to help or employees and coworkers who are eager to get involved.

Wednesday, November 24 (Moon in Cancer)   Mom or her surrogate in your life plays a part in the day's events. Or you may be nurturing someone else. Regardless, there's a strong home-and-hearth component to the day, right in time for Thanksgiving.

Thursday, November 25 (Moon in Cancer)   Happy Thanksgiving! In the celebration of a long weekend, remember to be appreciative of all that you have. Surrounded by good friends or family or even caring strangers.

Friday, November 26 (Moon in Cancer to Leo 2:01 a.m.) This moon forms a beneficial angle to Mars in Sagittarius. So you've got plenty of physical energy and the focus to see a project or anything through to the end. You have the big picture for sure and may only have to connect the dots to bring it all together. When the moon enters Virgo on Sunday, you'll have a clearer sense of everything.

Saturday, November 27 (Moon in Leo) Still looking for some end-of-the-year tax breaks? It's favorable to buy those big-ticket items now that Venus is direct. Do it before December 10, when Mercury turns retrograde in your sign, or after December 30, when it turns direct again. But that might be cutting it all a bit too close.

Sunday, November 28 (Moon in Leo to Virgo 5:34 a.m.) Here's the connect-the-dots day. Regardless of where your focus is, it's important to tend to details. Read the small print. Listen to your intuition. Quite often, you intuitively pick up things that your left brain misses or overlooks.

Monday, November 29 (Moon in Virgo) As you head into the last month of the year, do a retrospective, just as you did at the end of last month. Are you happy with where you are right this moment? What would you like to achieve during December? Start thinking about your goals for 2011.

Tuesday, November 30 (Moon in Virgo to Libra 8:16 a.m.) Mercury enters your sign. Except for the retrograde period, you'll enjoy this transit. Your mind is sharp, quick, organized, and focused. You may want to start organizing your New Year's festivities before Mercury turns retrograde on December 10. Otherwise, things are sure to change.

DECEMBER 2010

Wednesday, December 1 (Moon in Libra) Have you met your career goals for the year? If not, what can you do before the end of the year to move things closer to your goal? You'll be dealing with those kinds of questions today and may be talking about these very issues with coworkers and friends.

Thursday, December 2 (Moon in Libra to Scorpio 10:44 a.m.) The moon forms a beneficial angle to Mercury in your sign, bringing an intuitive element to your conscious thoughts. It's easier to plan and strategize now, and if you can do this in an intuitive way, taking your cues from your environment and the people around you, so much the better.

Friday, December 3 (Moon in Scorpio) The moon links up with Venus. Your love life, creativity, and even your kids play into the day's events. Intense experiences and emotions are the norm. You have the ability today to delve deeply into anything you do, read, think, investigate, and feel.

Saturday, December 4 (Moon in Scorpio to Sagittarius 2:00 p.m.) If the holidays are pressing down against you like a ton of bricks—shopping, guests arriving, plans, or whatever—today is perfect for getting off by yourself and putting things in order. In fact, tomorrow's new moon should bring more opportunities to do exactly that.

Sunday, December 5 (Moon in Sagittarius) The new moon in Sagittarius should usher in opportunities for overseas travel, education, and working behind the scenes in some capacity. Saturn forms a beneficial angle to this moon, indicating that these opportunities are serious and deserve your consideration. Uranus also turns direct in Pisces. The impact of this movement probably will be subtle, but you should notice a difference in your daily life experiences. Fewer snafus!

Monday, December 6 (Moon in Sagittarius to Capricorn 7:17 p.m.) Mercury turns retrograde on December 10, so start making backups of your computer files, finalize your travel plans and your plans for New Year's Eve, and buy whatever items you need for end-of-the-year tax write-offs. Since Mercury will be turning retrograde in your sign, be sure to have backup plans for everything!

Tuesday, December 7 (Moon in Capricorn)   Mars enters your sign today, joining Mercury and Pluto in your first house. This lineup of planets, particularly Mars and Pluto traveling together, really acts as a booster rocket for whatever you're doing. You're in a powerful position to get things done, to push your agenda forward, and to organize and implement. This is especially true from now to December 10, when Mercury turns retrograde.

Wednesday, December 8 (Moon in Capricorn)   With so many planets lined up in your favor today, you really have to work at making a wrong move! A partner—romantic or business—is helpful in whatever you're working on. Resist the urge to do it all yourself. Delegate.

Thursday, December 9 (Moon in Capricorn to Aquarius 3:32 a.m.)   Time to back up computer files, sign contracts, and finalize travel and New Year's Eve plans. Mercury turns retrograde in your sign tomorrow. It might also be a good idea if you can wind up your holiday shopping today, especially if you're buying expensive items. You don't want to be in the return lines on December 26.

Friday, December 10 (Moon in Aquarius)   Mercury turns retrograde in Capricorn and stays that way until December 30. You've got plenty of other good stuff going on, what with Mars in your sign, providing all the physical energy you need, and Venus still in Scorpio. The angle Mars and Venus make to each other is beneficial and should add smoothness and heightened sexuality to any romantic relationship.

Saturday, December 11 (Moon in Aquarius to Pisces 2:41 p.m.)   Today through Monday will be the last time this year that the moon hooks up with Jupiter and Uranus in Pisces. Take advantage of the energy while you can. Get into a creative project. Mend fences with a relative. Forgive, forget and move on.

Sunday, December 12 (Moon in Pisces)   Intuitively, you're right on the money about an issue or situation. But to convince someone else that you understand what's going on, you may have to gather facts to back up your intuition. Not a problem. You know exactly where to find what you need.

Monday, December 13 (Moon in Pisces)   Venus and the moon form beneficial angles to each other and to Mars, Pluto, and Mercury in your sign. This combination is so favorable to anything you do, think, or plan that things should manifest in a positive way despite Mercury's retrograde. You simply have to remain focused on your intents and desires.

Tuesday, December 14 (Moon in Pisces to Aries 3:15 a.m.) Today favors picking up last-minute holiday items or planning an office party or just generally trying to get things together for the holidays. You're the planner, and that's true whether you're planning at work or at home, and yes, today you're the problem solver as well.

Wednesday, December 15 (Moon in Aries)   Your ideas flow forth with such shocking ease that you wonder where they're coming from. Record them. When a creative tap like this one opens up, you want to be sure the ideas don't get away! Some of the ideas could be triggered by a conversation with a family member or with someone else in your personal environment.

Thursday, December 16 (Moon in Aries to Taurus 2:49 p.m.) Venus and the moon are opposed to each other. It's not as serious as it sounds, but can lead to excesses—hammering at an old issue, too much partying, losing sleep, and all the things many of us do around the holidays. Strive for balance.

Friday, December 17 (Moon in Taurus)   Despite yester-day's warning, the Taurus moon really is about enjoying your-self, in whatever form that takes. If you have children, then today may be their last school day until the New Year. Perhaps it's time to gather up the kids and enjoy yourself with them.

Saturday, December 18 (Moon in Taurus to Gemini 11:38 a.m.)   Right now, every planet except for Mercury is mov-

303

ing in direct motion. So despite Mercury's mischievousness, you're able to zip through your day at your usual pace. You connect with old friends through e-mail or a blog or chat room. Information is shared, and it happens to be exactly what you're looking for. Serendipity!

Sunday, December 19 (Moon in Gemini)   Haven't you earned a day off? Yes, you have. So pat yourself on the back, kick back, and get lost in a good book. Or go see a movie. Take a nap. Do whatever you want.

Monday, December 20 (Moon in Gemini)   Your local bookstore could be your favorite haunt today. Whether you're browsing or doing last-minute holiday shopping, there's something about the smell and feel and texture of books that excites you, that stokes your imagination. If you're buying for coworkers, make sure the books fit the people.

Tuesday, December 21 (Moon in Gemini to Cancer 5:22 a.m.)   Today's full moon in Gemini highlights something in your daily work routine. If you've applied for a new job or put in for a promotion, then today you may receive news about it. Saturn forms a wide but beneficial angle to this moon indicating that any offers or news you receive are solid, real and serious.

Wednesday, December 22 (Moon in Cancer)   Whether you're traveling for the holidays and staying close to home it's about this time every year (or sooner) when life gets busy. You flourish when you're busy. You even flourish in chaos. But you also like to call the shots, to be in control of the situation and today you may not be. Try not to obsess about it. Go with the flow. You'll be happier.

Thursday, December 23 (Moon in Cancer to Leo 8:51 a.m.
You may be wrestling with insurance and tax issues today. It's not what you want to do during the holidays, but best to get it out of the way so you can enjoy the rest of the holidays. Be forewarned that because Mercury is retrograde, you may be doing the same thing again on December 30.

Friday, December 24 (Moon in Leo) Whether you celebrate Christmas or not, it's a good time to take a look around and appreciate everything you have. Whether it's family, friends, a home, good health, or prosperity, be grateful. Show your appreciation for the people around you.

Saturday, December 25 (Moon in Leo to Virgo 11:15 a.m.) Merry Christmas! Whether you celebrate today or not, there's a need to pay attention to details. It may have to do with people's relationships to one another, how they treat each other, what they say or don't say. You may find yourself mediating or explaining.

Sunday, December 26 (Moon in Virgo) Avoid the malls. Sleep in. Burn off some of that energy from Mars in your sign. This could mean doing something physical—skiing, taking a walk, or going to the gym. Honor Jupiter's final fling in Pisces by giving back to your neighborhood or community in some way.

Monday, December 27 (Moon in Virgo to Libra 1:39 p.m.) If you go into work today, there will be a team effort of some kind to push through a product, agenda, or idea before the end of the year. If you've taken time off from work, you may have the same challenge facing you, but on the home front.

Tuesday, December 28 (Moon in Libra) You're the arbitrator today, the one who mitigates, the one who stands in the other person's shoes, feeling and seeing what he or she does. It deepens your understanding of the conflicts between people that are often founded on nothing more than misunderstandings.

Wednesday, December 29 (Moon in Libra to Scorpio 4:50 p.m.) The moon joins Venus in Scorpio and brings your creativity into sharp relief. Since Mercury will be retrograde until tomorrow, don't pitch ideas or submit any creative projects until December 31. Better yet, wait until next year.

Thursday, December 30 (Moon in Scorpio) Mercury turns direct. Before you rush to the phone or the computer to firm up plans for tomorrow night, if you don't have plans yet, wait until tomorrow morning, when Mercury is stabilized. If you don't want to wing it that way, then take your chances! But maintain flexibility. You'll need it.

Friday, December 31 (Moon in Scorpio)   Reflect back on the year. Then look forward. Standing where you are right this second, what would you change? There's no right or wrong answer. Only honesty is required!

HAPPY NEW YEAR!

SYDNEY OMARR

Born on August 5, 1926, in Philadelphia, Pennsylvania, Sydney Omarr was the only person ever given full-time duty in the U.S. Army as an astrologer. He is regarded as the most erudite astrologer of our time and the best known, through his syndicated column and his radio and television programs (he was Merv Griffin's "resident astrologer"). Omarr has been called the most "knowledgeable astrologer since Evangeline Adams." His forecasts of Nixon's downfall, the end of World War II in mid-August of 1945, the assassination of John F. Kennedy, Roosevelt's election to a fourth term and his death in office ... these and many others are on the record and quoted enough to be considered "legendary."

ABOUT THE SERIES

This is one of a series of twelve *Sydney Omarr® Day-by-Day Astrological Guides* for the signs of 2010. For questions and comments about the book, go to www.tjmacgregor.com.

COMING SOON

SYDNEY OMARR'S® ASTROLOGICAL GUIDE FOR YOU IN 2010

Brimming with tantalizing projections, this amazing single-volume guide contains advice on romantic matters, career moves, travel, even finance, trends and world events. Find year overviews and detailed month-by-month predictions for every sign. Omarr reveals everything new under the stars, including:

- Attraction and romance
- New career opportunities for success in the future
- Global shifts and world forecasts

...and much more! Don't face the future blindly—let the Zodiac be your guide.